THE FOCUSING ARTIFICE

THE
FOCUSING
ARTIFICE

The Poetry of Robert Browning

ROMA A. KING, Jr.

OHIO UNIVERSITY PRESS

Athens, Ohio
1968

To Austin Warren

Acknowledgments

I gratefully acknowledge the assistance given me by Park Honan, Gordon Pitts, Rainer Schulte, Sandra Smith, Robert Reid, and Jerry Trammell. I am also indebted to my graduate students at Ohio University and the University of Missouri at Kansas City, with whom I have engaged in a continuing dialogue about the poetry of Robert Browning ever since I began writing this book. Among us the role of teacher and student has constantly shifted, and I more often than not have been chief benefactor of our discussions.

❧

. . . to join in the discussion of value and disvalue, one must see five hundred convictions *beneath* oneself—behind oneself.

—NIETZSCHE

❧

What we do depends on what we are, but it is necessary to add also that what we are, to a certain extent, is what we do, and that we are continually creating ourselves.

—HENRI BERGSON

❧

   . . . being bound to trust
All feelings equally—to hear all sides:
Yet I cannot indulge them, and they live,
Referring to some state or life unknown.

—BROWNING, *Pauline*

❧

               Thus moaned
Man till Prometheus helped him,—as we learn,—
Offered an artifice whereby he drew
Sun's rays into a focus.

—BROWNING, *Parleyings*

❦ ❦ CONTENTS

PREFACE

❧ When I began work some years ago on *The Bow and the Lyre: The Art of Robert Browning*, I felt that critics had given too little attention to Browning's artistic achievements. The worst of the Browning Society era was over, but it was still widely assumed that Browning was an unpolished genius, more to be revered for what he said than for how he said it. My purpose was limited. I hoped to question the notion that there was a disjunction between Browning's matter and structure and to demonstrate, by detailed analysis of a few poems, that Browning's poetry, at its best, possessed the organic unity characteristic of all great art.

In the same year that my book appeared, 1957, Robert Langbaum in *The Poetry of Experience* gave us our first modern definition of the dramatic monologue, thus providing the necessary perspective from which Browning could be seen as poet rather than preacher or prophet.[1] Four years later, Park Honan published *Browning's Characters: A Study in Poetic Technique.*[2] Although his purpose differed from Langbaum's, he too was concerned about the development of character in Browning's poetry, and he demonstrated both in his argument and in his perceptive analysis of individual poems that Browning's significance lay primarily in his artistic achievements. These two important books prepared the way for the many excellent articles which have followed and today, perhaps for the first time, Browning is taken seriously by a great number of readers as a careful, conscious craftsman.

Now it seems to me, another kind of book is in order. I would like to go beyond the scope of *The Bow and the Lyre* to discuss not only the "art" of Robert Browning, but also what I call here, for want of a better single word, the "poetry" of Robert Browning. My interests are less in characterizing Browning's achievement in one genre, the dramatic monologue, than in understanding, intellectually and artistically, the diverse whole of his work from *Pauline* through *Asolando*. I am concerned, primarily, to describe and evaluate his achievements for what they are, and, secondarily, to relate Browning's poetry, both as it was influenced by and as it contributed to the developing modern tradition.[3]

The Focusing Artifice has some of the surface characteristics of a traditional introduction. I have intended that it be more than that, however. I assume that my readers have some familiarity with Browning's poetry, and my aim is less to introduce them to entirely new materials than to suggest the outline of a new perspective from which they may see the whole of Browning's poetry. It is frequently assumed that Browning's genius culminated in *The Ring and the Book* and afterwards went into radical decline.[4] As a result not only have a number of good poems gone unappreciated, but, more seriously, the whole of Browning's work has been seen in truncated and, therefore, distorted form. I propose that the poems most crucial to an understanding of Browning are *Sordello, The Ring and the Book, Fifine at the Fair,* and *Parleyings With Certain People of Importance in Their Day.*

These four poems cannot be regarded as isolated works, however, but rather must be treated as organic parts of Browning's entire achievement, each marking a significant state in the process of development which begins with *Pauline* and continues throughout his life. We must be careful, of course, when we use such words as *organic* and *development* not to suggest a greater sense of entity in Browning than actually existed. There was not one Browning, fixed and static, but many Brownings, the dynamic, changing, sometimes affirming, sometimes negating nature of whom his poetry stands as a record. It cannot be assumed that precisely the same man wrote both *Pauline* and *Parleyings*. When we attempt something so tenuous and precarious as to interpret Browning, therefore, we must be continually aware both of chronology and context.

Moreover, I want to maintain the integrity of the individual poem. Some adequate notion of Browning's "thought" might be achieved by taking lines out of context and arranging them into a thematic pattern. We would be on dubious ground, however, if we were to do so. We cannot assume that all statements in Browning's poetry represent equally the poet's own thought, or that the ideas which he maintained at one time represented his thought at all other times. Ideas have meaning in relation to the context in which they occur. Two statements which seem to say the same thing may prove upon closer examination to be wholly or partly contradictory. Their possible diverse meanings may arise from the point of view from which they are spoken or they may take on intellectual, emotional, and sensuous meanings as a result of the context in which they appear. Browning meant to communicate much more than what he called "naked thought" in his poetry. My purpose seems best served by treating the poems as artistic entities in an essentially chronological order.

In order to relate Browning to the developing modern tradition, one must be aware of the intellectual and cultural forces that helped shape his vision of reality. Browning, like other intellectuals in the early nineteenth century, found himself in a world of rapidly changing values and of spiritual uncertainty. Many competent scholars and critics have traced the reorientation of Western thought during the late eighteenth and early nineteenth century.[5] The change involved a transition from largely communal values to highly individual values. The old values derived from an order external to and independent of man. They were subject to man's rational understanding, however, and capable of being embodied in creedal statements and social institutions. A man of the classical world not only assumed a meaningful universe but accepted the pronouncements and institutions of his culture as its rational embodiment.

Although statement and institution might become corrupted by the errors of man, the avenues for achieving and expressing those truths were never entirely closed. The Christian required his revelation because of Adam's willful rejection of the eternal order, not because of his native alienation from it. The mission of the Church always was to restore the natural order and to reconcile man with God, from whom he had been tragically and unnaturally separated. For all practical purposes, then, preromantic man found his orientation—toward God, man, and self—in the statements and creeds of his culture and in the institutions of his own making.

In the late eighteenth century, however, this world view came to be questioned by a minority, small but significant because they were the thinkers and artists who were to reshape Western thought and culture. These early modern men came to feel that they had lost contact with God, the source of meaning and value in the classical world which they had inherited. The heavens that once declared God's glory had become ominously silent or, at best, perversely uncommunicative. God's disappearance undermined, also, the thought and institutions, those human embodiments of divine order and meaning, which previously had constituted man's most concrete reality, leaving him utterly disoriented.[6] Isolated from God, alienated from nature, bereft of values and uncertain of self, man was forced to seek reality within himself and to evolve from his own sense of consciousness a new set of values that were necessarily individualistic and subjective. The older values had given definition to the individual and pattern to his actions by imposing upon him a system derived from the external order which they reflected; the new values, emanating from within the individual, were to be used, in contrast, for imposing order and meaning upon the otherwise chaotic world. Thus, man's self, his "soul," as Goethe, Browning, and Baudelaire alike called it, became his chief concern.

As Carlyle pointed out, however, the self within exists less as an absolute entity than as a dynamic possibility.[7] Modern man faced the almost overwhelming task of creating values from a self that was paradoxically at once the source and the end product of his actions. Under the old dispensation the good life was possible although not easy; under the new, even its possibility was questionable. Man stood, as Browning's Childe Roland, in the midst of a plain on which the road back toward the past and the road toward the future were alike obliterated.

Perhaps it would be more accurate to say that for Browning and most of his contemporaries God was obscured rather than dead. Certainly Browning had not reached the nihilism that Nietzsche was to express later in the century. Browning held it probable that God would not again emerge in his old guise as transcendental law giver; he was confident that he would not appear again in any form in response to traditional modes of supplication and search. Browning early lost his faith in Enlightenment rationalism, political activism, religious institutionalism, and evangelical pietism. How was he to discover a meaning and value in life without these traditional aids? That search remained the central action of his poetic career.

His problem was twofold. Like all men, he had, first of all, to determine the process by which man developed the self-consciousness from which he might evolve values that would illuminate his world. This activity is inevitably an imaginative, creative one which demands that all men become artists to the extent of their powers, or perhaps more accurately to the extent of their willingness to act out those powers, great or small. Beyond this, however, the special artist—the poet, the painter, the musician—had another task. If he were to transcend the private, he had to create not only his own "soul" but an artifice capable of bringing together into a coherent vision which transforms the part into the whole and the merely private into the universal. These two problems are of course closely related.

At the height of his early career, looking back over his entire work but attempting particularly to clarify his objective in *Sordello,* Browning declared that his "stress lay on the incidents in the development of a soul." He obviously meant that he had attempted to depict that process by which a character achieves self-awareness. In *Fifine at the Fair,* he elaborates,

> *Alack, our life is lent,*
> *From first to last, the whole, for this experiment,*
> *Of proving what I say—that we ourselves are true.*

True, in context of the poem, clearly means real, authentic. In his last long poem he gives the idea of soul even sharper focus in a statement which brings inner and outer, metaphysical and material world together in a productive relation:

> *soul's first act*
> *(Call consciousness the soul—some name we need)* [*is*]
> *Getting itself aware, through stuff decreed*
> *Thereto (so call the body). . . .*

Becoming aware of one's self through the stuff of this body and the things of this world is the aim, conscious or unconscious, realized or unrealized, of Browning's *dramatis per-*

sonae. It is, indeed, for Browning the primary aim of all men.

In the three earliest poems, Pauline's poet, Paracelus, and to some extent Sordello attempt to possess God and to achieve self-realization immediately and wholly without material mediation. All fail. Sordello does come, however, to face the reality of his creaturehood and the limitations which that implies. He discovers that man's mind is limited and that he lacks capacity for immediate and total communion with God. Between him and the Infinite lies the obscuring reality of his own finiteness, a barrier that can neither be glossed over nor eradicated. By the time Browning finished *Sordello* he had discovered the general direction he was to pursue for the rest of his career.

Browning, characteristically, attempted to turn man's limitations into strengths. Although man must forego the perfect knowledge, the complete vision, he can realize some saving portion of Infinity through his finite faculties. The very fact that each of his efforts falls short of full realization provides incentive for his continuing to strive, to grow, to develop—in short, to remain spiritually alive, completely man. The dynamic rather than the static, the state of becoming rather than of being, shapes the amorphous gestalt from which Browning viewed human experience.

In his poetry after *Sordello,* Browning for a while gave up hope of achieving the total vision and contented himself with the patient observation and careful depiction of those fragments of Infinity permitted him. Multiplicity and diversity rather than completeness and singleness became his aim. Hence, the dramatis personae. Each of his men and women represents another fragment of the tantalizing but unattainable whole. Each records the personal search of a character for self. This is not to say that each of Browning's characters succeeds in discovering the nature of his being. Far from it. More often than not, Browning's poems seem to argue, man's real interests are obscured and tragically misdirected by pressures from dead conventions and institutions outside himself. His will is blunted and sometimes perverted by his human inadequacies. Actually, few of Browning's characters achieve wholeness, complete and satisfying self-realization. Nevertheless, we infer, even man's hostile, negating actions are perverse forms of his natural drive for self-completing action. Man's nature is to grow. In the dynamic state of becoming man achieves his highest manhood.

To describe this search—both his own and that of his characters—[8] was Browning's first concern; this desire shapes the vision that produced the great dramatic monologues, a creative effort culminating in *Men and Women* (1855) and *Dramatis Personae* (1864). Browning could not remain content, however, with capturing the isolated fragments. Increasingly, he became concerned to bring his men and women together in some pattern which would suggest, if not represent, a total vision of human experience. Such a vision might reveal a metaphysical ground for values, a common pattern for conduct. *The Ring and the Book* represents his first major attempt after *Sordello* to achieve this more comprehensive objective. Between these two works, Browning had learned much. He would not again make the mistakes of his youth. The structuring of life on the basis of a transcendental vision of God was for him no longer possible. (On one level *The Ring and the Book* is one of the most nihilistic poems of the nineteenth century.) Moreover, Browning had considerably improved his technique. What he had learned about creating character served him well.

Browning still had problems, in spite of his intellectual and artistic advances. To create a coherent, universal vision of human experience requires some perspective, some point of view, from which to work. Up to this point in his career, Browning had more or less evaded this dilemma.[9] Now he needed a system to bring his highly individual fragments into a whole. That he satisfactorily solved the problem is questionable. He had discarded the transcendental view of his youth; he was dissatisfied with his objective, fragmentary vision of men and women. At the same time, he rejected any externally applied system of organization that would violate their personal integrity. At times, he anticipates modern existentialism; indeed, he postulates as the ultimate reality something much like the "necessary fiction" of Wallace Stevens. His efforts to discover a ground for universal values are central in all his poetry beginning with *The Ring and the Book.* He comes closest to achieving his objective in *Fifine at the Fair* (1871) and *Parleyings With Certain People of Importance in Their Day* (1887). My second major aim in this book is to trace that struggle and to define, as nearly as I am able in the light of the evidence, the end to which it led.

Wallace Stevens has said, "Now that we no longer have religion we must look to poetry for life's redemption." Browning would not have made the statement in precisely those terms, but he would have understood Stevens' meaning, for he increasingly came to regard art as man's most— perhaps *only*—significant activity. He no longer held that art actually embodied the transcendental reality; he did assert that through the imaginative structures of art man experienced a sense of participating in meaning and value. In *Parleyings With Certain People of Importance in Their Day,* Browning created the image that embodies his understanding of the artist and his work and at the same time provides the best perspective from which to approach his poetry. Art, he declared, is the artifice, the glass, which brings the Infinite the refracted rays of the sun, into focus, reducing and unifying them so that they become meaningful and useful to man.

Although this image expresses Browning's conception of art more fully than any other, it still is not entirely satisfactory. Art, indeed, provides a point of view that aids us in our search for meaning and value. It provides incentive for and makes self-defining action possible. Nevertheless, we are not to assume that any work of art or, for that matter, any body of artistic works can reveal Truth absolutely and finally. To assume that it can belies one of Browning's deepest convictions, arrived at when he was working on *Sordello:* The created artifice must be as multifaceted and dynamic as that which it records. It is crucial to remember that it depicts an internal rather than an external order or process, man's perception of meaning and not Meaning itself.

The image of the glass becomes more comprehensive and satisfying in *Parleyings.* There Browning presents the poet as myth maker, the creator of the imaginative vision, and the poet's work as the artifice of his mythic rendering of that reality. Man needs myth since he is incapable of responding directly to the Infinite and unable to act out any Ideal. But the necessary myth is potentially dangerous. When it ceases to operate as myth, or imaginative illusion —as it so readily can and generally does—and becomes a proscriptive intellectual or religious system, it enslaves rather than liberates. All the dead creeds and institutions standing between men and themselves are poetic myths which, preserved beyond their usefulness, have been transformed into external systems and forced into services they were never intended to perform. Myth must function both to fix and to free, to order and to destroy, to orient and to disorient. It must, above all, remain the dynamic, everchanging, multifaceted expression in finite and concrete terms of man's ever changing sense of the Infinite.

Art significantly is not an analogy for or a symbol of the Infinite. Neither is it a platform from which man leaps from this world into another. On the contrary, art fixes firmly on this world, circumscribing man's activities, indeed, but at the same time imbuing his finite efforts with a boundless significance.

In brief, then, my primary purpose in this book is to show how Browning sought to display the development of the individual "soul," as both the source and end of values, and to declare his vision of human experience, portrayed through men and women as the poet brings them together in that unified pattern of artifice that is his art. My second purpose is to relate Browning's achievements to the developing modern tradition.

THE FOCUSING ARTIFICE

❦ ❦ ❦ CHAPTER I

"Soul's Precocious Start"

> . . . *our road*
> *Is one, our times of travel many; thwart*
> *No enterprising soul's precocious start*
> *Before the general march.*
>
> (*Sordello*, VI, *310–313*)
>
> *This life to feed my soul, direct, oblique,*
> *But always feeding!*
>
> (*Sordello*, VI, *355–356*)

❦ Neither modesty nor fear caused Robert Browning to publish his first poem, *Pauline*, anonymously. As early as 1833, he had chosen to make the interior life of a character, not that of the poet himself, the subject of his poetry. We can accept his statement to John Forster that *Pauline* was part of a "foolish plan" in which he hoped to "assume and realize I know not how many different characters" through "this poem, the other novel, such an opera, such a speech, etc., etc." Browning failed to complete this early ambitious scheme, but the fact that he conceived it suggests that from the beginning he thought of the poem as a "soul" study of an imaginary character.

Pauline and the two poems that followed, *Paracelsus* (1835) and *Sordello* (1840), bound together by a common concern, form the first stage in Browning's poetic career. Each is the story of a sensitive, creative young man that unfolds against a backdrop of disintegrating traditional values, which turns what might have been conventional rites of passage into spiritual struggles that are characteristically modern. Browning's young men ask not how soon they can maturely occupy their fathers' world but whether there is any longer a world to occupy. They look as aliens upon the immediate past with its dissolving certainties and crumbling institutions. They find in their present no external, defining structures to give them identity and purpose. The poems depict, with increasing clarity, the sense of isolation and frustration that the modern artist feels. Each attempts to trace the spiritual development of its central character as he gropes his way uncertainly toward self-understanding and self-expression. The three poems also illustrate Browning's own groping for a structure that would give organic expression to the development of a soul. In one sense, then, these are apprentice poems; on the other hand, in at least one of them, *Sordello*, Browning shows an intellectual and artistic maturity that places the poem among his finest achievements.

I ❦ *Pauline*

Browning's contemporaries agreed that in *Pauline* the young poet had failed. Today we are less eager to reverse their judgment than to understand what Browning was trying to do. *Pauline* recounts a typical Victorian "soul crisis," treating three stages in the poet's development: his childhood innocence; his falling away from faith; his return.

Admittedly hard to follow, the story, in broad outlines, is as follows: The poet addresses Pauline, his mistress-confessor, hinting vaguely of an evil of which he must purge himself. To Shelley, his "Sun Treader," he attributes, paradoxically, both his apostasy and, partly, his return. Proposing to cleanse himself by confession, he traces, in uncertain pattern, his loss of faith and his capacity to feel and love. Describing that period in his past when, having become skeptical and rationalistic, he felt his emotional life and his creative faculties atrophy, he writes now of his spiritual recovery, achieved with the help of Shelley and Pauline.

Browning seemed to realize that his early poem might be misunderstood. Through the persona Pauline, he comments following line 811:

> I fear indeed that my poor friend may not always be perfectly understood in what remains to be read of this strange fragment, but he is less suitable than any other to make clear that which of its very nature can never be any more than dream and confusion. Moreover, I do not know whether in trying better to coordinate certain parts one would not run the risk of destroying the only merit which such a unique work might claim, that of giving a fairly precise idea of the genre of which it is only a rough sketch. This unpretentious beginning, this stirring of passion which at first increases and then by degrees subsides, these transports of the soul, the sudden return upon the self, and above all that way of thinking which is peculiar to my friend make changes almost impossible. . . . I think that in that which follows he alludes to a particular examination which he once made of the soul, or rather his own soul, to discover the sequence of objects that it would be possible for him to achieve, each of which, having been obtained, was to form a kind of plateau from which he could perceive other ends, other projects, other pleasures which, in their turn, were to be

surmounted. What resulted was that unconsciousness and sleep would put an end to everything. This conception, which I do not fully understand, is perhaps as unintelligible to him as it is to me.

In one sense, at least, Browning understood perfectly what he wanted to do; he was less certain of his ability to do it. The tumultuous flow of experience which defies traditional logic and coherence helps to define his subject, the development of a soul; his method, an associationally related montage, communicates the sense of an experience.

"I believe in God, and truth, and love." This is the position he reaches at the end of the poem. But it is also that from which he started years earlier. In a traditional sense, the poem has no action; yet it is not static. Something happens. A Freudian might discover a death wish, a desire to return to the womb, a rejection of maturity and responsibility. Terrified by the responsibilities of manhood, the speaker seems to retreat to childhood. Pauline, initially his mistress, later comes to represent his mother:

> No more of this—we will go hand in hand,
> I will go with thee, even as a child,
> Looking no further than thy sweet commands.
>
> (947–949)

Early vowed to liberty and to social action (lines 417–428), the young man seeks solitary refuge at the end of the poem.

On another level, we must seriously consider his position at the end of the poem. That the two actions are imperfectly integrated thematically and artistically is a serious weakness. He returns to occupy once more, but on different terms, the ground he earlier surrendered. He goes back much as Wordsworth returned to the spot above Tintern Abbey, not sentimentally, to become a child again, but from his new perspective, to remake his past. Between this position and his earlier profession lies a body of experience. What once he passively accepted as part of his cultural heritage, he comes to possess as experience, thus turning abstraction into reality. The real, he suggests, lies not in the end of experience, not in formulations and institutions, but in experience itself, dynamically realized and presently felt.

That his final affirmation seems inconclusive (Pauline's comment suggests this) is part of its genuineness. Truth is dynamic, developing; it must not become static. His return is only the beginning; beyond lie "other ends, other projects, other pleasures, which, in their turn, were to be surmounted."

Perhaps readers have associated Browning too exclusively with the speaker of the poem. Browning is present also in Pauline, particularly in the comment just quoted, and in the poet, Shelley, under whose influence Browning early fell and to whom he pays homage in *Pauline*. Browning was embarrassed when his contemporaries failed to distinguish between himself and his character. Clearly he intended to identify himself wholly with no one persona; nevertheless, the speaker must reflect partially his own malaise. Like most sensitive men after the mid-eighteenth century, Browning's narrator discovered the sterility of reason and felt the collapse of his ideological and institutional world. Victim of what Carlyle called "dry as dust" reason, he could no longer believe in an ideal order, and with loss of faith went his capacity to love and to create. The speaker's problem (it was also Browning's, Wordsworth's, Coleridge's, Shelley's, and Carlyle's—Browning's friend Joseph Arnould referred to *Pauline* as Browning's *Sartor Resartus*) was to discover a new structuring principle that would make possible once more the life of the imagination.

His problem is less what to believe than how to believe. He realizes that the old certainties of Newtonian physics, Lockean psychology, and neo-Aristotelian philosophy (so perfectly reflected in the heroic couplet) are dead and that with their demise went the systematic thought and the social and religious institutions they sustained. Collapse of his early vision of a just society founded on reason has left him spiritually impotent. Toward his restoration Shelley performs dual roles. He is initially the apostle of reason and Utopia, whose views reveal to the young poet the irrationality of his childhood faith. All too soon he discovers, however, that the new hopes which Shelley inspired are equally indefensible, and his resulting despair over this dual loss leads to the unspecified aberrations for which he must confess:

> First went my hopes of perfecting mankind,
> And faith in them—then freedom in itself,
> And virtue in itself—and then my motives' ends,
> And powers and loves; and human love went last.
> (458–461)

Shelley, as the poem progresses, comes to symbolize the constructive force of love rather than reason.

Pauline performs multiple roles: mistress, mother, friend, alter ego, perhaps even God. Shelley as the constructive force of love merges with Pauline, to signify the yielding of reason to love, or rationalization to imagination.

The end of the action seems on the one hand to signal a rejection of maturity and, on the other, to assert a spiritual awakening. The problem results from confusion rather than complexity; Browning was uncertain of his purpose. At the conclusion of the poem, however, the speaker, impelled by love and the imaginative vision which it makes

possible, affirms anew his belief in God and truth and love
and sets out on a new venture that supposedly symbolizes
his spiritual recovery. The conclusion, ambiguous and
vague, fails to satisfy our expectations.

Both subject matter (the development of a soul) and
structure are original. Browning hoped to create a new
form in which a speaker, through confession, presented a
dynamic portrait of his inner life. The speaker begins in
the middle of his experience; he talks about it not as it
occurred, or as any fragment of it might have appeared at
the time it was occurring, but as he now experiences it and
as it is reconstructed by the present. This attempt to communicate the sense of the developing experience required a
new organization and a new expression. Browning sacrificed chronological order, narrative development, and lin-
guistic conventions, attempting to mirror structurally the
movement of consciousness itself. Occasionally he succeeds
brilliantly; too often he falls into vagueness and incoher-
ence.

The poem is addressed to Pauline, to Shelley, to God,
and to the reader. Although it is not a mature monologue,
it anticipates some of the elements that characterize
Browning's later achievements.[1] A speaker addresses an auditor, in this case several auditors. The creation of Pauline,
in spite of her insubstantiality, is a genuine triumph. Her
presence makes the confession possible and also helps produce a sense of immediacy.

The reception of the poem in 1833 was a disappointment to Browning. Among his critics, almost all of them
unsympathetic, John S. Mill alone was helpful. Mill's
notes, scribbled in the margins of his copy of the poem and
intended as material for a review that he never wrote, fell
into Browning's hands with salutary results. Browning was
particularly jolted by the following: "With considerable
poetic power, this writer seems to me possessed with a

more intense and morbid self-consciousness than I ever knew in any sane human being." Mill obviously interpreted *Pauline* as straight autobiography, referring to it on one page as a "psychological history of himself." It is often said that this remark changed Browning's way of writing, transforming him from a subjective into an objective poet. This is not quite accurate. If we accept Browning's statement of intention (the truth of which is borne out by the poem), he meant *Pauline* to be objective. Moreover, he remained interested in the inner life of his characters; to the end of his life he used his own ideas and experiences as materials for his poems. He did realize, however, that if he were convincingly to dissociate himself from his personae he had to develop a more skillful manner of writing.

In an introduction to the 1868 edition of the poem, Browning wrote:

> The thing was my earliest attempt at "poetry always dramatic in principle, and so many utterances of so many imaginary persons, not mine," which I have since written according to a scheme less extravagant and scale less impracticable than were ventured upon in this crude preliminary sketch—a sketch that, on review, appears not altogether wide of some hint of the characteristic features of that particular *dramatis persona* it would fain have reproduced: good draughtsmanship, however, and right handling were far beyond the artist at that time.

I know of no better comment on the poem. Browning rightly realized its significance and its limitations. He learned much from *Pauline,* and, although he was unable to formulate his statement about it until much later, undoubtedly he turned to his new poem in March, 1833, a wiser and more mature poet.

II ❦ *Paracelsus*

That new poem was *Sordello*. The new effort was obviously intended to correct the weaknesses of *Pauline* and to say effectively what earlier he had bungled. Again Browning's subject was the developing soul of a poet, but in order to avoid charges of "morbid self-consciousness" he chose as his speaker a historical figure, Sordello, the late twelfth-century Mantuan poet whom Dante referred to as having created the Italian language. Sordello obviously appealed to Browning because he tried to create a language, a mode of communicating an illusive, complex truth, and also because he failed.

In spite of Browning's eagerness to dissociate himself from his persona, he soon must have realized that he was writing autobiography. After working on the poem for almost a year, he abandoned it temporarily for a trip abroad. When he returned to London, he may or may not have resumed work on *Sordello*. By October, however, he had begun *Paracelsus*, another poem about the development of a soul, but in this case his subject was not only a historical figure but a scientist rather than a poet, Paracelsus (1493–1541), the Swiss-born alchemist and physician.

Paracelsus was the first of Browning's many characters borrowed from the Renaissance. His frequent pillaging of the period for subjects and characters has caused some critics to assume that he enjoyed intellectual and spiritual affinity with the age. Actually, however, Browning had little genuine historical perspective, and all his characters, whether they are from the Middle Ages, the Renaissance, or some later period, have much in common.[2] They bear names from the past and they inhabit the exterior world of another age, but intellectually and spiritually they are consistently Browning's contemporaries, if not Browning himself. He says of *Paracelsus* that the liberties he has taken with the historical figure are trifling. He is deceived. The actual time of the poem is the early nineteenth century; the central character is young Robert Browning. Once again we must read the poem against his own intellectual background.

The character's problem is one which the historical Paracelsus would not have understood: how to relate his rational and emotional faculties so as to achieve Truth, not as an abstract formula but as an experiential reality. He is frustrated by attempts to apprehend the infinite through the finite. *Paracelsus* in theme and tone is as modern as *Pauline*. Although *Pauline* is overtly confessional and *Paracelsus*, on the surface, is dramatic, the difference is more apparent than real. The pseudo-dramatic exterior of the latter merely obscures its basic confessional nature. Browning makes it clear that *Paracelsus* is no ordinary play. In his preface, he writes that

> it is an attempt, probably more novel than happy, to reverse the method usually adopted by writers whose aim it is to set forth any phenomenon of the mind or the passions, by the operation of persons and events; and that, instead of having recourse to an external machinery of incidents to create and evolve the crisis I desire to produce, I have ventured to display somewhat minutely the mood itself in its rise and progress, and have suffered the agency by which it is influenced and determined, to be generally discernable in its effects alone, and subordinate throughout, if not altogether excluded. . . .

Although the structure helped Browning obscure his presence in the poem and discouraged the misinterpretation from which *Pauline* suffered, it is not organic to his real purpose. He is interested, as he states, in the "mood" of his character in "its rise and progress," not in the action evolving from character, situation, setting, and event.

Paracelsus, like *Pauline,* depicts an inner, not an external, action.

At the beginning, Paracelsus undertakes a journey, both symbolic and literal. "I go," he says, "to prove my soul." This statement implies two significant concepts. Paracelsus must, first, prove to himself that he actually exists; that is, he must discover within himself the source for values that he no longer finds in the institutions of his culture, in Festus' church, for example. He must, second, pursue a course of action that will translate those potential values into concrete reality. He wishes, he says, to serve man through knowing, but by "knowing" he clearly does not mean ratiocination. Paracelsus begins where the hero of Pauline leaves off. In the following lines he both describes truth as an emanation from within rather than an imposition from without and suggests the means by which the potential may be translated into the actual:

> *Truth is within ourselves; it takes no rise*
> *From outward things, whate'er you may believe:*
> *There is an inmost centre in us all,*
> *Where truth abides in fulness; and around,*
> *Wall within wall, the gross flesh hems it in,*
> *Perfect and true perception—what is truth;*
> *A baffling and perverting carnal mesh*
> *Which blinds it, and makes error: and, "to know"*
> *Rather consists in opening out a way*
> *Whence the imprison'd splendour may dart forth,*
> *Than in effecting entry for the light*
> *Supposed to be without.*
>
> (I, 726–737)

The significance of these lines lies in the radical shift from the objective to the subjective, from the external to the internal. Although Paracelsus' pilgrimage does not terminate in the discovery of an objective grail, something outside himself that gives shape and meaning to life, something does happen. Precisely what that is I shall discuss later. It is enough to observe now that he must make the journey in order to prove his soul and to release the inward splendors. Action in Browning's poetry, often interpreted as muscular reflexes of a healthy body that Browning mistook for spiritual vigor, becomes the means for releasing the light that illuminates man's path and guides his course.

The stages through which Paracelsus moves constitute the action of the poem. It is a process, a "mood" in its "rise and progress." In *Paracelsus,* Browning again used many of the devices that he employed in Pauline. Here, however, he depicted his persona more clearly, using him with greater skill as the consciousness through which we see the thought and action of the poem. The auditors, too, are more clearly conceived and more organically related to the central action. The pseudo-dramatic form enabled Browning to avoid some of the amorphousness of *Pauline.* The external action, although by no means a series of related events, is sharper and clearer than that in the earlier poem.

Browning remained interested in presenting the actual sense of an internal movement, and in order to achieve this end he employed external action more effectively. He treated external action as it was "discernible in its effects alone, and subordinate throughout, if not altogether excluded." In traditional drama, action within a character develops simultaneously with and parallel to external action. A breakdown in one signals a corresponding breakdown in the other. Browning rejected this identification of the two, declaring his interest to be exclusively in the internal. External action ceased to be agent and became effect, subject not to causal operation of a temporal and spatial world but to the unpredictable undulation of "mood," of consciousness on its elemental level. This notion of action, revolutionary in 1834, is an unquestioned assumption among artists today.

The inner life of the character can best be traced, Browning believed, by presenting him in successive moments of crisis, each of which brings a new, perhaps temporary, vision that makes it possible for him to act once more. Browning's Paracelsus moves from one such self-confrontation to another, achieving through painful stages his final vision. Browning relates inner and outer world but turns the traditional pattern upside down, finding within the character a unity and coherence based upon psychical rather than physical laws.

In the beginning, Paracelsus is young, rebellious, unfeeling. He affirms his belief in God, and he states, with obvious sincerity, that he wishes to serve mankind. He is over-ambitious, so preoccupied with the sublime that he is careless of the humble love of his old friends, Festus and Michal, and disdainful of ordinary human beings. He rejects all past knowledge and the institutions through which it is transmitted. This in itself is not a fault, however; indeed, if Truth does reside wholly within man, as Paracelsus affirms, he is justified in his impatience with external restraints imposed upon him by his society. His error lies rather in the assumption that he can apprehend God immediately and fully. On such a solitary quest, however, he sets out; he would possess all Truth and serve all mankind.

Browning fails to record events between Paracelsus' departure from Würzburg in 1512 and his arrival in Constantinople in 1521, a hiatus in external action characteristic of Browning's method throughout the poem. Although eliminating the events themselves, he shows their effect upon Paracelsus, who, discouraged, comes to question the reality of his original vision and the meaningfulness of his journey. "I sicken," he says in despair, "on a dead gulf streaked with light/ From its own putrifying depths alone" (II,

175–176). At this psychological moment, Aprile, the poet, enters.

Aprile, too, has tried and failed to serve mankind, but through love rather than knowledge. Apparently by love Aprile means something closer to artistic imagination than to human affection. Like Paracelsus, however, he has pursued the abstract ideal, scorning the finite means through which he might have realized a genuine affection. Dying, he discovers his mistake. Man, the finite creature, can possess infinity, he realizes, only in fragments and through some mediating structure. If he could start over, he muses, he would begin with the lowliest forms and gradually work toward that union with God which he had attempted to grasp immediately and entirely. Assuming in Paracelsus a wholeness that is not actually there, he pays him homage:

> My king! and envious thoughts could outrage thee!
> Lo, I forget my ruin, and rejoice
> In thy success, as thou! Let our God's praise
> Go bravely through the world at last! What care
> Through me or thee? I feel thy breath . . . why, tears?
> Tears in the darkness—and from thee to me?
>
> (II, 612–617)

This unselfish gesture toward Paracelsus is an act of complete abnegation, of perfect human love. Through it the discouraged Paracelsus glimpses a new vision and finds a new impulse to action. He aspires again.

He goes to Basel where, as teacher, he attempts to realize Aprile's idea, but to his great frustration he can feel only contempt for the stupidity and wickedness of his pupils. Becoming bitter and cynical, he experiences once more a sense of failure and futility. Finally, driven from Basel, he sends for Festus. Obviously drunk, he pours out his tortured soul, displaying a shocking coarseness and cynicism. He takes perverse pleasure in the hatred of the rabble, and he invites Festus' scorn:

> *Do you not thoroughly despise me, Festus?*
> *No flattery! One like you needs not be told*
> *We live and breathe deceiving and deceived.*
> *Do you not scorn me from your heart of hearts,*
> *Me and my cant, my petty subterfuges—*
> *These rhymes, and all this frothy shower of*
> *   words—*
> *My glozing self-deceit—my outward crust*
> *Of lies, which wrap, as tetter, morphew, furfair*
> *Wrap the sound flesh?—so see you flatter not!*
> *Even God flatters! but my friend, at least,*
> *Is true. I would depart, secure henceforth*
> *Against all further insult, hate, and wrong*
> *From puny foes: my one friend's scorn shall brand*
> *   me—*
> *No fear of sinking deeper.*
>
> (IV, 633–646)

As he earlier aspired for the heights, he now covets the depths. But he cannot rest even there. The old compulsion remains, and once more he is driven forth, resuming his quest. But, renouncing the asceticism of his youth, he now pledges himself to revel and sensual delight. Still again he aspires.

By the time we reach Book V, the issues are clear: How can Paracelsus break through the barriers of his own finiteness and of the conventions and institutions imposed upon him to release the "imprison'd splendour" within? How can he relate rational and emotional faculties to achieve infinite Truth? He needs a renewed vision, another Aprile, to help him reconcile the discrepancies less between love and knowledge than between his ideal conception of what man ought to be and what he has found man actually to be. It comes, not through a Festus or an Aprile but as a divine visitation. All creation, he perceives, from the lowest form to the sublimest spiritual manifestation, is united by common life and aspiration. Progress is the law of the spiritual and of the physical world. All creation, including man, is in a flux of continuing realization and increasing perfection. Not all men have achieved the same stage of development. Some few, like Paracelsus, are out ahead. Lesser men follow. All, nevertheless, reach toward perfection. Even man's stupidities and wickednesses are perverse expressions of the divine impulse toward progress. Men, Paracelsus discovers, can be loved for their potential and pitied for their incompleteness. This new insight provides motive for loving those he previously scorned. Finally, he attains.

At this point, we see Festus from a new perspective. A lesser man than Paracelsus, he nevertheless has his own beauty and goodness. Sitting by Paracelsus and waiting for him to regain consciousness, Festus says, in words that recall Aprile's,

> *I am for noble Aureole, God!*
> *I am upon his side, come weal or woe!*
> *His portion shall be mine! He has done well!*
> *I would have sinn'd, had I been strong enough,*
> *As he has sinn'd! Reward him or I waive*
> *Reward! If thou canst find no place for him,*
> *He shall be king elsewhere, and I will be*
> *His slave forever!*
>
> *(V. 406–413)*

These are audacious words, indeed, for the timid Festus. Obviously, he too has undergone development. He no longer stands in passive awe before formalized knowledge and established institutions. He challenges the very foundations of the theology by which his life has been governed. Here, as lover, he identifies himself with his beloved, willing even to be damned for his sake. Paracelsus represents those terrifying few who lead; Festus the many who follow. Each achieves his own perfection.

In *Paracelsus* Browning achieves a resolution to his problem by tour de force. The solution, however, contradicts his earlier assumptions about truth. Having failed to release the "imprison'd splendour," Paracelsus is saved by a vision that comes from without. It was inevitable, therefore, that Browning would return to question the validity of the mystic vision by which Paracelsus is saved. As an intellectual commitment and an artistic device, it could not long satisfy him. It did enable him, however, to bring *Paracelsus* to a conclusion, although in doing so he perhaps compromised his essential vision. Browning's contemporaries, however, recognized no inconsistency and, in spite of Browning's later remarks, showered him with praise. In an article published in the *New Monthly Magazine,* March, 1836, John Forster wrote, "Without the slightest hesitation we name Mr. Robert Browning at once with Shelley, Coleridge, and Wordsworth. He has entitled himself to a place among the acknowledged poets of the age." The young poet naturally was gratified by their praise. For the next several years he was to identify himself as "the Author of *Paracelsus.*"

III ❧ *Sordello*

The *Sordello* that Browning finally published in 1840 outraged his contemporaries. Even those who had praised *Paracelsus* were baffled, sometimes angered, by the new poem. Prior to the publication of James Joyce's *Ulysses* in 1922, *Sordello* held undisputed title to being the most obscure work in the English language. Since 1922, readers have become familiar with Joyce's techniques, and his prose, while losing none of its complexity, now seems considerably less obscure. *Sordello,* however, remains an enigma to most readers. Only the few, Ezra Pound perhaps most notable among them, have returned to give the poem the kind of patient, sympathetic reading that Joyce's novel has received. *Sordello,* we are discovering very slowly, does make sense when we read it for what it actually is.[3]

That *Sordello* is difficult, often obscure, cannot be denied. Part of the difficulty is inherent in the materials Browning used. The poem is based on the shadowy life of a thirteenth-century Italian troubadour. Born in Mantua around 1189, Sordello achieved fame both as a poet and a warrior before meeting an early, perhaps violent, death. The historical Sordello was aligned with the Ghibellines, the emperor's party, in their struggles against the Guelphs, the Pope's party. The historical record is fragmentary and confusing. Browning's retelling of the story reflects both.

More to the point, however, the obscurities of *Sordello* reflect both Browning's youth and uncertainty and his reader's unreadiness or unwillingness to accept the new complex form which he was creating. The poem's weaknesses are apparent. DeVane, in his account of Browning's composition, demonstrates that the young poet grasped his subject only slowly.[4] The complexity of the subject as it eventually emerged tested Browning's intellectual grasp and his technical faculties severely. In *Sordello,* Browning was attempting to solve what Peckham has called "The dilemma of the nineteenth century" [5] and, at the same time, to forge a literary structure organic to his new vision of reality. He was consciously experimenting. He obviously regarded his new poem as a break with his past. Early in the poem he addresses the spirit of Shelley, whose presence is felt everywhere in *Pauline* and *Paracelsus:*

> *thou, spirit, come not near*
> *Now—nor this time desert thy cloudy place*
> *To scare me, thus employed, with that pure face!*
> *I need not fear this audience, I make free*
> *With them, but then this is no place for thee!*
>
> (*I, 60–64*)

The inconclusiveness of *Pauline* and the contradictory mysticism of *Paracelsus* no longer seemed tenable, and apparently he felt that he had to free himself from the influence of Shelley before he could achieve intellectual and artistic maturity and independence. In *Sordello,* he seems to say, he will treat the problem honestly and uncompromisingly in his own way.

Groping for his real subject and consciously attempting to create a new structure, Browning proved less than a master of the situation. His attempt to achieve colloquialness and economy in expression, to mirror structurally the flow of consciousness, and to communicate the immediate sense of an experience often made demands that he was incapable of meeting fully. These failures were felt both by Browning and by his readers, often to the dismay of the latter.

Nevertheless, *Sordello,* with its immaturities, remains one of the great poems of the nineteenth century. Along with *The Ring and the Book, Fifine at the Fair,* and *Parleyings With Certain People of Importance in Their Day,* it is essential to an understanding of Browning.

Sordello is a decided advance conceptually and technically over the two earlier poems. Like *Pauline* and *Paracelsus, Sordello* is a soul study; like them, also, it depicts a character in search of identity. In *Sordello* Browning handles point of view more skillfully than in the earlier poems. In *Pauline* the narrator and the persona are the same; in *Paracelsus* the narrator ostensibly disappears and the persona speaks dramatically. Neither point of view seemed adequate to Browning's purpose. In *Sordello,* Browning uses both a narrator and a persona in a dialectical relation with each other. The narrator, not a passive storyteller but a participant in the action, both relates events and takes part in them, speaking from a continually shifting perspective. Thus, in *Sordello,* Browning assumes an intellectual stance that he maintained throughout his career. The dying Sordello undoubtedly reflects Browning's own view:

> *Vain ordinances, I have one appeal—*
> *I feel, am what I feel, know what I feel*
> *—So much is Truth to me—What Is then? Since*
> *One object viewed diversely may evince*
> *Beauty and ugliness—this way attract,*
> *That way repel, why gloze upon the fact?*
> *Why must a single of the sides be right?*
> *Who bids choose this and leave its opposite?*
> *No abstract Right for me—*
>
> (VI, 437–445)

That Sordello states this skeptical view possibly to justify an action which his conscience condemns in no way invalidates it. The fact that a truth may damn as well as save only heightens Sordello's problem—and Browning's.

The more complex point of view makes possible a subtler, more sophisticated action. Much of the so-called obscurity in the poem results from the reader's assumption that it is a simple account of Sordello's story. It is a great deal more. Actually it is the record of two developing souls, Sordello's and the narrator's. By having two participants in the action and by permitting each to assume shifting positions, Browning enriches and complicates the poem. Obviously, Sordello is presented less as a historical figure than as a recreation of Browning's imagination: at once historical and imaginary, ancient and modern, both Browning's subject and his mouthpiece. At the same time, the speaker does not fully represent Browning's own views. The dialectical exchange ostensibly between character and narrator perhaps actually occurs within Browning himself. In *Sordello*, Browning continues through dramatis personae a search for identity and direction. Here he succeeds—as he did not in the earlier poems—in obscuring his own identity.

The action of the poem may seem unfinished in one sense. At the conclusion, the speaker claims ironically that he has told Sordello's story, achieving what he originally set out to do. We are not convinced that he has or that, if he had, the story would have satisfied our expectations. The speaker also interests us, and we want to know what happened to him. He becomes part of the story too.

The inconclusiveness here is intentional, functioning thematically and structurally as it did not in *Pauline*. The real action arises from the relation between the speaker and Sordello and must remain unfinished. For it to achieve stasis would defeat Browning's purpose. The "development of a soul," the phrase Browning uses to describe his intent, is ambivalent. The word *develop* both denotes a process and describes a quality. The awakening soul remains the developing soul. It never can achieve finality. *Sordello*, the poem, nevertheless, has wholeness in that it satisfyingly presents one movement in that larger, never-ending action.

I shall first describe and interpret the stages through which Sordello passes and then explore the more complex meanings that arise from the relation between him and the speaker. Sordello is seen in a number of situations: his detached childhood at Goito; his first spiritual awakening, when he sings before Palma, and his subsequent disillusionment; his initial, naïve, and disastrous excursion into political action; his withdrawal once again to Goito; his second venture into the world and the series of disorienting experiences that follow—his new vision of suffering humanity (related as the speaker's but intended as Sordello's also), his resolution to serve mankind, his new conviction that the Guelphs, his old enemies, not the Ghibellines, his friends, represent the interest of the people, his disappointment with Salinguerra, and his effort to divert him to the Guelph cause, and, finally, that experience which brings on his last crisis—Salinguerra's unexpected choice of him as the new leader of the Ghibellines and his discovery that he is the old man's son.

Each stage in his development causes him to recognize as an illusion one more of the principles upon which he has tried to structure his life: romantic nature, pure art, abstract thought, social and religious institutions, political action. His sense of isolation and frustration increases until finally, faced with an apparent impasse, he breaks under the tension.

He describes his inner life suggestively as a fluid, unshaped, but tumultuous body of water, waiting for some external force to give it structure and direction, as the moon governs the currents of the sea:

> The real way seemed made up of all the ways—
> Mood after mood of the one mind in him;
> Tokens of the existence, bright or dim,
> Of a transcendent all-embracing sense
> Demanding only outward influence,
> A soul, in Palma's phrase, above his soul,
> Power to uplift his power, this moon's control,
> Over the sea-depths, and their mass had swept
> Onward from the beginning and still kept

> Its course; but years and years the sky above
> Held none. . . .
>
> (VI, 36–46)

Sordello's painful realization that he is without direction
mirrors more accurately the dilemma of the nineteenth
century than of the thirteenth. Sordello asks—and in vain—
for guidance from some power outside himself. In his despair, following his realization that no such divine illumi-
nation is forthcoming, he reaches the depth that Paracelsus
experienced just before his vision. For Sordello, however,
there is no vision, and soul

> in foam-showers spilt,
> Wedge-like insisting, quivered now a gilt
> Shield in the sunshine, now a blinding race
> Of whitest ripples o'er the reef—found place
> For myriad charms; not gathered up and, hurled
> Right from its heart, encompassing the world.
>
> (VI, 51–56)

These lines describe both the state of Sordello's soul and
the mirroring structure of the poem. This brilliant, cascad-
ing, splitting, quivering, shifting movement of water parallels the flow of his consciousness. The long complex sentences, distorted syntax, enjambment, broken rhythmic
movement, condensation of thought, ellipsis, associationally related asyntactical elements, omission of transitional
elements between sentences and paragraphs, disregard for
chronological time, and the resulting violation of traditional ordering of structural elements are all parts of
Browning's attempt to give the reader an immediate sense
of the developing experience.

In light of *Sordello*, the speaker of *Pauline* appears particularly immature. His retreat from the world solves no

important problem. His affirmation is not convincing. Nor can Sordello accept Paracelsus' vision. Sordello remains painfully aware of his disorientation and isolation. Unable to retreat and lacking clear vision, how, he asks himself, can he act? Being a poet, he knows, involves him with the world and with men and women. His problem is that no conceivable act and no possible relationship are adequate to his spiritual need. He is eventually reduced to a psychological impasse that destroys him.

While Sordello struggles, the speaker maintains a steady flow of comments at once sympathetic and detached, understanding and critical. Ostensibly, he speaks primarily to the long-dead poet or to some unidentified audience, perhaps the reader of the poem. Actually, he addresses himself, attempting through words to explore and perhaps understand his own problems. Sordello is his foil. Like him, the speaker is aware of a breakdown in conventional values, in normal modes of communication, of the obvious impurity of every human motive and the inadequacy of every human action: in short, of the impossibility of embodying infinite aspiration in finite forms. The resulting malaise he describes as "a dim vulgar vast unobvious grief/ Not to be fancied off" (VI, 149–150). "External power!" he exclaims, and adds skeptically, "If none be adequate . . . ?" This is the fear that undermines his confidence and renders him impotent. As Sordello hesitates between the course dictated by his conscience and that opened to him by Salinguerra's action and Palma's revelation (both equally impossible), the voices of the two poets, narrator and subject, merge into a single, ambivalent, cacophonous chorus that betrays the sense of futility which both feel.

The speaker survives Sordello. Following his account of Sordello's death, he becomes the center of the action, a shift in perspective which places his relation to the work as a whole in a new light. Obviously he is more than narrator. He reflects upon Sordello's destiny, understanding and sympathizing with him but eventually withdrawing from him sufficiently to speak ambivalently about his death. This act of objective detachment marks an advance in his spiritual development.

He recalls that Palma observed what she thought was a smile of triumph on the dead poet's lips. There is also the crushed badge on the floor to signify that Sordello refused to compromise his conscience. Nevertheless, we are made to understand, his was a costly victory. Sordello is dead, having neither written his poem nor saved his people—in short, without having achieved identity. The breach between the ideal and the real is as great as ever. His example offers no real help. Unlike Paracelsus' death, his is less than complete victory. Some such thought must prompt the speaker's remarks. Salinguerra in ways scorned by Sordello had done more than he to reconcile Guelphs and Ghibellines. Dante, later, was to write the poem that refused to yield itself to Sordello's efforts. In retrospect, Eglamor, of whom both speaker and Sordello earlier were contemptuous, receives his most sympathetic comments. Eglamor at least fulfilled his nature to the extent of his capacities. His ability to love enabled him to act out his identity.

Sordello, rather than Eglamor or Dante, however, is Browning's subject in this poem precisely because he failed. He embodies the problem that remains central in all Browning's poetry: How can one in the absence of certain truth and unambiguous choices perform soul-developing action that becomes in itself a spiritual and moral end? How can one communicate infinite vision through finite means? The speaker is concerned less to solve than to define the problem. He projects his own frustrations upon a remote and quasi-historical figure in order to see them more clearly and objectively. The detachment he finally achieves permits him to analyze his problem and to develop at least one stage beyond Sordello. In the end he is able to pinpoint Sordello's difficulty, his inability to act:

> *Thus had Sordello ta'en that step alone,*
> *Apollo had been compassed—'twas a fit*
> *He wished should go to him, not he to it*
> *—As one content to merely be supposed*
> *Singing or fighting elsewhere, while he dozed*
> *Really at home—and who was chiefly glad*
> *To have achieved the few real deeds he had*
> *Because that way assured they were not worth*
> *Doing, so spared from doing them henceforth—*
> *A tree that covets fruitage and yet tastes*
> *Never itself, itself. . . .*
>
> (*VI, 832–842*)

His own efforts at least will not terminate in that self-destroying impasse.

With its obvious weaknesses, *Sordello* is not only superior to *Pauline* and *Paracelsus* but significant in its own right. The long period of introspection during which Browning wrote *Sordello* was crucial in his career; his technical experimentations were decisive. He came to understand the nature of his problem: the need for self-realization and the difficulty of achieving meaning and value in a world from which the traditional God had departed. He freed himself from the influence of the early Shelley and from the transcendental idealism of his own youth; he came to speak, although still haltingly, in a voice that was his own. The real Browning is certainly present in the earlier poems, but his image is blurred; in *Sordello* it emerges with surprising clarity. Browning was later to mature but never to change essentially. Putting the vague romantic *angst* of *Pauline* and *Paracelsus* behind him, the ironic, ambivalent poet of *Sordello* achieves a sense of direction enabling him to undertake seriously the journey that becomes his poetic career.

CHAPTER **II**

In Search of Form: The Dramas

> Columbus died almost without seeing it;
> and not really knowing what he had
> discovered. It's life that matters, nothing
> but life—the process of discovering, the
> everlasting and perpetual process, not the
> discovery itself, at all.
>
> (Dostoevsky, *The Idiot.*)

❧ Before Browning finally published *Sordello,* he had already witnessed the production of his first play. With that new sense of reality that *Sordello* records, Browning must have felt that drama provided the most promising mode of expression for his ambivalent, dialectical, ironic view. Indeed, Browning had always considered himself a dramatic poet. In his preface to *Paracelsus,* a literary form of the drama, he distinguished between the dramatic poem and the stage play. The poem he professed not quite to understand, but he asserted confidently that the nature of the drama was evident to everyone. Browning's interests seemed adapted to dramatic expression; he professed to understand the requirements of the drama.

Nevertheless, when he turned from the poem to the stage, he demonstrated less competence than we might expect.

Already interested in the theater, Browning required little urging from William Macready, the famous actor-manager, who first suggested to him that he write a play. Browning immediately interrupted his work on *Sordello* in 1836 to write *Strafford,* thus beginning an effort to write for the stage that continued for ten disappointing years. During this time he wrote eight plays: *Strafford* (1837), *Pippa Passes* (1841), *King Victor and King Charles* (1842), *The Return of the Druses* (1843), *A Blot in the 'Scutcheon* (1843), *Colombe's Birthday* (1844), *A Soul's Tragedy* (1846), and *Luria* (1846). Of these only two were produced during the forties: *Strafford* and *A Blot.* Nevertheless, only *Pippa Passes, A Soul's Tragedy,* and *Luria* were written without a stage production in mind.

Despite Browning's enthusiasm, his obvious dramatic sensibility, and, initially, the encouragement of influential friends, including Macready, Browning never wrote a successful stage play. The causes for his failure are not merely personal. Most of the major writers of the nineteenth century, many of them masters of the dramatic monologue, wrote unsuccessfully for the stage. To attribute their failure to their slavish imitation of the Elizabethans is at best a partial explanation. It is scarcely more convincing to say that the romantic view was essentially lyrical rather than dramatic. Both suggestions contain elements of truth that require considerable amplification in light of the literary milieu of the early nineteenth century. What nineteenth-century drama needed was a new structure capable of expressing a new concept, essentially modern, of dramatic action.

The subject of Browning's plays throws significant light upon his own intellectual and spiritual maturation and at the same time suggests the primary reason for his failure in the theater. Many of his plays involve political or social revolt. All were concerned with an individual's loss of direction and of values. Browning was obviously preoccupied with the disintegration of the state and of the culture that it embodied. His interests, however, were in neither the relative merits of diverse systems nor in the restoration of any system from which a meaningful order would emanate. There is, indeed, something rotten in Browning's Denmark, as there is in Shakespeare's, but Browning was unable to approach his problem from Shakespeare's perspective. For Shakespeare, the purging of the kingdom and the restoration of a meaningful order were both desirable and possible. His *Hamlet* ended not with the death of the young hero but with the triumphal entry of Fortinbras. Hamlet was lost, but society was saved. The gain is not merely political but also personal and social; the means exist once more through which human values may be realized.

For Browning, on the other hand, the rottenness of his society signaled not merely a corruption which required purging but a death that was not subject to resuscitation. His characters, in contrast to Shakespeare's, have no external order, actual or potential, to give meaning to the existences. Each, living in an essentially alien universe, must search, alone, within himself for an identity and for those new values that self-realization makes possible. Browning's plays, as a result, are studies not in a universal moral order but in individual soul development; they delineate an action in character, to use Browning's own words, rather than characters in action.

Browning carried to the theater both his interest in the development of the internal life of a character and the conviction that man's self-realization would be achieved—if it were achieved—without aid from an externally imposed set of values. The traditional dramatic forms, therefore, designed to convey action and to embody those values that result from man's harmonious relation with the natural order of the divine creation, were inadequate for his purposes. Unfortunately, Browning did not clearly realize his problem.

I ❧ *Strafford*

In early 1837, Macready expressed his disappointment with Browning's first attempt, writing in his diary on March 19: "Read Strafford in the evening, which I fear is too historical; it is the policy of the man, and its consequence upon him, not the heart, temper, feelings, that work on this policy, which Browning portrayed—and how admirably." We do not know precisely what this first version of the play was like, but we can assume that it contained even less character in action than the version that was finally produced. During the weeks in which the play was in production, Macready tried hard—often with opposition from Browning—to correct what he considered obvious mistakes. At one point he records in his diary that he and Forster "went over the play *Strafford,* altered, omitted, and made up one new scene" (April 5). He pressed Browning to make further changes but became increasingly disillusioned with the playwright, concluding shortly before the production, "Looked at Browning's alterations of the last scene of *Strafford*—found them quite bad—mere feeble rant—neither power, not nature, nor healthful fancy—very unworthy of Browning" (April 23). Browning for his part became increasingly irritated with Macready, and by the time the play opened it was clear that writer and producer were working toward opposing goals. Browning's frustrations were intensified by the fact that he was less certain than Macready about what he wanted.

It would be absurd to argue that Browning's first play might have been good if Macready had not tampered with it. At the same time, it is clear, also, that no changes Macready could make would improve it.

Strafford is the story of two men, Strafford and Pym, each dedicated to what he considers the good of England. Strafford identifies the good with King and monarchy; Pym, with the people and popular government. Both maintain their cause with difficulty. Strafford is frustrated by Charles' weakness and duplicity; Pym, by the treachery of many of his followers and by his love for Strafford, now his enemy. Superficially, the conflict is ideological and political; the external action details the complicated maneuvering of men determined to control the government. On this level, the play is hopelessly confused.

Actually, however, Browning's real concern is elsewhere. He is interested in Strafford and Pym not as representatives of opposing causes but as human beings undergoing internal conflict. He needs both characters to express the action of the play. Strafford alone might indicate that Browning was defending Charles and monarchy (an absurdity); Pym alone, that he was supporting popular government) not at all a certainty). By introducing both, Browning focuses upon a psychological rather than a political problem. The struggle between the two universalizes the conflict within each, dissociating it from any particular intellectual or moral stance. On the level of action in character, the purpose of the play is remarkably clear.

Browning brings the two together at the end of the play, after Pym has secured Strafford's death sentence. Pym speaks:

Have I done well? Speak, England! Whose sole sake
I still have laboured for, with disregard
To my own heart,—for whom my youth was made
Barren, my manhood waste, to offer up
Her sacrifice—this friend, this Wentworth here—
Who walked in youth with me, loved me, it may be,
And whom, for his forsaking England's cause,
I hunted by all means (trusting that she
Would sanctify all means) even to the block
Which waits for him. And saying this, I feel
No bitterer pang than first I felt, the hour
I swore that Wentworth might leave us, but I
Would never leave him: I do leave him now.
I render up my charge (be witness, God!)
To England who imposed it. I have done
Her bidding—poorly, wrongly,—it may be,
Will ill effects—for I am weak, a man:
Still, I have done my best, my human best,
Not faltering for a moment. It is done.
                                    (V, ii, pp. 303–304)[2]

Pym's self-defense is less that he has achieved a worthy end
than that he has done his best. Strafford replies:

I have loved England too; we'll meet then, Pym,
As well die now! Youth is the only time
To think and to decide on a great course:
Manhood with action follows; but 't is dreary,
To have to alter our whole life in age—
The time past, the strength gone! As well die now.
When we meet, Pym, I'd be set right—but now!
Best die. Then if there's fault, fault too
Dies, smothered up. Poor grey old little Laud
May dream his dream out, of a perfect Church,

In some blind corner. And there's not one left.
I trust the King now wholly to you, Pym!
And yet, I know not: I shall not be there:
Friends fail—if he have any. And he's weak,
And loves the Queen, . . . oh, my fate is nothing—
Nothing! But not that awful head—not that!
                                                    (V, ii, p. 305)

Strafford, weary and disillusioned, claims victory only for not having betrayed "that awful head." His struggle is less clear than Pym's. There are moments when his devotion seems more to a man—an unworthy man—than to an ideal. To love Charles more than Pym and his children appears perverse. Yet Strafford's devotion is to Charles the symbol rather than to Charles the man, to an obligation rather than to a whim:

        Then, Lucy, then, dear child,
    God put it in my mind to love, serve, die
    For Charles. . . .
                                        (III, ii, p. 254)

Charles is less significant as an object defining the nobility of Strafford's action than as a means of focusing and releasing his energies, making possible an action which in itself becomes noble.

Both men achieve victory, manhood with honor, not by the choices they make (they make different choices) but by choosing; not by the deeds they perform (they follow diverse courses) but by doing. We are asked to admire both. Strafford with his lost cause (in Browning one may achieve moral victory by pursuing a lost, even a "wrong" cause, e.g., "The Statue and the Bust") is no less heroic than Pym. Soul battles, Browning seems to say, are fought within the individual, not in some external arena. This is what Browning means by action in character rather than character in action. Charles, who refuses to commit himself to any course, is the lost soul.

Browning's real problem in *Strafford* was structural. Emphasizing action in character, he imposed upon himself a task he did not fully understand and for which he did not have the skill. The result was a compromise that neither pleased Macready nor met the needs of his subject.

II ❧ *King Victor and King Charles*

In spite of his temporary discouragement following the failure of *Strafford*, Browning was at work two months later on a new play, *King Victor and King Charles*. When he finished it we are not sure, but two years later, September 5, 1839, Macready refers to it in his diary: "Read Browning's play on Victor, King of Sardinia—it turned out to be a *great mistake*." Browning's subject is again historical. King Victor, who has held his throne by guile and brutality, is at last caught in his own duplicity and decides, in order to save himself and perhaps his kingdom, to abdicate in favor of his weak son, Charles. Obviously, he intends to repossess the crown once the crisis is over. Charles, however, much to everyone's surprise, with the help of his strong wife, Polyxena, proves a wise and just ruler. When his father a year later demands return of the crown, Charles refuses. Victor then plots to repossess it by force, and Charles has him arrested as a traitor. The old king, obviously shaken by his son's unexpected firmness, is forced to humble himself. Charles then gives the crown that earlier he has refused to have taken from him, reversing the situation at the beginning of the play: Charles is now giver; Victor, recipient. The experience is too much for the old man and he dies. The curtain goes down with the implication that Charles will once more become king, having demonstrated both strength and generosity.

The concept is dramatic. But Browning is less interested in "a terrible event without consequences" (Browning's preface) than in character. His theme, the development of Charles, is significant; his conflict, between the characters and within character, is potentially theatrical.

Critics agree with Macready: the play fails. In some respects, however, it is an advance over *Strafford*. Honan rightly observes that "the prosodic and imagistic elements that had been sacrificed in *Strafford* are to some extent recovered in *King Victor,* and without a return to the undramatic and rather lyrical type of speech of *Paracelsus*" (*Browning's Characters,* 59). There are other structural gains also. The play relates crucial situations in the development of Charles' soul, situations less important in themselves than for their effect upon character. The most promising thing about *King Victor* is that Browning eliminates much of the irrelevant external action that cluttered *Strafford*. There is a closer relation in *King Charles* between inner action and external form. What Browning needed was a new flexible structure that would embody dramatically the action in character that was his concern. He was handicapped not merely by a failure of imagination but by the external pressures of tradition and contemporary taste. The structure remains an inadequate expression of the dramatic action.

III ✤ *The Return of the Druses*

Browning's next play, *The Return of the Druses,* was announced as nearly ready with the publication of *Sordello* in

1839. It was finished by the summer of 1840, for on August 3 of that year, Macready wrote, "Read Browning's play, and with deepest concern. I yield to the belief that he will *never write again*—to any purpose. I fear his intellect is not quite clear." We know that Macready had lectured Browning on the shortcomings of *King Victor* and we suspect that among other things he complained about the play's lack of action. At any rate, Browning appears determined not to fail again in that respect. *The Return of the Druses* contains more spectacular and violent action than any of his earlier plays.

It is the story of Djabal, who, to free his people, the Druses, and to win the love of Anael, proclaims himself the reincarnation of the god Hakeem. At first he justifies this deception as the means to a good end, but he comes finally almost to believe that he is indeed the god. He arranges for Venetian ships to take the Druses to Lebanon and prepares for their departure by plotting the assassination of the tyrannical prefect. When he enters the ruler's chambers, however, he finds him already dead; Anael stands over him with a bloody sword. She had done the deed to make herself worthy of her god-lover. When Djabal confesses his deception, she recognizes that her act is mere human violence, not part of a divine plan. Conscience-stricken and disappointed, she accuses Djabal before the Druses. As they are about to renounce him, she falls dead at his feet. The credulous Druses assume that Hakeem has stricken her for blasphemy and prostrate themselves before Djabal. He, assuming once more the role thrust upon him, directs his people to the Venetian ships and then stabs himself.

Ironically, while Djabal and Anael are destroying themselves, the freedom of the Druses is achieved for all practical purposes without their aid. Djabal's old friend, Loys de Dreux, arrives on the island as the new prefect, fully dedicated to liberal government.

The personal tragedy of the characters is only loosely related to the political fate of the people. In such plays as *Oedipus Rex* and *King Lear,* the fate of the hero and that of society are identical. Even when the hero meets death it is a sacrificial death resulting paradoxically in a new life for both society and himself. Unlike the older dramatists, however, Browning does not necessarily identify the fate of the individuals with that of society. His concern is primarily with character and only incidentally with politics and social reform. The Druses are liberated, indeed, but finally this seems relatively unimportant. We are more concerned about the dead Anael and Djabal. As a result, Djabal's last speech, "On to the Mountain! At the Mountain, Druses!" seems mere rhetoric. Anael is dead; as he speaks, Djabal is dying. Their deaths are pointless, not sacrificial. The deliverance of the Druses comes only indirectly through their suffering. The return of Loys as prefect makes the latter action of the play unnecessary, a mere trick of chance.

Clearly the central action, and consequently our concern, is the destruction of the characters. Djabal summarizes his problem:

> *Ah, was it thou betrayedst me? Then, speak!*
> *'Tis well—I have deserved this—I submit—*
> *Nor 'tis much evil thou inflictest—life*
> *Ends here. The cedars shall not wave for us—*
> *For there was crime, and must be punishment.*
> *See fate! By thee I was seduced—by thee*
> *I perish—yet do I, can I repent!*
> *I, with an Arab instinct thwarted ever*
> *By my Frank policy,—and, in its turn,*
> *A Frank brain thwarted by my Arab heart—*
> *While these remained in equipoise I lived*
> *Nothing; had either been predominant,*
> *As a Frank schemer or an Arab mystic*

I had been something;—now, each has destroyed
The other—and behold from out their crash
A third and better nature rises up—
My mere Man's-nature. And I yield to it—
I love thee—I—who did not love before!

(V, p. 18)

This is not a tragedy of fate. It is a modern psychological drama. Like Sordello, Djabal is destroyed by inaction. He is at odds with himself as a result of his antithetical Arab-Frank nature. He talks about crime and punishment, but by his attitude toward repentance he demonstrates that these terms are for him psychological rather than moral. Although his language is vaguely religious, his final vision is humanistic. His plight is that victory—his new manhood—is purchased at so high a price. By the time he understands his situation it is too late. Anael is destroyed by unendurable inner conflicts, and Djabal kills himself, his suicide symbolizing the death of the spirit that has already occurred.

Browning's error is not that his subject fails to achieve tragic proportion. His was not the tragic vision. What he has to say, however, is significant in its own right and worthy of its own kind of dramatic treatment. Browning's weakness, here as elsewhere, lies in his inability to create a new structure capable of expressing precisely that action which is his concern. His borrowed external actions and techniques are inappropriate.

IV ❧ *A Blot in the 'Scutcheon*

Stung by Macready's rejection of his previous two plays and prepared to make whatever compromises necessary to see his next work produced, Browning wrote *A Blot in the 'Scutcheon* during the fall of 1840. His subject matter is in certain respects derivative, particularly of *Romeo and Juliet* and *Much Ado About Nothing*. He wrote Macready:

> "The luck of the third adventure" is proverbial. I have written a spick and span new Tragedy (a sort of compromise between my own notion and yours—as I understand it, at least) and will send it to you if you care to be bothered so far. There is *action* in it, drabbing, stabbing, et autres gentillesses,—who knows but the Gods may make me good even yet? [3]

Precisely. It is the most disappointing, because the most perverse, of Browning's plays. "Compromise" is scarcely the word to describe his work. In this play, Browning capitulated completely to what he thought Macready wanted, creating for him an external "action" which negated any good his original idea might have contained.

In spite of its Shakespearean echoes and its traditional claptrap, *A Blot in the 'Scutcheon* contains the germinal idea of a new drama. It contrasts an old morality based upon abstractions and conventions with a new morality of motive rooted in the subjective life of a character. Its central concern is not the death of the star-crossed lovers but the act of self-discovery within Tresham.

Earl Tresham, possessor of a blotless 'scutcheon, is in the process of betrothing his sister, Mildred, to the esteemed young Earl Mertoun when he discovers that she entertains a suitor nightly in her chamber. Wishing to right things, Tresham apprehends the furtive suitor, who proves to be young Mertoun himself. Tresham slays him without giving him opportunity to argue the purity of his illicit love. Tresham then carries the news of Mertoun's death to Mildred. In a scene in which Browning shows unusual insight into character, Tresham both bares the details of his horrible deed and betrays by implication his own incestuous love for Mildred. With compelling irony, Browning redirects the condemnation until he that condemns is condemned, he that judges is judged. The family 'scutcheon is marred less by the erring Mildred than by the righteous, selfish older brother. At last Tresham achieves insight:

> *Had I but heard him—had I let him speak*
> *Half the truth—less—had I looked long on him,*
> *I had desisted! Why, as he lay there,*
> *The moon on his flushed cheek, I gathered all*
> *The story ere he told it! I saw thro'*
> *The troubled surface of his crime and yours*
> *A depth of purity immovable!*
> *Had I but glanced, where all seemed turbidest*
> *Had gleaned some inlet to the calm beneath!*
> *I would not glance—my punishment's at hand.*
>
> (III, ii, p. 15)

Once again enlightment comes too late. Overcome by emotion and having lost will to live, Mildred falls upon Tresham's neck. She is scarcely dead when he too is seized, a victim of poison he has taken earlier.

Tresham defends traditional moral and social values at the cost of three lives. In the play, morality is subjected to a new, humanistic standard. What first appears right proves wrong, and what wrong, right. Mertoun and Mildred talk about "sin" and "punishment," but clearly their error is more imagined that real, their punishment more the reflexes of convention than judgment of universal moral law. Browning repeats the position he took in *Strafford* and *The Return of the Druses*. Within themselves, Tresham realizes, Mertoun and Mildred remain pure, something he can no longer claim for himself. If there is tragedy in their unfortunate end, it comes less from their offense against goodness than from their disregard of social convention. Their predicament has neither pity nor terror, as Aristotle used those terms. The real sinner is the "righteous" Tresham.

Browning's defense of the lovers is not sentimental, although his play often falls into sentimentality. Mildred is not the golden-hearted prostitute of popular romance. Browning does not suspend all moral law, offering instead of judgment the soft heart as a guide to conduct. Rather he seeks a new and more relevant definition of morality. The ultimate morality, he seems to say, stems from something that the character *is* rather than from abstractions and conventions imposed upon him. Mildred is justified because in the deepest sense she is right, not because she is young, has no mother, and is forgotten by God.

Very little of this comes through the melodramatic situations and traditional structure. Having decided upon "drabbing, stabbing, et autres gentillesses," he has no alternative but to follow through. The conclusion is absurd, but at least it is consistent with the rest of the play. In this performance, Browning seems less victim than willing collaborator. Macready kept the play for two years before finally producing it in 1843. Browning was rewarded by seeing it run for three nights.

V ❧ Colombe's Birthday

The failure brought to a climax the quarrel between Browning and Macready, and the two parted, not to speak again for many years. Consequently, Browning's next play, *Colombe's Birthday,* was written for Charles Kean and his wife. Unable to agree with Kean on a production date, however, Browning published it unacted, as No. VI of *Bells and Pomegranates* in 1844.

At the opening of *Colombe's Birthday,* Colombe, Duchess of Juliers and Cleves, is virtually prisoner of her own palace guard. Under their control, she has served a year as Duchess. We learn immediately that Prince Berthold is en route to the palace with authority to assume rule of her duchy. Into this crisis comes Valence, a Perseus-like figure, to love and save her. He suffers a momentary setback when Prince Berthold offers Colombe his hand and the prospect of remaining Duchess. Browning provides her a choice between a useless life as a figurehead duchess and a meaningful life as a human being, loved and loving. We are asked to assume that a moral issue is at stake, and perhaps in Browning's mind there is, but the issue is never clearly defined or dramatically presented. The play never quite comes to life. Browning avoids the worst defects of *A Blot in the 'Scutcheon* but again fails to achieve a new dramatic form or to equal the psychological depth and complexity which makes *King Victor* potentially interesting.

VI ❧ *Pippa Passes*

The misfortunes of *A Blot in the 'Scutcheon* in the theater were both disappointing and discouraging to Browning. He never again wrote with any real conviction for the stage. After *Colombe's Birthday,* he wrote two more plays, but they, like the earlier *Pippa Passes,* were not intended for the theater. Of these three, two—*Pippa* and *A Soul's Tragedy*—are most interesting. Although neither is really stageworthy, both suggest that when Browning freed himself from the demands of the early nineteenth-century theater and permitted his imagination free play, he came close to realizing the dramatic vision that was increasingly to dominate creative minds through the rest of the nineteenth century and into the twentieth.

Looking back upon his earlier work in 1885, Browning spoke of great changes taking place in the theater and pondered momentarily what he would do if he were beginning again under circumstances more favorable to experimentation than those of the thirties and forties. In a letter to Lawrence Barrett, February 3, 1885, he wrote,

> When I look back to the circumstances under which the piece [*A Blot*] was brought out in London—forty-two years ago—I may well wonder whether,—if my inclination for dramatic writing had met with half so much encouragement and assistance as you have really gratuitously bestowed on it,—I might not have gone on, for better or worse, play-writing to the end of my days; and the conditions of the stage were so much simpler then than at present, that it would not follow necessarily that, because I constructed a piece then with a view to its performance in the little Haymarket Theatre, I should not now attempt to employ more elaborate means to an end than seemed advisable when an audience was rather "all ears" than "all eyes."
>
> (Hood, *Letters,* 235)

Actually, in 1885 great changes had not occurred on the English stage, and Browning remained unfamiliar with developments in Europe. What specifically he had in mind is not clear, nor is it certain how he would have altered *A Blot.* He does say that he would have made it more visual and less auditory, a suggestion that might have tremendous implications for a dramatist. In *Pippa Passes* and *A Soul's Tragedy,* plays not written for Macready, however, we find some interesting suggestions of possible directions that Browning's work might have taken under different circumstances.

Griffin and Minchin suggest that *Pippa Passes* was conceived as a "direct contrast to *Sordello.*" [4] Certainly the idea for the play came to Browning while he was finishing *Sordello,* and the little silk weaver is the antithesis of the self-conscious poet. The play also seems a reaction against the theater of William Macready. Browning resented Macready's attempts to rewrite *Strafford* and was disappointed by its treatment on the stage. He was perhaps working at the same time on *Pippa Passes, King Victor,* and *The Return of the Druses.* In the last, as we have seen, he compromised with popular expectations in a way that must have disturbed his conscience. It was perhaps some compensation to work on *Pippa* without having to please either Macready or an audience for which he had developed contempt. The result is a bold, experimental, and in some ways exciting new work. In this play, as in nothing he had written up to this time, idea and structure work together to create a total vision of life.

Character and action are Browning's most challenging problems. *Pippa* has no traditional protagonist and no continuous external action. A play lacking these elements was indeed novel in 1841; in fact, *Pippa* was not generally regarded as a play at all. That it is a significant play, however, James P. McCormick has persuasively argued.[5] I agree.

Who or what is Pippa and how does she function in the dramatic action? The title provides a clue by focusing not on Pippa herself but on her action, her "passing." Actually, we are not concerned with Pippa; she is not a very interesting person, if indeed she is a person at all. She is neither the protagonist nor the idealization of what man ought to be. She is simple, ignorant, sometimes misguided, and at best only partially admirable. Certainly, the good she accomplishes is the result of unconscious rather than conscious action. Pippa, as I shall show, is more, a force, an impetus to action, than a character.

Nor is any other person in the play a heroic protagonist. Each is an individual upon whom Pippa exerts an irresistible influence. McCormick is right I think, when he suggests that in this play Browning is interested less in a character than in a community of characters. I think we might go so far as to say that Browning is concerned with a composite character—man, Everyman—conceived as so complex and so at odds with himself that he can be portrayed—on the stage, at least—only as a cast of characters. He tries to depict how such a person responds to life through normal human pursuits—love, art, religion. Just as the title emphasizes Pippa's passing rather than her being, the treatment of character focuses upon man's act of responding rather than upon the object to which he responds or even the ends to which his action leads.

In *Pippa,* Browning displays man in his characteristic responses to love—physical, maternal, and divine. By concentrating on this one area of experience, he makes his subject more manageable theatrically without, at the same time, excluding other relevant experience. Indeed, talking profoundly about love, he inevitably talks about the other human concerns—here, specifically, about art and religion.

Although Pippa functions decisively in the play, she is still part of the composite personality, working within more than outside the characters. Her meaning is relative; her singing is significant primarily for the meaning that the various characters, in their specific and immediate situations, give it. She brings them no new insights but rediscovers within them that which they have lost or are in danger of losing; she helps them to understand something they have not understood or have understood only partially. Sebald feels guilt, Jules aspires to the ideal, Luigi feels compelled to kill the Austrian emperor, the Monsignor recognizes moral obligation, *before* Pippa makes her appearance.

Her role is that of innocence—that pre-fall simplicity that makes spontaneous, impulsive action possible. Innocence is not meant as a synonym for goodness. Pippa's innocence is in itself amoral. Let us recall that Browning wrote *Pippa* partly as a by-product of *Sordello*. In contrast to Pippa, the other characters, like Sordello, are consciously involved in social and moral situations that make conflicting demands on them, rendering them incapable of decisive action. Given the dilemma in which each finds himself, what action can he possibly take? Each is in danger of psychological and moral paralysis. Pippa functions as a primitive, anti-intellectual force. She reduces the complexities of a situation largely by ignoring its contradictions. Sebald's affairs, for example, are hopelessly entangled, indeed, but God is in his heaven. This is enough. Pippa's impulsiveness cuts through sophisticated rationalization, worldly wisdom, and encourages action on a basic level. Pippa is important less because she helps them make the "right" choice than because she enables them to make any choice. Their action is in itself their salvation.

Browning says, then, that man escapes oversophistication by recapturing innocence. He does not offer Pippa alone, however, as the salutary alternative to Sordello, nor does he propose Rousseauistic primitivism as the antidote to modern complexity. The choice he offers is no simple alternative. Ottima and Sebald, Jules and Phene, Luigi, and the Monsignor are all firmly established in a social and intellectual world to which Browning gives reality and permanence. Man must find his salvation in the world. Paradoxically he must become Sordello and Pippa simultaneously.

For much of his external action, Browning borrows once again from the popular melodramatic tradition. Each episode in the play might have come directly from one of the successful dramas of his time. But Browning handles them, the "drabbing, stabbing, et autre gentillesses," less objectionably than in *A Blot*. *Pippa* is no more a nineteenth-century melodrama than *Hamlet* is an early Elizabethan revenge play. The drama is plotless; the external action is episodic; the characters enter briefly and depart. Superficially there is little save the wispy figure of Pippa to hold the play together. Yet underneath the tempestuous surface there is a current of significant action that moves simultaneously in two directions.

First, there is the action within each episode. In each, for one reason or another a character reaches a point of stasis. Sebald yields once again to the hypnotic charms of Ottima; Jules makes a traditional but meaningless gesture; Luigi surrenders to his mother's rationalizations; even the Monsignor considers compromise with the Intendant. Each needs a fresh perspective, which Pippa offers. The definition of action as a good in itself is neither immoral nor even amoral, but it is untraditional. *Pippa* is as enigmatic as *A Blot*. The play neither condemns nor approves adultery, murder, deception, and theft. Its moral import—as Browning conceived morality—can best be seen by the "good" influence Pippa has on each of these characters.

Her song awakens and intensifies Sebald's guilt. It makes him see Ottima not as his great white queen, magnificent in sin, but as a repulsive flesh-and-blood female. He expresses his reaction to the new image in one of the most powerful speeches in dramatic literature:

> *My God! and she is emptied of it now!*
> *Outright now!—how miraculously gone*
> *All of the grace—had she not strange grace once?*
> *Why, the blank cheek hangs listless as it likes,*
> *No purpose holds the features up together,*
> *Only the cloven brow and puckered chin*
> *Stay in their places—and the very hair,*
> *That seemed to have a sort of life in it,*
> *Drops a dead web!*
>
> (*Part I, p. 6*)

Two symbols are especially effective. Ottima is emptied of a "strange grace"; so is Sebald. Her hair appears a web, an image which, coming at the end of the description, summarizes the passage, making Ottima the snare in which Sebald is hopelessly entangled. He attempts to commit suicide, an act that from a traditional point of view is immoral. Is this the good to which he has been brought? Actually, the good lies not in the outcome of the deed but in the fact that Sebald, in whom conscience and will were deadened, lives again, exists as a morally aware creature capable of choosing and acting. He escapes the damnation of spiritual and moral nonexistence.

The end of the episode is ambivalent. A seemingly repentant Ottima cradles Sebald's head on her breast and consoles him: "There, there, both deaths presently." I do not know how to interpret literally Sebald's last speech, but symbolically it is a powerful expression of destruction:

My brain is drowned now—quite drowned: all I feel
Is . . . is at swift-recurring intervals,
A hurrying-down within me, as of waters
Loosened to smother up some ghastly pit—
There they go—whirls from a black, fiery sea.

(Part I, p. 7)

This destruction is also, paradoxically, his salvation. To possess power to damn oneself and to know that one is doing it is to exist on a spiritual level higher than that of the spirtually unaware.

The Jules–Phene episode ends ambivalently also. Perhaps Jules may go to "some unsuspected isle in the far seas!" and there, working in his new medium, succeed in painting his newly conceived Ideal. Nothing, however, assures us that he will. Yet this does not seem really important. Jules understands what is happening to him. Browning's somewhat sketchy account of Jules' awakening in the first edition is elaborated and clarified in the collected edition of 1849:

> *Look at the woman here with the new soul,*
> *Like my own Psyche's,—fresh upon her lips*
> *Alit, the visionary butterfly,*
> *Waiting my word to enter and make bright,*
> *Or flutter off and leave all blank as first.*
> *This body had no soul before, but slept*
> *Or stirred, was beauteous or ungainly, free*
> *From taint or foul with stain, as outward things*
> *Fasten their image on its passiveness:*
> *Now, it will wake, feel, live—or die again!*
> *Shall to produce form out of unshaped stuff*
> *Be art—and, further, to evoke a soul*
> *From form, be nothing? This new soul is mine!*
> *(1849 ed., Part II, pp. 201–202)*[6]

"My own Psyche's," "This new soul is mine." Like Sebald's speech ostensibly describing Ottima, this is less a portrait of the object than of the observer. Suddenly, he, Jules, the artist, exists—a responsible, choosing, acting individual. He can never again be satisfied with his old conventional marble forms. Even if he retires to "Some unsuspected isle" he will take with him his new sense of reality. Even if he fails to paint a masterpiece, he has willed one. This is enough for his salvation.

Luigi listens to Pippa's song and hears in it the voice of God, bidding him kill the Austrian emperor, and is awakened from his spiritual lethargy. The Monsignor alone is inspired to a conventionally moral action.

Obviously, Browning intends that the voice of Pippa be that of a "good spirit," but, we may well ask, in what way is

it good? It is good because it returns man to a state of innocent simplicity, enabling him, in a world of frustrating
complexity and oversophistication, to make moral choices
and to act. Even though it does not direct him toward traditionally "good" goals, it makes him capable of moral action and therefore of creating a significant life. Insofar as
action within the episode is concerned, Browning is entirely
successful.

There should also be an action generated by the interaction of episodes upon each other. We expect forward movement. Browning makes some effort to provide this. The
progress of the play from morning to night might signify a
transition from the light of innocence to the dark of
knowledge, but this seems hardly possible. Pippa is the
only innocent of the play, and she ends her day no more
aware or wise than she began it. Moreover, the tone of the
play requires that we interpret the conclusion of each episode as a triumph in some sense. The transition from morning to night suggests a continuous and circular rather than
horizontal movement. At the end of the play we begin
again, morning following night and night following morning. Life is measured by its intensity rather than by its concrete achievements. By doing what one can and should do,
Pippa by singing and the Bishop by judging, each achieves
his own kind of perfection. This is the sense in which all
service ranks the same with God, and this circular movement is the structural pattern which best symbolizes such
a vision of life.

There is also a progression from passionate to marital to
maternal to divine love. But here, too, the end seems
scarcely an end, for Browning clearly indicates that love for
God and love for man are in no wise mutually exclusive.
Even the love of Ottima and Sebald has its divine potential. Jules' idealism and Luigi's dedication to freedom become steps toward divinity once they are activated by

Pippa's song. The Monsignor saves himself by saving Pippa.

The significant action should result from the arrangement of episodes in a pattern of spiraling intensity. Browning attempts to achieve drama by arranging materials in a nonsequential order, a device he was to use so effectively in *The Ring and the Book*. The result is—or should be—a circular and vertical movement rather than a horizontal one, an amplification and intensification of thematic and emotional elements of the subject rather than a progression in time from beginning through middle to end.

Browning is less successful in *Pippa* than in *The Ring and the Book*. The episodes in the play at first may seem less repetitious than those in the poem. Actually, this is not the case. The incidents in the poem are roughly the same, but the points of view—the inner lives, Browning's souls, which apprehend and interpret them—are different. In each new book we get a fresh approach to the subject. In the play, the incidents are different, but the point of view is the same, and the result is repetitious and monotonous.

In *The Ring and the Book* the climactic book comes where we expect it—at the end. The book itself, however, is not what we expect. Browning's daring act of giving Guido a second speech after the Pope has pronounced judgment is boldly dramatic. *Pippa* is devoid of such surprises, and as a result its structure seems contrived.

Browning seems, nevertheless, to know partly what he is doing. He tries to make the final episode climactic by choosing the important Monsignor as his central figure, by placing divine love in terminal relation to the loves of the preceding episodes, and by making Pippa's safety a major concern. His efforts are unsuccessful. The first episode remains the most interesting. After it, everything is anticlimactic.

In summation: each of the incidents is interesting in itself but together they fail to form a dramatic pattern of increasing tension. Nevertheless, *Pippa* is Browning's best play. In this bold departure, he demonstrated himself the precursor of the modern theater, especially in his handling of theme and character, in his conception of action as circular and vertical, and in his structural innovations. If Browning could have seen this play sensitively produced in a sympathetic imaginative theater, he might have eliminated its weaknesses. Such good fortune might have backdated the revival of the stage in England by several decades.

VII ❦ *A Soul's Tragedy*

Browning's other significant drama came at the end of his playwriting career. He conceived the idea for *A Soul's Tragedy* as early as ˙842 but did not publish the play until 1846. He never intended it for the stage; indeed, he never thought very highly of it. He wrote Elizabeth Barrett on February 11, 1846:

> For the "Soul's Tragedy"—*that* will surprise you, I think. There is no trace of you there,—you have not put out the black face of *it*—it is all sneering and *disillusion* —and shall not be printed but burned if you say the word—now wait and see and then say! [7]

Miss Barrett disagreed with Browning's judgment. So do most modern critics. *A Soul's Tragedy* is less a theater piece than *Pippa,* but at the same time it is more than a poem like *Paracelsus.* Both its prose and verse have the unmistakable rhythm of the speaking voice and the colloquial tone of conversation. Further, Browning's concept in *A Soul's*

Tragedy is essentially dramatic rather than lyrical. Here as in none of his other plays, with the possible exception of *Pippa Passes,* he establishes a meaningful relation between characters and uses situation and setting as an organic part of the dramatic movement. His success in this play results from certain innovations that anticipate a new theater.

In 1842 Browning described the play as a "wise metaphysical play (about a great mind and soul turning to ill). . . ." [8] By the time he published it in 1846, however, his concept of the central character, Chiappino, had enlarged. Chiappino had become a "mind and soul" too complex to be fully delineated in a single stage figure. Symons observed that the other characters in the play "serve to set off the main figure." [9] Honan refers to Ogniben as an "aspect of Chiappino's own character" (*Browning's Characters,* 98), and McCormick calls him Chiappino's conscience (990).

We could say that Luitolfo too is part of Chiappino. In short, Browning's original "mind and soul" has become a composite personality brought to focus and given dramatic credibility in the person of Chiappino, in whom the central action takes place. The fragmentation of Chiappino into several characters provides a dramatic means of expressing externally an internal action; the presence of Chiappino as a single figure within whom the conflicts converge gives to the play a unifying element that *Pippa* does not have. *A Soul's Tragedy* makes an advance toward a new structure capable of embodying action in character.

There are indications also that Browning has at last grasped the importance of situation as an organic part of dramatic movement. In *A Soul's Tragedy* he reduces the number of important scenes to two, avoiding the confused overcrowding of his earlier plays. Each is relevant to the development of character. The first comes at the end of Act I when Chiappino sacrifices himself for his friend; the second, at the end of Act II when at last he understands that he has betrayed his ideal. Neither comes of esoteric revelation, as in *Paracelsus,* but of situation. Perhaps here for the first time Browning achieves convincingly the psychological realism that distinguishes his later works.

These two crisis moments are related thematically, psychologically, and structurally. The first, Browning calls the poetry of Chiappino's life, and the second, the prose. These are not absolute terms, however, one designating pure idealism and the other total cynicism. Nor is the poetry and the prose in which they are written entirely pure. The first frequently merges into conversational statement and the second into impassioned expression. The resulting movement resembles that of *Pippa*—it is dialectical rather than horizontal.

The play is a complex organization of dramatic ambivalences, reversals, and surprises. No part of it remains static for long. Chiappino, Browning's "hero," is neither great nor little, but both. He seems at first self-centered, self-pitying, whining—an altogether unpleasant character. His "idealism" appears phony, for he rails without discrimination against the society that allegedly abuses him and against Luitolfo who befriends him. While Luitolfo intercedes with the Provost for him, Chiappino belittles his efforts and makes love to Luitolfo's betrothed, Eulalia.

In contrast, Luitolfo appears brave, generous, sensible. Our image of a "bad" man and a "good" man, however, is shattered almost as quickly as it forms. Luitolfo, becoming involved in an argument with the Provost, loses his temper and strikes him what appears a fatal blow. In the crisis that follows, he acts as we would expect Chiappino to act. Forgetting his lover and his friend, he is concerned only to save himself. Chiappino, on the other hand, shows a nobility contrary to all that we have observed in him previously. After arranging for Luitolfo's escape, he dons his old friend's clothes and faces what he thinks is an angry mob. Chiappino is obviously both the embittered idealist and the generous man of action, at once the Chiappino and the Luitolfo of the opening scene.

Events as well as characters constantly present themselves in a new light, from a fresh and seemingly contradictory perspective. The mob that Chiappino faces is friendly, not hostile; eager to award, not punish; Chiappino's act proves self-advancing, not self-sacrificing. And eventually we learn that the Provost was merely injured, not killed.

By the beginning of Act II, Chiappino has assumed a different role or, perhaps more accurately, has shifted emphasis from one to another aspect of his character. Ostensibly, he retains his idealistic goals, but he compromises with the "human situation." He will accept the office of provost, he rationalizes, as a means to an otherwise unattainable end. It might seem at first that he is either self-deceived or utterly perverted. Yet there is enough truth in what he says to convince him that his new course is wise and good and, also, to win some sympathy from the spectator.

At this point Ogniben enters to play the role of doppelgänger. He is at once advocate and prosecutor, simultaneously confirming Chiappino's practical wisdom and condemning his particular action. Chiappino errs less in his assessment of the human situation than in his understanding of his own motives. Once more, Browning redefines traditional morality. The ideal, indeed, is incapable of human realization; the ideal society has no earthly counterpart. Chiappino is wrong, not in recognizing this but in using it to cover his own selfish grab for power. He suffers the temptations of all Browning's politicians. What he learns eventually is not that all human government is wrong but that manipulators of governments are in danger of self-deception and damnation (as was Djabal). Browning's play is a statement about a "mind and soul" and the mainsprings of its being rather than about a human system.

At this point we might ask in what sense the play is a tragedy. Does Chiappino actually come to a tragic end? Clearly it was better that he achieve a modicum of self-realization and forego his ambition to become provost than that he continue on a course of self-deception and unwilled hypocrisy. Rather let us say that his tragic error is in failing to maintain that moment of heroism when instinctively he offered his life for his friend. That he did not—could not—is the tragedy of Chiappino and of man. Such poetry is fragile and of brief duration. It is inevitably followed by the prose of everyday human existence. Being man is at best ambivalent. Chiappino has no choice. The prose of his life is part of the human condition. In 1846, this somber reality struck the young Browning, who was just emerging from his youthful idealism, as "all sneering and disillusion." His play, however, does not validate his judgment.

Chiappino's triumph is that he comes to understand himself and to reject the action that would make him a complacent partner of all the errors inherent in the human system. Browning attempts to give us this process of discovery while it is yet in the process of forming, through the interchange between Chiappino and Ogniben. Thus he externalizes in the two characters an action within the one.

Eulalia's role in Chiappino's development is less active than Luitolfo's and Ogniben's. She has her part less as a person than as an object. She is in the first act for Chiappino to make love to and thus betray his friend; she is in the second for him to reject and thus confirm his loss of human values as he becomes increasingly a part of the system.

In *A Soul's Tragedy* and *Pippa Passes* Browning anticipated the modern stage. Continuing to focus on the internal life of his characters, he further developed a structure potentially capable of expressing his sophisticated, ambivalent views. The fragmentation of the traditional tragic hero into multiple characters was a real step toward modernity. The concept of action as a dialectical relation between idea, situation, and character or parts of character was a significant move toward a new, flexible, dramatic structure capable of expressing action in character.

Having said this in defense of the play, I must, nevertheless, confirm the traditional view that the play fails as a stage piece. The second act is too long—too long as a whole and too long in the separate speeches. The dramatic tension that results from the dialectical arrangement of situation and character is more a promise than a reality. The credibility of the play is undermined by an unfortunate mixture of styles. *A Soul's Tragedy* is essentially intellectual and abstract (as much modern drama is); its basic structure should be suggestive and symbolic. At moments, however, it is disturbingly realistic. That Browning had this problem should not surprise any student of modern theater. Ibsen had difficulty in making the transition from the narrow realism of his early middle plays to the deeper, richer symbolism of the later works. McCormick observes that when, at the end of *A Soul's Tragedy,* Ogniben assumes a being of his own, the dramatic movement crumbles (990). Indeed, Ogniben is a problem from the moment he enters. He constantly threatens to step out of the role of doppelgänger to become a person in his own right. As such he is always an intruder. The conclusion of the play, as critics tirelessly point out, is amusing—but it is artistically wrong. The action has ended some lines back, and Ogniben's assumption of character leaves us with irrelevant questions about his future and that of the city, when the play is about the mind and soul of Chiappino—the tragedy of the prose of human existence.

After the long humorless early poems it is good to see Browning expressing his natural sense of humor. He had yet, however, to integrate seriousness and humor into the single complex, ironical vision that we find in later poems such as "Bishop Blougram's Apology."

VIII ❧ *Luria*

Browning's last play, *Luria,* is in a category by itself. Unlike his earlier plays, it was not written for the stage, and unlike *Pippa* and *A Soul's Tragedy* it lacks even potential strength. In a letter to Elizabeth Barrett, February 26, 1845, Browning outlined his intentions for *Luria*:

> That "Luria" you enquire about, shall be my last play—for it is but a play, woe's me! . . . Luria is a Moor, of Othello's country, and devotes himself to something he thinks Florence, and the old fortune follows—all in my brain, yet, but the bright weather helps and I will soon loosen my Braccio and Puccio (a pale discontented man), and Tiburzio (the Pisan, good true fellow, this one), and Domizia the Lady—loosen all these on dear foolish (ravishing must his folly be), golden-hearted Luria, all these with their worldly-wisdom and Tuscan shrewd ways; and, for me, the misfortune is, I sympathize just as much with these as with him.
>
> (*Love Letters,* I, 26)

By 1846 Browning had grown weary not only of the theater but of *Luria.* One year after he began work on the play, he was still uncertain about major elements of the plot and characterization. Many of his problems were never solved. The play has neither external nor internal action, neither achievement nor promise.

His primary failure is in the character of Luria. He was handicapped, I think, by being unable to dissociate his own Moor from Shakespeare's. The surface similarities between the two serve only to emphasize Luria's superficiality. We accept Othello's love for Desdemona and we understand why he murdered her and stabbed himself. Luria, however, loves not a woman, not even a city, but the illusion of a city. We are not convinced. We are willing to accept a man's devotion to an ideal if it is motivated psychologically, but Luria's devotion to what he thinks is Florence never seems real. As a result, his suicide appears just another mistake in a series of mistakes. Browning fails to render dramatic the conflict between Moorish heart and shrewd Tuscan ways even more noticeably than he failed to give substance to Djabal's struggle between Arab instincts and Frank mind.

IX ❧

Clearly, Browning's attempts to write for the theater were disappointing. None of his plays is stageworthy today, and only two are promising. The reasons for his failure should be fairly clear by now. His intellectual interests are obvious. He emphasized social and institutional instability and the consequent disintegration of values, but his concerns were not political or social. He was disturbed rather by the alienation of his characters and the meaninglessness of their lives in the absence of traditional values. From the time of the Greeks until the late eighteenth century, drama was thought to imitate an action based upon a fixed order of reality and values external to man. Upon this assumption Aristotle gave action supremacy among dramatic elements. Browning too recognized the importance of action but redefined the term by giving it a new referent. Dramatic action no longer mirrored an external order (fate, God, moral law) to which a character must relate himself; rather it illuminated the internal life of a character. Action for Browning was the character's attempt to achieve self-realization and to arrive at pragmatic values without reference to an external natural order. Browning stumbled into a new literary era with a revolutionary concept of action in character without fully comprehending the radical nature of what he proposed. For the old term *imitation,* he, as a part of the literary current of his day, substituted *discovery* and *expression.*

The dramatic conventions—the structure of the play and all the techniques of production, including the theater itself—that Browning inherited had developed through the centuries as a corollary of the drama that Aristotle described. They were not only inadequate but devastating for Browning. Partly because he was uncertain of himself and partly because of pressure from outside, he usually attempted to contain his action in character in old forms. His intent and execution were at cross purposes. However, the rare exceptions, particularly *Pippa* and *A Soul's Tragedy,* make him a significant precursor of modernism in the theater. Browning needed, above all, to clarify his ideas and to create a new dramatic structure for expressing them. But that required a sympathetic theater and a cooperative audience. He had neither.

When a playwright of today creates a character, he has a century of experimentation and achievement to draw upon. He succeeds where Browning failed not necessarily because he has a more dramatic imagination or a greater structural facility but because he works within a living tradition and for a sympathetic stage. Browning was for all practical purposes working in a vacuum. The old forms were decadent, and the new ones were just being created.

❦ ❦ ❦ CHAPTER III

The Development of a Soul

> . . . my stress lay on the incidents in the development of a soul: little else is worth study.
>
> (Preface to *Sordello*, 1863.)

> *I count life just a stuff*
> *To try the soul's strength on, educe the man.*
> *Who keeps one end in view makes all things serve.*
> *As with the body—he who hurls a lance*
> *Or heaps up stone on stone, shows strength alike,*
> *So I will seize and use all means to prove*
> *And show this soul of mine you crown as yours,*
> *And justify us both.*
>
> (*In a Balcony.*)

❦ The dramas were obviously exploratory and ultimately unsatisfactory. They reveal, on the one hand, Browning's lack of faith in external forms and institutions and his consequent search for new, subjective values, and, on the other, his experimental efforts to develop a form suited for depicting action in character, the development of a soul. He was unable to shape the drama to his purpose. He came increasingly to realize that the short dramatic poem provided the mode of expression best suited for delineating his men and women. The structure had the additional advantage also of providing precisely the limits within which Browning was best prepared to work at this time. For approximately twenty-two years, 1842–1864, he devoted himself primarily to the development of the short dramatic poem, producing in that genre what many critics still consider his most significant work.

In 1842, he published *Dramatic Lyrics;* in 1845, *Dramatic Romances and Lyrics;* in 1855, *Men and Women;* in 1864, *Dramatis Personae.* In 1850, he published *Christmas-Eve and Easter-Day,* two relatively long poems but, nonetheless, intellectual and artistic products of this period.

That Browning experimented throughout these years is clear from the titles of his works. Their one constant is the word *dramatic,* either explicit or implied; otherwise, they vary from lyrics to romances to personae. Browning displayed the experimental and tentative nature of his classifications by shifting poems from one category to another. No one would argue that his final placement is entirely satisfactory.

Browning's short poems, then, defy rigid classification.[1] They are often referred to loosely as dramatic monologues and judged by arbitrary standards supposedly essential to that genre: speaker, auditor, setting, situation. Clearly, however, many of Browning's finest achievements among the shorter poems are deficient in one or more of these formal characteristics. Any critical approach to the poems that is based upon abitrary systems is doomed to failure. Each poem must be judged for what it is.

Browning himself stated, in his introduction to the first edition of *Dramatic Lyrics,* precisely what he meant by *dramatic:*

> Such Poems as the following come properly enough, I suppose, under the head of "Dramatic Pieces;" being, though for the most part Lyric in expression, always Dramatic in principle, and so many utterances of so many imaginary persons, not mine.

This does not mean, of course, that Browning remains always aloof from his poems, but rather that he gives character precedent over idea and formal structure. The poems are about men and women who undergo potentially soul-developing experiences.[2] The character, the persona, therefore, is the one constant in these poems. Other structural devices are present when they are required. Although most of the poems have an auditor, actually or by implication, none is required a priori by Browning's definition of *dramatic*. Depending upon the poem, the nature of the experience to be revealed, and the circumstances surrounding it, the auditor may be clearly defined (as in "Andrea del Sarto") or he may be a mere shadow (as in "My Last Duchess"). In others, particularly in the lyrics and the narratives, he may almost disappear, becoming an indefinite "you" or reader-understood. In every case, however, the auditor's significance lies in his relation to the inner life, the "soul" of the character. Browning's use of other devices, such as setting and situation, is governed by the same principle. My point is that each of Browning's poems must be studied as an organic unit, subject to the laws of its own nature (the character being depicted) and not to any arbitrary notion of an ideal structure.

When Browning fails, as he sometimes does, it is less often the result of inept handling of a preconceived structure—such as the monologue—than of his failure to grasp clearly and to reflect wholly the internal action of his character. In "Saul," for example, he seems unable to decide whether he is writing a soul study of the King, presenting symbolically the mystical vision of David, or developing an analogical argument for the existence of a God of love. As a result, the poem fails structurally, not because it is not a monologue but because it is consistently no one thing.

It should be emphasized, as I have already stated, that Browning's men and women undergo *potentially* soul developing experiences. Not all by any means arrive at self-realization to become fully developed souls. Many, including the famous Duke of Ferrara, for example, achieve only self-revelation. The reader sees that of which the character remains unaware. Actually, Browning's characters are constantly deceived and thwarted either by their own limited capacities—their imperfect knowledge and infirm will—or by outside forces—dead traditions and stultifying systems. Browning's lovers, worshipers, and artists, more often than not remain unaware or only partially aware of selfhood, and, consequently, unawakened or only partially awakened to the fulness of life. Their failures affirm at once man's need for and his difficulty in achieving self-realization.

For the sake of discussion, the poems of this period may be grouped in almost any manner so long as the scheme of organization is clearly understood to be only a temporary convenience. In the following, I shall refer especially to the lyric; the character study, popularly called the monologue; the straight narrative; the framed narrative (a story related by a character who is uninvolved or only obliquely involved in the story); and the dialogue.

I ❦ *Dramatic Lyrics*

Browning gave the title *Dramatic Lyrics* to the fourteen poems he published in 1842, four years before he brought to an end his unsuccessful attempt to write stage plays. That the term was not entirely successful he acknowledged when in the collected edition of 1863 he permitted only four of the poems to remain under that title. He transferred seven to *Dramatic Romances* and three to *Men and Women*. His reasons for his final placement are not always clear. One wonders, for example, why "My Last Duchess" was not included in *Men and Women,* and why "Porphyria's Lover" became part of *Dramatic Romances* while "Johannes Agricola," its companion piece, became part of *Men and Women*. Such unanswered questions merely emphasize the danger of approaching Browning's poems with a rigid notion of formal structure.

Browning is concerned in *Dramatic Lyrics* with the same themes that he was trying to develop in the dramas. Although the early short poems are primarily character studies, they lack in general the psychological depth Browning was to achieve later in *Men and Women* and *Dramatis Personae*. In 1842, he had not yet perfected the technique of totally subordinating idea, setting, and situation to the delineation of the inner life of the persona. In many of these early poems Browning concentrates quite obviously on those external restraints—national characteristics, social conventions, religious systems, traditional moral codes—that thwart man's efforts for self-realization.

In *Dramatic Lyrics,* Browning groups a number of poems in pairs, joining them obviously for the diverse perspectives that together they provide on a particular theme: "Italy" and "France" (later called "My Last Duchess" and "Count Gismond"); "Camp and Cloister" (later called "Incident of the French Camp" and "Soliloquy of the Spanish Cloister"); "Queen Worship" (later called "Rudel to the Lady of Tripoli" and "Cristina"); "Madhouse Cells" (later called "Johannes Agricola in Meditation" and "Porphyria's Lover").

The first pair offers contrasting views of love and marriage: "My Last Duchess," that of a corrupt Renaissance

Italian nobleman; "Count Gismond," that of a chivalric Provençal knight. "My Last Duchess" displays a maturity of conception and technique beyond that evidenced in any other poem in the collection. In it, Browning depicts the gradual revelation of the inner life of the Duke. He, not his last duchess, is the subject of the poem. The point of view is rigidly that of the speaker. Auditor, situation, and setting are used as aids through which the Duke's sordid life is revealed. Externally the action relates to a proposed marriage between the Duke and a wealthy commoner represented by the auditor. The reader, however, never becomes really involved in this external action. He is scarcely aware when the poem is over that the Duke and the envoy have reached no stated agreement. Does the Duke marry the girl or not? It really does not matter. Infinitely more interesting is the Duke himself. The action by which his character is gradually revealed moves steadily from the opening statement to the final three lines, which bring into sudden, sharp focus the image which we have watched emerge:

> *Notice Neptune, tho',*
> *Taming a sea-horse, thought a rarity,*
> *Which Claus of Innsbruck cast in bronze for me.*
> (54–56)

Neither merely a decoration nor an illustration of the Duke's love for art, these lines provide a summarizing image that serves the same purpose as a concluding epigram in a didactic poem. We readily identify the Duke with the god (always remembering that we see through his eyes), symbol of egotism and power, in an act of subjugating the seahorse (any threat to his godlike sway over people and things) by brute strength. The artistry of the object suggests a certain perverse beauty in the Duke and explains partly why we have been temporarily captivated by him. Upon reflection he is likely to seem repugnant. It also invites, upon reflection, a certain judgment: ironically the Duke has achieved his "godhood" and his "beauty" at the expense of his humanity. He has been rendered bronze.

"Camp and Cloister" contrasts French and Spanish sensibility as Browning interprets them. He expresses his antipathy for the ascetic life, counterpointing camp against cloister. He makes no defense of war but asserts simply that it is easier to achieve heroism on the battlefield than in the monastery. He identifies morality with action, displaying distrust of institutions and systems. He contrasts the speaker of "Soliloquy of the Spanish Cloister" with his peer, the simple Brother Lawrence, and particularly with the boy of "Incident of the French Camp." Brother Lawrence somehow retains a simple innocence, resisting the institutionalism that has reduced the speaker to a hateful, lustful, Pharisaical old man. In Freudian overtones, Browning asserts the insidiousness of a system that prevents man from being less than whole. "Soliloquy of the Spanish Cloister" is a study of an unpleasant character, but unlike "My Last Duchess" it is not entirely successful. We know from the beginning that the monk is a nasty fellow, unredeemed by a single virtue, and consequently we are not even momentarily caught by the magnificence of his evil. The poem, as a result, appeals one-dimensionally, forcing us to judge it by standards that reveal its partiality. The reader cannot become interested in a character so thoroughly depraved; he can only condemn.

Johannes Agricola, in "Madhouse Cells, I," is less repugnant, although he asserts an equally unacceptable theology. The difference between the poems lies in the fuller, more ambivalent conception of Agricola, who argues a theology of predestination with such intensity and passion that he commands some sympathy. We respond emotionally if not intellectually, attracted to him on one level while we are repelled on another. The relation between this poem and its companion, "Porphyria's Lover," is tenuous. In contrast to Johannes, whose world is wholly determined, that of Porphyria's lover is essentially godless. His last line, "And yet God has not said a word," could mean that the silence signifies either God's nonexistence or his indifference; more likely, however, it means that on some basis relevant to the speaker alone his act has received cosmic sanction. At any rate, we are drawn into a highly subjective world, so eccentric as to justify the title under which Browning placed the poem.

In "Porphyria's Lover" we witness a deed not in the process of occurring but as it appears to have occurred in a reconstruction made some time later by the speaker. Whether his account is factual is unimportant; actually, the reconstruction permits the speaker to distort the facts to form a more nearly perfect image of his twisted soul. He tells how he strangled Porphyria in order, he says, to preserve the good moment of bliss that he feels when she sits before his fire and cradles his head upon her breast. In his strength, he has done what in her weakness she resisted. We suspect other and less flattering motives. Throughout the first part of the poem, even in the reconstruction, she displays strength, assuming the active role in an affair in which he remains passive. He resents her strength, although perhaps subconsciously. This fact becomes clear after he strangles her:

> *I propped her head up as before,*
> *Only, this time my shoulder bore*
> *Her head, which droops upon it still.*
> (*49–51*)

In this change of stance, he seems to say that through his deed he has righted things and assumed the normal masculine role. Perhaps this conviction lies beyond the silence which he interprets as God's affirmation.

Two other poems in this early volume deserve special comment: "Waring" and "In a Gondola." Browning addressed "Waring" to his old friend Alfred Domett, who had emigrated to Australia. It is a warmly moving tribute to a friendship. At the same time, however, the poem seems to be more about Browning than about Domett. It expresses attitudes and themes that we know Browning himself held: a sense of failure and a hope for better things, eagerness for recognition, contempt for writers of the establishment, conviction that contemporary arts were trivial and ineffectual. Browning makes Waring an almost legendary figure, another Paracelsus, wandering over the earth exploring all things through diverse modes: poetry, painting, music. He displays love for solitude and reticence to reveal his inmost self. He concludes with a defense of art as a means of awakening life.

"In a Gondola," melodramatic, perhaps sentimental, is nevertheless a clear presentation of Browning's early conviction that life is measured in intensity rather than in time; that goodness is fidelity to one's inmost being rather than conformity to external code. In this poem, as in so many others, Browning ignores traditional moral views. A young man and his married lover talk through a clandestine meeting, which ends with his murder by the offended husband and his companions. We are made to sympathize with the couple, accepting their rendezvous as right and rejecting the husband's revenge as wrong. Although defying external codes, they remain true to their inner beings, asserting the supremacy of love over social and moral conventions. The point is less that Browning defends a Bohemian morality than that he emphasizes the subjective basis for goodness. Moreover, he has created his characters with such conviction that we become interested primarily in their development and only secondarily, if at all, in abstract moral issues. The young man summarizes in the last lines:

> *It was to be so, Sweet, and best*
> *Comes 'neath thine eyes, and on thy breast.*
> *Still kiss me! Care not for the cowards! Care*
> *Only to put aside thy beauteous hair*
> *My blood will hurt. The Three I do not scorn*
> *To death, because they never lived: but I*
> *Have lived indeed, and so—(yet one more kiss)—*
> > *can die.*
>
> > (*XV*)

It is a triumph for Browning's artistry that we are convinced that the young man has indeed lived—and well—less by the explicit statement of these lines than by the sensuous and emotional persuasiveness of the poem that has preceded them.

II ❦ *Dramatic Romances and Lyrics*

Dramatic Romances and Lyrics, 1845, contained the earlier lyrics and twenty-one new poems. Browning again suggested his uncertainty over the proper description of his dramatic pieces by expanding the title of his new volume. Even this attempt, however, proved unsatisfactory, and in the collected edition of 1863 he transferred thirteen of the new poems to *Dramatic Lyrics,* six to *Dramatic Romances,* and two to *Men and Women.*

In these poems, as in the earlier lyrics, Browning continues to concentrate on the external restrictions that hinder a character in achieving self-realization. He displays a wider intellectual and artistic interest, however. He avoids the somewhat simplistic arrangement of poems into antithetical pairs, a practice which encourages psychological over-simplification and a concentration on theme rather than character development, and begins to focus more specifically upon the internal process by which a character is brought to a moment of self-realization. He still has not achieved the mastery that was later to distinguish his handling of men and women, however. For the sake of discussion the poems may be divided into three formal groups: the love lyrics, the romantic narratives, and the character studies. With one exception, "Night and Morning," the lyrics and romances require scant attention. In addition to the character studies, which do deserve careful consideration, there is another poem, "The Flight of the Duchess," which, belonging to no one group, merits special attention.

a

"Night and Morning" (later called "Meeting at Night" and "Parting at Morning") is one of Browning's best lyrics. The speaker is a persona; the poem, a lyrical description of an inner action. It presents the experience of love from one possible perspective—the sensuous. The external action is only indirectly related to the meaning of the poem. Browning is less interested in the escapade than in the experience of sensuous love itself. The poem is a series of images related more by association than by rational ordering of events. It is a full assault upon the senses advanced through diction, sound, rhythm—all the structural devices at Browning's command. The obvious sexual symbolism is sensuous and emotional; the reader is swept by an irresistible undulating movement, created visually and orally, from the boat, across the field, to the dark room where the woman waits—from the first image to the climaxing phrase, "two hearts beating each on each." Significantly, "Meeting at Night" contains no complete sentence. Its meaning is a-logical and a-syntactical.

Midway through the poem there is a break in the structure to indicate a lapse of time. The final section begins on the following morning. The intense excitement is gone and the "startled little waves" no longer "leap in fiery ringlets." The speaker's inner calm is suggested by the first complete sentence in the poem, "Round the cape of a sudden came the sea." The nocturnal experience which at the moment of its occurrence was so absorbing has passed, and now, the man, satisfied, is drawn back into a "world of men."

Unlike "Night and Morning," the other love lyrics in these two early volumes, "Cristina," "Rudel to the Lady of Tripoli," and "The Lost Mistress," speak of frustrated love. They fail to achieve sensuous intensity and emotional genuineness. Among the romances, there is a small group of narrative poems, "How They Brought the Good News," "The Glove," "The Boy and the Angel," which enjoy considerable popular acclaim but are not central to Browning's major artistic achievement.

b

The more fully developed character studies include "Pictor Ignotus," "The Tomb at St. Praxed's," "Sibrandus Schafnaburgensis," "The Laboratory," and "The Confessional." Loosely called monologues, these poems differ markedly in structure, reminding us once again of the amorphous nature of Browning's shorter poems.

"The Confessional," like "Porphyria's Lover," is the speaker's reconstruction of an action. The girl, in this case, shapes the action, limiting the view to include only that which she is capable of seeing and is willing to divulge, or that which she unwittingly implies. In the strict sense there is no auditor (only an indefinite "you"), so that the conflict is solely internal. Although she professes to expose the priests and bishops, we soon realize that condemnation of them is only part of her "confession." The title is ambivalent. It refers obviously to the booth in which she was betrayed by her priest but also to an act of self-recognition that the poem never states (the point of view, after all, prohibits such a statement) but clearly implies. The conflict is less between the girl and the priests than within herself, between her conscious protestation of innocence and her subconscious awareness of guilt. The latter, along with her sense of personal loss and her disillusionment, accounts for the emotional intensity and hysterical tone of the poem. To us, clearly, and to her also, more than she is willing to acknowledge, the "lie" is equally theirs and hers. Ironically, she simultaneously exposes them and herself. She discovers, without rationalizing the fact, that evil exists both in the world and in her own heart. She is both the betrayed and the betrayer.

In "The Laboratory" a woman talks to a chemist while he compounds a poison with which she hopes to destroy her rivals. The action is reported as it happens, involving both a conflict within the speaker and a complex of interaction between speaker and auditor-situation-setting. The setting makes possible the ironic contrast between the speaker's outward fastidiousness and her inner chaos: "But brush this dust off me, lest horror it brings . . ." (47). The auditor, at the end of the poem, makes explicit something that has been implicit throughout. When the girl demands that he kiss her—"on my mouth if you will!"—we realize that her murderous desperation culminates years of frustration caused by her diminutive size, her physical unattractiveness, her neglect by men, her sexual frustration.

"Pictor Ignotus" details a soul development in another form. Here we have neither a reconstruction nor an exchange between speaker and auditor. Although Pictor Ignotus addresses an undefined "ye" at the beginning of the poem and the "youth men praise so" at the end, he really speaks to himself. His conflict arises between his artist desires to embrace life joyfully and creatively and his monk fear to assert himself; between the painter's yen for man's approval and his fear that, loving the world more than heaven, he will lose God's; between his need for the world's praise and his fear of its abuse. These conflicts come together in the image:

> *Glimpses of such sights*
> *Have scared me, like the revels thro' a door*
> *Of some strange House of Idols at its rites.* . . .
> *(41–43)*

Forced by fear and timidity to deny himself the world, he ironically loses heaven also. His life is lived superficially and externally, and his reward is in kind. His heart sinks; his paintings die. There is perhaps envy and some spite in his attitude toward the youth; yet there is also frustration, pathos, and honest searching in his final queries: "holds their praise its worth?" (The risk of spiritual damnation and personal humiliation.) "Tastes sweet the water with such specks of earth?" For the painter both the splendors and the specks of the world are equally real; ironically, he pays for the specks without enjoying the splendors. His is the tragedy of a man, unlike the speaker of "In a Gondola," who was afraid to live and remained in every sense an unknown, unrealized, painter.

"Sibrandus Schafnaburgensis" emphasizes the importance of life as direct experience and illustrates Browning's considerable gift for satiric humor. In the poem, Browning satirizes pedantry as a perversion of the creative forces of nature, counterpointing the narrowly cultivated mind and spirit against the compulsion toward life and the creativity which he sees in nature:

> *All that life, and fun, and romping,*
> *All that frisking, and twisting, and coupling,*
> *While slowly our poor friend's leaves were swamping,*
> *And clasps were cracking, and covers suppling!*
> *As if you had carried sour John Knox*
> *To the play-house at Paris, Vienna, or Munich,*
> *Fastened him into a front-row box,*
> *And danced off the Ballet with trousers and tunic.*
>
> *(VIII)*

"The Tomb at St. Praxed's," later called "The Bishop Orders His Tomb at St. Praxed's Church," is one of the finest achievements among these early poems.[3] The title as Browning revised it for the 1849 edition provides the first clue to its meaning. In what sense does the Bishop *order* his tomb? The apparent discrepancy between what he demands and what he gets suggests the unifying irony of the poem. Employing a fully developed character, a set of real auditors, and a rich setting and situation, Browning is able to establish conflicting views of the Bishop: that arising from the facts of the poem and the narrower, more subjective vision which the Bishop has of himself. The action is to effect a kind of junction between the Bishop's illusions of himself as a commanding figure capable of controlling people and things and the contrasting fact, apparent to all but the Bishop, of his mortality and, eventually, his inability to command at all. The poem presents a self-revelation that eventually forces the Bishop to accept a reality paradoxical to the illusion under which he has lived.

The poem is epitomized in a series of reversals, that of the contrast between his imagined and his actual tomb being the most apparent. The ordered tomb symbolizes the values he considers enduring, a curious mixture of paganism and Christianity, both material and sensual; and the confidence with which he orders it, his illusion of personal power. The ineffectuality of his order and his revised vision of the tomb—

> *Stone—*
> *Gritstone, a-crumble! Clammy squares which sweat*
> *As if the corpse they keep were oozing through—*
> *(115–117)*

bring him abruptly to face the inevitable. Perhaps the most effective reversals have to do with his personal relations— with Gandolf, his mistress, and his sons. In the beginning, the dying Bishop is exalted and Gandolf is humbled; in conclusion, the Bishop is humbled and Gandolf is relatively exalted. His mistress becomes a tantalizing memory, real only as a reminder that once he took her from Gandolf. Accustomed all his life to respect and obedience from his subjects, he issues his last orders to them only to discover that he no longer has power to secure his demands. Having rejected his sons during his lifetime, he is in his death rejected by them. It is a devastating confrontation. The Bishop, however, is incapable of real insight and, consequently, of the regeneration characteristic of the tragic hero; he lacks the capacity for nobility. Indeed, he is another of Browning's characters who significantly remain nameless. His only redeeming quality is a stoical acceptance of the inevitable. He might have whined but does not. "Well go!" he says, "I bless ye." Lest we take this final benediction to mean more than it does, Browning permits the old man to return in the last lines to speculations which in-

dicate that his confrontation with reality has not brought
spiritual awakening:

> *And leave me in my church, the church for peace,*
> *That I may watch at leisure if he leers—*
> *Old Gandolf, at me, from his onion-stone,*
> *As still he envied me, so fair she was!*
>
> (*122–125*)

The associational relation of elements in a frequently
a-syntactical structure presents with masterly precision the
development of internal action which often occurs on a
preconscious level. The skillful manipulation of other
structural devices, particularly sound and rhythm, binds
the elements of the poem into a unit. It is one of Browning's great triumphs.

c

Neither a monologue nor a simple narrative, "The
Flight of the Duchess" is a special dramatic form required
for the poem that Browning writes. The speaker, who is
not the subject of the poem, tells a story in which he is not
a chief participant. He is, nevertheless, necessary to the
poem's meaning, as I shall indicate. The poem is concerned
less with the development of a specific soul than with the
conditions under which souls develop. The title provides
the first clue to its meaning, focusing our attention less on
the Duchess than on her flight, upon an action more than
upon a personality. Instead of showing us what it feels like
to experience liberation after bondage, Browning invites
us to contemplate, emotionally as well as intellectually, the
complex ramifications of spiritual bondage and liberation.
Seeing the Duchess as we do, from a distance and through
the eyes of another character, we sympathize with her and

rejoice in her escape. This point of view makes possible an intellectual and moral reaction that would have been highly improbable were we permitted to see the action from her perspective. At the same time, the carefully controlled dramatic structure prevents the poem from becoming a philosophical or moral tract.

To understand the Duchess' act fully, we need a more complex perspective than her consciousness alone provides. We need also the view of other participants: the Duke and his mother reveal the deadening effects of traditional structures upon those who submit passively to them; the speaker, the potential of the few to find realization within the structures; the Duchess, the need of the many to seek new life in flight from them.

The speaker helps shape our way of seeing the Duchess. His mundane reality contrasts with her romantic flight, sharpening and intensifying its outlines, increasing its plausibility and transforming what might have been merely an escape from physical bondage into a spiritual liberation that assumes a mythic quality. His description of the gypsy tribe and of the scene between the old crone and the young Duchess gives the events a mysterious depth. We accept them for more than they actually are precisely because he does. Presenting these mysteries through the eyes of a man capable of belief and awe, Browning gives them reality, gaining our acceptance of a situation we would ordinarily reject. The physical escape of one human from a brutal husband comes to signify a universal spiritual liberation.

The literal conflict of the poem is between the court and the caravan, the Duke and the gypsy queen. The one represents restricting social structures; the other, the mysterious call to life, unstructured and free. The one is safe and deadening; the other, vaguely glimpsed, mysterious, alluring. The one produces dukes and duchesses and an occasional retainer who achieves manhood in spite of his surroundings; the other, at once alluring and frightening, promises freedom and self-realization.

Not everyone can hear the life call. The Duke and his mother, unaware of life outside their narrow confines, a reconstructed imaginary medieval estate, remain oblivious. Their conduct is at once ludicrous and terrifying. Browning humorously satirizes them but, at the same time, shows that their antics are frightening. Unable to recognize men beneath the medieval masquerade, they are monstrously inhumane. They abuse the young Duchess without being aware of their cruelty. They have been rendered incapable both of seeing and feeling. The past that Browning rejects here was not necessarily bad when it was past, but it is bad now because it imposes alien patterns upon the present, thwarting man's awareness and his capacity to act spontaneously.

There are some few who do not need to hear the call that lured the Duchess. The speaker achieves humanity by remaining and fulfilling his obligation within the court. The Duchess, however, is no retainer. Aware of the sham of the court, she must throw off traditional bonds—even that of her marriage—and follow the old mysterious gypsy into an unknown wilderness. To stay dutifully at the court would be for her a sin against selfhood, an immoral act. Her flight is significantly vague, not a charted journey to a definite place. We do not know where she goes or what she does. Neither is of much importance. The ecstasy she feels when she leaves is unrelated to any tangible code or object but comes from some inner vision which we cannot glimpse directly. That ecstasy rather than any specific destination is her reward.

Asserting at the end of the poem that once he has fulfilled his obligation to his master, he will go out and seek the Duchess, the retainer emphasizes, unconsciously, the unknowable destination awaiting the courageous who seek self-realization. We do not believe he will find her. His statement also reminds us that such journeys are made alone. The Duchess did not need and could not have used his services even if he had been willing to desert the Duke and follow her.

III ❧ *Christmas-Eve and Easter-Day*

After *Sordello* none of Browning's characters attempts to possess Truth immediately and totally. Sordello had learned that man of necessity was confined to searching for Infinity through his limited faculties and in the finite stuff of this world. The paradox of his condition is a central problem for most of Browning's men and women in the plays and the early lyrics and romances. Their problem was Browning's also. It was one for which he could find no satisfying intellectual solution. His dilemma reached a climax when in the early 1840's he began work on a poem based on the Old Testament figure, Saul. The material itself—part of a well-known, cherished tradition—called for a kind of solution that Browning was unable at the time to accept. To treat Saul as he had treated other historical characters, Sordello, for example—and this is obviously what he was inclined to do—would distort a story that was a fixed part of sacred tradition. Browning's own intuited sense of reality and his artistic interests were brought into conflict with his materials and with the expectations they imposed upon him. Eventually he gave up the project and published the fragment of a poem in 1845. Elizabeth Barrett, with whom he began his correspondence shortly before he despaired of finishing "Saul," directed him in the months following toward a solution which at least gave him temporarily a point of view from which to continue his work. In *Christmas-Eve and Easter-Day*, published in 1850, he affirmed his belief in the Christian doctrine of the Incarnation, a concept which we do not find in his earlier poetry. Such a position provided Browning a prototype of the realization of the Infinite within the finite and, by asserting that love was the law of creation, gave him a ground for values and a motivation for his men and women. That the orthodox doctrine of the Incarnation conflicted with views expressed in *Paracelsus* and *Sordello,* he was aware. In fact, in the revised *Paracelsus* which appeared in 1849, Browning converted Aprile into an Incarnationalist by adding to his final speech the following lines:

> *Man's weakness is his glory—for the strength*
> *Which raises him to heaven and near God's self,*
> *Came spite of it: God's strength his glory is,*
> *For thence came with our weakness sympathy*
> *Which brought God down to earth, a man like us.*
>
> (*II, 663–670*)

(As an aside, we should note here that Browning dropped these lines from the 1863 *Paracelsus,* an act the significance of which we shall see later. Browning was apparently unaware at the time of the possible conflict between an orthodox conception of the Incarnation and his persistent idea that order and meaning were imposed upon the world by man and not upon man by systems external to him. He did later come to realize this problem.)

Christmas-Eve and Easter-Day and "Saul," the completed version of which was published in *Men and Women,* seem Browning's response to Elizabeth Barrett's urging that he speak out in his own person rather than through *dramatis personae.* They represent, no doubt, his effort to become the objective-subjective poet that she held up to him as an ideal—an ideal he elaborates upon in his essay on Shelley written in 1851.[4] Nevertheless, personal as it is, "Christmas-Eve" could not have pleased Miss Barrett—Mrs. Browning by the time the poem was published—completely. The poem remains dramatic, at least on the surface, and the point of view is ambivalent. The speaker eventually casts his lot with the Evangelicals but remains aware of their shortcomings, even of their absurdities. He rejects Roman Catholicism, finding in its ritual a deterrent to personal communion with God but at the same time admiring its devotion to love and regretting that he must forego the beauty of its liturgy. He is attracted by the richness of Christmas-Eve Mass in St. Peter's as obviously as he is repelled by the bareness of the chapel service. He is totally repelled, however, only by the German professor, whose rationalism excludes both love and beauty and thus kills the spirit. He rejects Catholicism because it imposes an unnecessary barrier between man and God, but he condemns rationalism because it renders communion with God and fellowship with men—self-realization—impossible on any terms. He accepts Evangelicism, with all its weaknesses, and with reservations that he does not make entirely clear, because unencumbered by either intellectualism or ritualism it offers man greatest freedom in his personal quest for God. The speaker echoes many of Browning's own views, but "Christmas-Eve" is not "R.B., a poem" (*Love Letters*, I, 17). The speaker maintains a life of his own, speaking with a detachment and humor that saves the poem from becoming dogmatic.

In a sense, "Easter-Day" is a companion piece to "Christmas-Eve," but it is a very different kind of poem. It is not a monologue that fails; neither is it a straight philosophical poem. The distinctive treatment of the speaker and auditor, both perhaps aspects of the same character, and the ordering of events and concepts argue that it belongs to a genre of its own. The centrality of idea makes it other than a monologue, and the psychological dimensions of the expressed thoughts render it other than a philosophical poem. "Easter-Day" anticipates such great dialectical studies as "Bishop Blougram's Apology," *Prince Hohenstiel-Schwangau, Fifine at the Fair,* and *Parleyings With Certain People of Importance in Their Day.* In all these poems conflicting ideas are turned into emotional and sensuous symbols of soul struggle.

Christian dogmas—the Incarnation and the Resurrection—are only superficially the subject of the poem. Browning's more basic concern is his new perception of the meaning and mode of believing, not the specific beliefs themselves. The poem is ostensibly a dialogue between two men, one who finds belief easy and the other who finds it difficult. Actually, the dialectical argument seems to occur within the single man. The poem is divided into two main parts. The speaker first states and then examines as an abstract proposition his thesis: "How very hard it is to be/ A Christian!" (sections I–XIII). He then shifts ground and speaks subjectively of believing as an experienced rather than rationalized reality:

> *and I asked,*
> *Fairly and frankly, what might be*
> *That History, that Faith, to me—*
> *—Me there—not me, in some domain*
> *Built up and peopled by my brain,*
> *Weighing its merits as one weighs*
> *Mere theories for blame or praise,*
> *—The Kingcraft of the Lucumons,*
> *Or Fourier's scheme, its pros and cons,—*
> *But as my faith, or none at all.*
> *'How were my case, now, should I fall*

> *'Dead here, this minute—do I lie*
> *'Faithful or faithless?'*
>
> (386–398)

The speaker's real concern is to explore the superficiality of belief as intellectual assent to a rational proposition and to suggest, in contrast, the apocalyptic nature of believing as a commitment of the entire self to an assumption that can be accepted only as a matter of faith.

Believing is considerably more radical than either right belief or moral effort. The speaker contemptuously dismisses an easy popular faith held "Only to give our joys a zest," insisting that genuine belief is

> *Quite other than a condiment*
> *To heighten flavours with, or meant*
> *(Like that brave curry of his Grace)*
> *To take at need the victuals' place. . . .*
>
> (337–340)

He examines and discards as ineffectual a faith based upon the belief that God may be discovered either in his creation ("as Plato cries/ He doth") or through the processes of reason. The kind of evidence available to man—history, his own sense of need, the dogmas of the Christian church —fail to satisfy precisely because their appeal is so limited. Addressing man's mind and ignoring other areas of his being, they are partial and superficial. They result in easy belief.

Beginning with Section XIV, the speaker approaches believing as an act of total commitment, an involvement not only of man's mind but of his will and affections. He postulates a Christianity based upon personal encounter rather than intellectual proof, upon commitment rather than belief. He recounts an experience in which he met the risen

Christ. Whether the experience was actual or imagined he is not certain. Perhaps, he says, it is not important. He is convinced, however, that whatever its actual origin its reality will be doubted by others:

> if my words in you
> Find veritable listeners,
> My story, reason's self avers
> Must needs be false—the happy chance!
> While, if each human countenance
> I meet in London streets all day,
> Be what I fear,—my warnings fray
> No one, and no one they convert,
> And no one helps me to assert
> How hard it is to really be
> A Christian, and in vacancy
> I pour this story!
>
> (354–365)

In this direct encounter with the Divine (a Christ not in heaven but present, near and within him; not of the past or future but of the Now), he saw his past life from a totally different perspective and realized to his great shame that his prior commitments to religion were not only partial but basically dishonest. That moment of personal encounter proved apocalyptic. It brought all eternity to focus upon him at that one moment in time; it became his personal Day of Judgment, a fact no longer a single event in remote history but a present and continuing experienced reality. He became an individual forced to respond to an utterly unreasonable, irrational demand for total commitment. He found himself in that position which Kierkegaard describes as a simple, clear-cut "either-or." That total, unrelenting, uncompromising demand constitutes the difficulty of being Christian.

From this sobering consideration, the speaker passes to another, equally demanding question: how can man make such a total commitment? He considers and discards such traditional modes as nature, art, and mind. Each of these fails because it is not capable of achieving that perfection short of which man remains incomplete, unsatisfied. Confronting the human paradox of the uncompromising demand made upon him and his finite capacity to respond, he cries in near despair, "Then, (sickening even while I spoke)/ 'Let me alone!' " (890–891). This state of realized helplessness is the prelude to self-discovery. The apprehension of Truth not as an abstraction but as a total experience can come only through feelings and passions—through love. Religion is a response of person to person. By love Browning means more than mere sentiment, of course. Love comprehends a complex of faculties and permits a personal commitment of the complete self on an existential level. It unifies thought and emotion and permits man to realize both in experience. It transforms belief into believing.

In the last section of the poem, the apocalyptic experience behind him ("Was this a vision? False or true?"), the speaker returns to the practical problem of realizing his new insights in everyday living:

> *And so I live, you see,*
> *Go through the world, try, prove, reject,*
> *Prefer, still struggling to effect*
> *My warfare; happy that I can*
> *Be crossed and thwarted as a man,*
> *Not left in God's contempt apart,*
> *With ghastly smooth life, dead at heart,*
> *Tame in earth's paddock as her prize.*
> *Thank God she still each method tries*
> *To catch me, who may yet escape,*

> *She knows, the fiend in angel's shape!*
> *Thank God, no paradise stands barred*
> *To entry, and I find it hard*
> *To be a Christian, as I said!*
>
> (*1019–1032*)

His victory is that he has been delivered not from doubt and hardships but from a "ghastly smooth life." He is no longer the tame prisoner in earth's paddock.

Clearly "Easter-Day" is not a rational defense of the speaker's—much less Browning's—belief in the Incarnation and Resurrection. Both dogmas are made concrete and permitted to function symbolically as expressions of Divine Love to which man can make that total commitment which is demanded of him. Mrs. Browning obviously understood her husband only partially when she said:

> I have complained of the *asceticism* in the second part, but he said it was "one side of the question." Don't think that he has taken to the cilix—indeed he has not—but it is his way to *see* things as passionately as other people *feel* them.[5]

IV ❦ Men and Women

There are fifty-one poems in *Men and Women*, representing a rich variety of subjects and forms. In "Transcendentalism: A Poem in Twelve Books," even though the speaker is a dramatis persona, Browning describes some of the defining characteristics of his new poems. Drawing a contrast between the philosopher Boehme, who wrote "naked thoughts," and the Magi John of Halberstadt, "who made things Boehme wrote thoughts about," he declares that song, not instruction, is the end of art. By song he means more than lyrical expression or words capable of musical annotation. He refers to the mode of expression that transcends rational statement and, by uniting intellect with emotion and sense, communicates meaning beyond that of ordinary language. The poet is a magician, not a philosopher; a maker, not a sayer. He illuminates rather than instructs. His method is dramatic and symbolic. Browning at his best in this volume creates men and women, permitting them through their lives to describe symbolically a portion of human experience. Together they provide a complex, ambiguous, often ironic statement about the meaning of human existence.

Ezra Pound called *Men and Women* the most interesting poems of the Victorian era. Browning's popular reputation still rests primarily on them. And, indeed, by consensus, they represent the full maturing of his powers in the short dramatic form.

This volume may be linked with his earlier works by considering " 'Childe Roland to the Dark Tower Came' " as an amplification of the theme of "The Flight of the Duchess." Both are spiritual journeys: the one depicts the happy beginnings of a journey; the other, the journey itself. "Childe Roland" takes up from a different point of view where the earlier poem leaves off. "The Flight of the Duchess" is reported as it appears to an outsider's limited view, and the action is cast within the sequential frame of commonplace reality. "Childe Roland" is a montage of personal experiences described by the traveler himself within a highly a-logical, symbolic frame.

These two poems make complementary comments upon man's need to achieve identity. In the former the end is obscured: it may or may not confirm objectively the internal meaning of the poem. In the latter, the meaningless-ness of the end is apparent: a discovery that emphasizes the meaningfulness of the action itself. Childe Roland travels a road that has no earthly destination; his visual and emotional experiences have no material counterpart. His journey is within; the horrors he experiences, described in the poem as though they were externally real, are objective approximations of his inner life. They are unified symbolically and associationally rather than logically and sequentially. The poem is a negation of external meaning, the cry of a soul cut off from God, from nature, from objective values. It presents with an almost overwhelming reality the personal disorientation felt by many of Browning's earlier heroes. It depicts the paradox of man's striving without hope, of his need to create meaning when no meaning exists. The intense frustration that this absurdity creates is communicated sensuously and emotionally in savagely violent imagery. Finally, the poem expresses less a new discovery than a new perspective from which an evolving system of values emerges. At the end of the journey there comes a "click/ As when a trap shuts" (Stanza 29), and burningly it comes upon him all at once, "This was the place!" There are no fairy towers, no sleeping beauties to rescue, no giants to fight, no tangible victories to win. It is not clear in the poem precisely what lies before Roland. Our attention shifts radically from outer world to inner world, and we are absorbed by what Roland experiences. This he describes with unmistakable accuracy. Suddenly he sees himself not as conqueror but as victim, the hunted rather than the hunter: "The hills, like giants at a hunting, lay,/ Chin upon hand, to see the game at bay,—" (Stanza 32). With the disintegration of the romantic image of himself comes a new sense of values. He blows the horn not as a challenge to an external enemy but as an assertion of his defiant manhood. He knows nothing will happen, yet he must blow. It is the act of blowing in face of the nothingness outside him that gives his act moral significance. The act itself is his triumph. In one flash of insight he sees before him

> *the lost adventurers my peers,*
> *. . . ranged along the hill-sides, met*
> *To view the last of me, a living frame*
> *For one more picture! in a sheet of flame*
> *I saw them and I knew them all.*
>
> (*Stanzas 33–34*)

In spite of this dismal realization, for the first time he expresses a mood close to ecstasy: "And yet/ Dauntless the slug-horn to my lips I set/ And blew" (Stanza 34).

The title of the poem is significant. The word *childe* designates a young man in training to become a knight. The poem is the record of a man's maturing. In the ironic reversals from conqueror to victim, from external action to internal self-realization, from objective end to action itself, the medieval quest is transformed into a modern spiritual pilgrimage.

"The Statue and the Bust" is related thematically to "Childe Roland." It is an interesting if not a good poem. Browning appears here to condemn the failure of the Great-Duke Ferdinand and his lady, "A bride the Riccardi brings home," to secure love by eloping with each other, although both are married. It is only partly true, however, that he defies traditional morality. He dissociates the various elements in the situation, using one and ignoring others. He is concerned with the couple's failure to act, not with the outcome of their action; with the motive, not with their deed. Not love of virtue but lethargy keeps them from adultery. Neither good nor bad, they remain "moral" but spiritually dead. For such as they, a statue and a bust is more faithfully representative than flesh and blood bodies. Their crime is "the unlit lamp and the ungirt loin" (247). Moreover, here, as in "Childe Roland," Browning focuses upon action itself rather than upon its end, implying that goodness may find itself in conflict with moral codes.

Morality is active, finding validity in motive rather than in end. These traditionally "good" people, Browning says,

> *see not God, I know,*
> *Nor all that chivalry of His,*
> *The soldier-saints who, row on row,*
>
> *Burn upward each to his point of bliss—*
> *Since, the end of life being manifest,*
> *He had cut his way thro' the world to this.*
>   *(223–228)*

Throughout his life Browning was concerned with three subjects: love, art, and religion, approaching them from first one and then another perspective, finding in the responses of his various characters both the diversity and the unity of all human experience. Through his characters, each with his own perspective, Browning described the complex, ambiguous, ironic nature of Truth, suggesting that man reaches for, partially seizes, never grasps completely the whole. He remains a seeker, attempting, succeeding only in his resolution to continue the attempt, to ensnare the eternal in the temporal.

a

Love is central in Browning's scheme of values, and yet he writes of no subject with greater hesitancy, with more ambiguity. He treats romantic love sometimes as physical passion ("Meeting at Night"), sometimes as Platonic worship ("Rudel to the Lady of Tripoli"), sometimes as spiritual union ("By the Fireside"), and always as being illusive and transient. Most of Browning's lovers are thwarted and frustrated.

In "By the Fireside," addressed to Elizabeth Barrett and

only thinly disguised as a monologue, Browning describes, more clearly than in any other of his poems, the relation between man and woman as an interdependent physical and spiritual union. He speaks through an old man who talks slowly and discursively, his mood and manner suggesting the placidity of his soul. Although he ostensibly addresses his wife, Leonor, the poem is more a meditation than a monologue. Indeed, so nearly perfect is the understanding between the lovers that words are dispensable. The speaker, knowing that his wife will understand, feels no compulsion to convince her, relying less upon direct statement than upon a melange of moods, images, and scenes to produce the sense of union between them. The long peaceful moment (time seems almost to stop and ancient Greece to merge with the apocalyptic future) provides the perspective from which, looking both forward and backward, he surveys their pilgrimage together from its beginnings ("we two drew together first/ Just for the obvious human bliss" [Stanza 29]) to its divine culminations ("So the earth has gained by one man more,/ And the gain of earth must be Heaven's gain too" [Stanza 53]). He describes with awe the moment that transformed their lives:

> *But you spared me this, like the heart you are,*
> *And filled my empty heart at a word.*
> *If you join two lives, there is oft a scar,*
> *They are one and one, with a shadowy third;*
> *One near one is too far.*
>
> *A moment after, and hands unseen*
> *Were hanging the night around us fast;*
> *But we knew that a bar was broken between*
> *Life and life: we were mixed at last*
> *In spite of the mortal screen.*
>
> *(Stanzas 46–47)*

That moment fixes their destinies and justifies their lives; it remains real but its immediacy is gone. There is a faint sadness in the fact that the old man sits now by the fireside reading "Not verse now, but prose," recalling but no longer experiencing the ecstasy of youthful love.

In the 1860 volume Browning placed "Any Wife to Any Husband" immediately after "By the Fireside," encouraging the reader to accept one as an ironic comment on the other. There is a similarity of language in the two poems. The wife, echoing the husband's language in "Fireside," says:

> But now, because the hour through years was fixed,
> Because our inmost beings met and mixed,
>   Because thou once hast loved me—
>
>   (Stanza 9)

The characters in the two poems might even be the same, the listener in the one becoming the speaker in the other. The woman in "Any Wife to Any Husband" displays qualities not suspected in the silent soul partner whom we see only through the eyes of the husband in "By the Fireside." When she speaks she throws new light both upon herself and her husband. She listens to his protestations of faithfulness skeptically and fearfully. Unlike him, dissatisfied with the moment, she wishes to secure also the future. Anticipating a time, perhaps after she is dead, when he will betray her, she tries to be heroic but fails. Her doubts act as a barrier between them, preventing each from entering wholly into a relation with the other. Their love is threatened less by the future than by the present, by the woman's doubts as much as by the man's possible unfaithfulness. The danger lies in something more subtle and elusive than a simple overt act. Personal reservations which make it impossible for either to enter fully, trustfully, into the experience of the moment prevents the fulfillment of a relation which began with a meeting and a mixing of their inmost beings. Their pilgrimage flounders short of the divine consummation imagined in "By the Fireside." The pathos of the failure is that neither is really responsible. "Had but love its will," she laments (Stanza 1), things would be different. She would trust and he would never wander, not even in imagination. But love does not have its will here, as in so many of Browning's poems.

"Two in the Campagna," one of Browning's finest short poems, explores the same theme. The young man aspires toward union with his mistress:

> *I would I could adopt your will,*
> *   See with your eyes, and set my heart*
> *Beating by yours, and drink my fill*
> *   At your soul's springs,—your part, my part*
> *In life, for good and ill.*
>
> (Stanza 9)

But here, too, love does not have its will, being thwarted by incomprehensible forces which neither man nor woman can control:

> *No. I yearn upward—touch you close,*
> *   Then stand away. I kiss your cheek,*
> *Catch your soul's warmth,—I pluck the rose*
> *   And love it more than tongue can speak—*
> *Then the good minute goes. . . .*
>
> *Just when I seemed about to learn!*
> *   Where is the thread now? Off again!*
> *The old trick! Only I discern—*

> *Infinite passion and the pain*
> *Of finite hearts that yearn.*
>
> *(Stanzas 10 and 12)*

Both "A Woman's Last Word" and "A Lovers' Quarrel" relate a pathetic incident in which a good relation is severed by some cause which remains undefined, is perhaps undefinable. In one a woman and in the other a man speaks his bewilderment that a thing so rare as love can be destroyed so easily. The woman teases, cajoles, flatters, and, finally, bribes, offering to place herself, flesh and spirit, in her husband's hands if he will cease arguing and merely love her; she finds herself incapable, however, when the moment comes:

> *That shall be to-morrow*
> *Not to-night:*
> *I must bury sorrow*
> *Out of sight:*
>
> *—Must a little weep, Love,*
> *—Foolish me!*
> *And so fall asleep, Love,*
> *Loved by thee.*
>
> *(Stanzas 9–10)*

The man despairs of normal reconciliation, wishing for them both an isolation so terrible that they would be forced in desperatiom to seek solace in each other. It doesn't come.

"Love Among the Ruins" is a romantic statement of a young man who, because of innocence, can conclude "Love is best." He has not yet learned the mysterious secret, "the old trick," which mars happiness in "Two in the Campagna," "A Lovers' Quarrel," "Any Wife to Any Husband," and "A Woman's Last Words."

"Evelyn Hope" is an aging man's macabre expression of his idealistic love for a young girl under circumstances which cause us to question his mental health. "The Last Ride Together" is less a love poem than a philosophical lyric. The speaker, like many of Browning's lovers, is thwarted, but he scarcely feels the loss of a woman or the ache of a broken relation. He accepts his rejection with surprising ease. That and the last ride he requests are only pretexts for a meditation upon time and eternity. Life is a riding, he concludes, an end in itself rather than a means to an end. Eternity is found in the good moment rather than in a heaven that comes when the gallop is over.

Browning treats love as many things and from many points of view. Most of his lovers, however, are frustrated and unhappy, their vision of an ideal love a tantalizing dream which only intensifies the pain of their unfulfilled longings.

b

Browning's poems on art and artists may be approached through a discussion of "How It Strikes a Contemporary." The poem sketches a poet not as he actually is but as he is seen by a contemporary. The speaker, a young man of mode, talks about a poet whom he has only seen and whose work he does not understand. He offers a series of impromptu, fragmentary, suggestive impressions rather than a full, consistent portrait. The poem implies more than it states.

The speaker tries to account for the impression the poet has made upon his peers, an impression not explained by external evidence. In spite of his detailed description and his various speculations, the poet remains a mystery, paradoxical and contradictory. The metaphors used to explain the poet are relevant and enlightening, but singly and as a group they fail to express the obvious full meaning of the poetic office. The speaker fails to establish a relation between the man and his work; indeed, to understand what his work is.

The speaker is handicapped by his external approach. His failures, ludicrous at times, confirm Browning's own distrust of the biographical approach to art (recall, for example, "House" and "At the 'Mermaid' "). "How It Strikes a Contemporary" on one level satirizes the imperceptiveness of his contemporaries and, on another, affirms the exalted office of the artist. The poet whose vision in some inexplicable way captures the infinite within finite forms surpasses rational explanation. The artist is a man of mystery whose real business is with God. His impact upon society, although certain, is indirect and, finally, immeasurable.

This sketchy figure, significant beyond appearance, is the prototype of all Browning's artists. Browning speaks about art indirectly through his personae permitting each to represent a partial and tentative insight into a subject that can be wholly understood and communicated by no single man. Through his *Men and Women,* however, certain attitudes and ideas emerge. The artist is obliged first to seek his own soul. His greatest failure is a loss of identity (in "Andrea del Sarto," "Master Hugues," and to some extent in "Fra Lippo Lippi"), a failure to understand himself and his relation to the Ideal.

His problem is increased, of course, by his inability to discover any structuring pattern in the universe outside himself and his consequent need to evolve his own meaning and value. Browning's artists remain lonely figures, men and women whose business, as Browning puts it, is with God. His immediate objective is to save his own soul, neither to please nor to redeem the social order. Although Browning senses some relation between the private vision and the social structure, the precise nature of that connection remains tenuous in his monologues. In *Men and Women* society appears most often in the role of villain, thwarting man's efforts to understand himself. Through the creative act, the artist attempts to free himself from the restricting patterns imposed upon him and to achieve the freedom to grow toward self-realization.

In "Old Pictures in Florence" Browning prefers early Renaissance painters (Giotto with his unfinished bell tower, for example) over Greek artists. That the Greeks achieved perfection is their failure:

> [*You*] *grew content in your poor degree*
> *With your little power, by those statues' godhead,*
> *And your little scope, by their eyes' full sway,*
> *And your little grace, by their grace embodied,*
> *And your little date, by their forms that stay.*
> *(Stanza 12)*

"What's come to perfection perishes," he continues, (Stanza 17), reiterating a characteristic aesthetic maxim. The marred, unfinished forms of early Renaissance art point beyond themselves to a vision that transcends formal expression. The Greek flaw becomes Giotto's glory, affirming by implication what can never be made explicit. For Browning, imperfections, distortions, and incompletions become technical devices, to be cultivated, not avoided, because they point beyond themselves, saying the unsayable. Basically, Browning shared Ruskin's views about Gothic art but emphasized their aesthetic rather than moral implications. In this respect his position seems more modern than Ruskin's.

Two of the poems are about music: "A Toccata of Galuppi's" and "Master Hugues of Saxe-Gotha." The theme of the former is the power of music to dissipate romantic illusion; its action, the disenchantment of the speaker, a provincial Englishman. He holds a romantic view both of ancient Venice and of himself. Into his world of illusion comes the music of Galuppi "like a ghostly cricket" (Stanza 12) to remind him of human limitations and transience, bringing him a devastating new insight:

> "Dust and ashes!" So you creak it, and I want the
>   heart to scold.
> Dear dead women, with such hair, too—what's
>   become of all the gold
> Used to hang and brush their bosoms? I feel chilly
>   and grown old.
>
> (Stanza 15)

Music is equally enlightening and destructive in "Master Hugues." The poem is a monologue about the speaker, a church organist who delights in his technical skill, and about an imaginary composer who wrote elaborate fugues. It details the speaker's discovery of the emptiness of both the music and his performance. The organist wants to believe that those complex musical structures, like the spider webs on the ceiling of the church, obscure a gold beneath. He comes to realize, however, that "not a glimpse of the far land/ Gets through" those forms (Stanza 24). The structures are symbolic of the "traditions, inventions" to which the composer has given his devotion; they obscure rather than reveal vision. Master Hugues and his disciple, like Pictor Ignotus, refuse the saving vision.

Browning uses light as unifying symbol, the poem beginning in the small glow of a candle and ending in darkness;

he reinforces this basic symbol by having the speaker descend from the choir loft down the "rotten-planked rat-riddled stairs" (Stanza 29). Part of his meaning is communicated through an ironic tone produced by the juxtaposition of the comic and grotesque, with the chilling sense of nothingness that increasingly "o'ershrouds" the speaker. The last line structurally embodies the idea and emotion of the poem, "Do I carry the moon in my pocket?"

Men and Women contains two great monologues in which painters are speakers: "Andrea del Sarto" and "Fra Lippo Lippi." Browning's continuing effort to depict the artist who fails reaches near perfection in "Andrea." The poem traces the subtle, complex, psychological process by which a man comes through self-realization to recognize his failure as lover, artist, and man. Andrea's speech is at once a dialogue with his wife, the beautiful but soulless Lucrezia, and a dialectical argument with himself. On one level, he humiliatingly barters with his wife for a few minutes of her time and, on the other, struggles against the self-realization which threatens to crumble his illusion of himself as husband and painter.

Andrea is an especially poignant figure because his vision exceeds his power to achieve: he desires a relation with Lucrezia beyond his capacity to demand (and perhaps beyond hers to give) and an artistic realization within his technical powers but beyond his spiritual reach. His tragedy is to know at once what he aspires to and what, in contrast, he can achieve. Ironically, he has insight and sensibility to feel the loss of that which he cannot grasp; his technical skill highlights rather than mitigates his spiritual poverty. The distance between aspiration and capacity, which he subconsciously feels, becomes increasingly overt as he talks. He senses the contradictions within himself. He both desires and fears the light, resents and welcomes the snare; he is at once the aspiring lover-painter and the "weak-eyed bat" compulsively seeking the dark. He is drawn to and repelled by Lucrezia.

He comes eventually to understand himself but can only accept and endure, not remedy his situation. He speaks rightly of himself as a "half-man" and "faultless painter." Lucrezia's "soulless" beauty and his sterile relation with her ("You love me quite enough, it seems to-night" [257]) define the limits of his capacities; the soulless perfection of his paintings delineates his artistic reach ("Ah, but a man's reach should exceed his grasp" [96]). Finally, darkness descends upon the world outside and upon Andrea within. Yielding to self-destroying impulses, he symbolically seeks refuge upon Lucrezia's breast, ironically reversing the relation suggested by his earlier metaphor: "Your soft hand is a woman of itself,/ And mine the man's bared breast she curls inside" (21–22). He finds in his token possession of her physical beauty some compensation for all the glory he has lost; he exchanges the half-hour she sits and holds his hand for the evening she is to spend with the lover who waits outside. Andrea comes to accept the reversal of roles that he initially rejected. Lucrezia calls, not he; she is the assertive and he the receptive member of the pair. Acquiescing finally in his own personal and artistic mediocrity, he accepts his state:

> . . . the whole seems to fall into a shape
> As if I saw alike my work and self
> And all that I was born to be and do,
> A twilight-piece.
>
> (46–49)

Nowhere does Browning work more surely than in this poem. Nowhere does he create a more fully realized character, a more nearly self-contained poem. "Andrea del Sarto" comes close to Browning's objective to create "things" rather than to write thoughts about them.

In "Fra Lippo Lippi," another of Browning's artists rationalizes his failures. In many respects Fra Lippo contrasts with Andrea. The essentially passive Andrea is married to a beautiful and sensual woman; the virile, masculine Lippo is a monk. Where Andrea fails, Lippo succeeds all too readily. Andrea is debilitated by an emptiness of soul; Lippo is possessed of a powerful upsurge of life (physical and spiritual), which creates tension between his own impulses and the expectations imposed on him by the world. Like many of Browning's characters, he struggles for self-realization, or "soul," against contradictory external forces—religious, social, artistic traditions. His conflict is expressed as a series of paradoxes: the world and the Garden; the street and the monastery; the sportive ladies and the Virgin; animal indulgence and holy reverence. He rejects the exclusive claims of each in search of wholeness that integrates body and soul. As in "Andrea del Sarto," the life and work of the man are inextricably bound together. Lippo's paintings reflect his physical gusto, his spiritual aspiration, his compromises. At the beginning, Lippo, obviously tipsy, is caught in that section of town "Where sportive ladies leave their doors ajar" (6). He attempts with unbecoming jocularity and crudeness to bribe, threaten, and wheedle his way out of a bad situation. Our first impression is not good, but as the poem develops we are forced first to modify and finally to alter our opinion. Lippo becomes increasingly sober, complex, serious. The poem ends, however, not in triumph but in compromise as Lippo disappears into the dusk of dawn. The movement of the poem is from sensuality to idealism to compromise. Lippo is unable to escape entirely the spiritual and artistic stereotypes which the external world presents for his emulation; he is unable to reconcile within him the claims of body and soul that seem at once mutually supporting and contradictory. At best his efforts at self-realization are only partially successful. The picture he proposes to paint as penance for his "night out" is a summary symbol of his final compromise. His vision focuses first on the Blessed Virgin and then on "a sweet angelic slip of a thing" who "puts out a soft palm" to lead him into the "celestial presence" (370–372). The two never merge into one figure capable of representing that wholeness which he seeks.

In "Andrea del Sarto" the deepening dusk symbolizes Andrea's progressive deterioration. In "Fra Lippo Lippi" light is also symbolic. The poem begins in darkness and ends in murky dawn. The progression toward a little light contrasts Lippo's partial salvation with Andrea's lostness. At the same time, however, the weakness of light suggests also Lippo's failure to integrate completely the monastery and the street into one clear and affirmative vision.

c

Robert Browning considered all activities religious which granted man a momentary vision of the infinite through finite action and form. The process of acting and making were in themselves devotional, so that, in a sense, Browning's lovers, poets, painters, musicians, seekers were as preoccupied with God as were his priests and philosophers. It is, therefore, misleading to call one group of Browning's poems religious, inferring that others are not. Certain poems, however, deal more explicitly than others with religious problems. There are three such works in *Men and Women* which deserve special notice: "Cleon," "Bishop Blougram's Apology," and "An Epistle Containing the Strange Medical Experience of Karshish, the Arab Physician."

"Cleon" represents superficially a clash between Greek

humanism and Christianity.[6] Browning's concerns, however, are less theological and moral than psychological.
Neither arguing the superiority of Christianity nor deplor-
ing Cleon's rejection of it, he presents Cleon's soul struggle
between paradoxical tensions: sensitiveness to beauty and
awareness of its fragility; joy in physical love and increasing debility; respect for intellect and growing awareness of
its limitations; love for art and realization that the fabri-
cated can never substitute for the actual; desire to eternal-
ize time and a sense of its transience; instinctive need for a
revealed religion and inability to accept one. In the course
of the poem, Cleon assumes first one stance and then another, finding peace in none. First he is the acclaimed poet
and then the rationalistic philosopher; finally, unable to
reconcile these contradictory roles and realizing that in
neither alone can he find the meaning he seeks, he brings
the whole man into focus. He sees that, having exhausted
the resources of body and mind, he needs a new vision, a
new impetus to action:

> *Long since, I imaged, wrote the fiction out,*
> *That he or other God, descended here*
> *And, once for all, showed simultaneously*
> *What, in its nature, never can be shown*
> *Piecemeal or in succession. . . .*
>
> (115–119)

> *It is so horrible,*
> *I dare at times imagine to my need*
> *Some future state revealed to us by Zeus. . . .*
>
> (323–325)

When the new vision comes, however, in the form of St.
Paul's Christianity, he cannot accept it. He *cannot*—the
imperative constitutes his tragedy—on the one hand, be-

cause of psychological and cultural barriers, and, on the other, because of intellectual and moral limitations, inescapable parts of the "human condition" as Browning understands it. Browning's triumph in this poem is neither argumentative nor inspirational, but artistic. He presents the immediate sense of Cleon's frustration, his paradoxical outreach and his limitations.

"Bishop Blougram's Apology" details an argument between a worldly nineteenth-century Roman Catholic bishop and a young journalist, Gigadibs, a self-professed literary man, a free-thinker, an idealist, who assumes that the Bishop is either a fool or a knave. He hopes in the course of the evening to trap the churchman into a confession that he can turn into a sensational literary expose. It is soon clear, however, that the Bishop is neither fool nor knave. Arguing on Gigadibs' own premises—which he himself recognizes as ultimately inadequate—he easily reduces the young man's intellectual pretensions to nonsense and, at the same time, demonstrates the pragmatic superiority of religion over agnosticism even on rationalistic grounds. His argument is a tour de force, an apology addressed solely to Gigadibs. As the final statement of the Christian religion it is unsatisfactory, not because it is false but because it is partial. The Bishop understands its limitations precisely:

> "I justify myself
> On every point where cavillers like this
> Oppugn my life: he tries one kind of fence—
> I close—he's worsted, that's enough for him;
> He's on the ground! if the ground should break away
> I take my stand on, there's a firmer yet
> Beneath it, both of us may sink and reach."
>
> (997–1003)

The apology, nevertheless, serves its immediate purpose, the devastation of Gigadibs, and, incidentally, reveals spiritual depths in the speaker that correct our initial impression of him as superficially worldly:

> *Just when we are safest, there's a sunset-touch,*
> *A fancy from a flower-bell, some one's death,*
> *A chorus-ending from Euripides,—*
> *And that's enough for fifty hopes and fears*
> *As old and new at once as Nature's self,*
> *To rap and knock and enter in our soul,*
> *Take hands and dance there, a fantastic ring,*
> *Round the ancient idol, on his base again,—*
> *The grand Perhaps!*
>
> (182–190)

That Browning, too, considered the Bishop's apology partial is clear from his postscript. The Bishop's clever casuistry has destroyed the young man's illusions and sent him off to Australia in search of a new and, we hope, more authentic life. Browning suggests that something more positive than argument is needed, however, to give that life substance:

> *Just a week*
> *Sufficed his sudden healthy vehemence. . . .*
> *And having bought, not cabin-furniture*
> *But settler's-implements (enough for three)*
> *And started for Australia—there, I hope,*
> *By this time he has tested his first plough,*
> *And studied his last chapter of St. John.*
>
> (1006–1014)

In "An Epistle," Karshish, the Arab physician, writes to his master Abib about his trip into Palestine. His ostensible purpose is to report scientific information, but the larger part of the letter is devoted to an unscientific account of the strange case of a man, one Lazarus, who claims to have been raised from the dead by a Nazarene physician of his tribe. This fact Abib would like to report with scientific objectivity, along with his observations on spiders, gum tragacanth, and scalp disease, but he is unable to do so.

Obviously, his experience has profoundly disoriented him. He is bewildered and embarrassed by an instinctive, emotional response to a situation at odds with both his reason and his preconceived notions. We sense the tension almost from the beginning. After the short opening formalities and his perfunctory report on his findings, both of which establish the limits within which he ordinarily thinks and acts, his tone changes radically. He takes up the subject of Lazarus with thinly disguised enthusiasm:

> *I half resolve to tell thee, yet I blush,*
> *What set me off a-writing first of all.*
> *An itch I had, a sting to write, a tang. . . .*
> (65–67)

We realize immediately that the necessity to understand and to reconcile his contradictory responses to this event is his only purpose for writing. Forcing himself to communicate with his skeptical old master seems, no doubt, a discipline capable of restoring his reason and reordering his world. It works only partially, however. For the epistle as it is finally shaped is less a report to Abib than the personal record of an intense inner struggle. Its concerns are psychological rather than scientific; its method, dialectical rather than expository.

In the main body of the poem, Karshish attempts to obscure the real issue; nevertheless, he speaks with ambivalent skepticism and belief, contempt and sympathy. What he rejects rationally he embraces emotionally; throughout, there is a tense interplay between conscious and unconscious. The result is a seemingly irreconcilable conflict. At any rate, Browning's purpose is to communicate a sense of the conflict rather than to enunciate its resolution. In this poem, as in so many others, Browning appears willing to sacrifice ideological and moral completeness to psychological intensity. To the very end he subordinates statement to internal action.

"An Epistle" is less conclusive than "Cleon," a poem it resembles in many respects. The main difference in the two is less in theme than in character. Cleon, it is clear, will reject Christianity and all other challenges to new life. Karshish, although noncommittal, remains open-minded, capable of action:

> *The very God! think, Abib; dost thou think?*
> *So, the All-Great, were the All-Loving too. . . .*
> *The madman saith He said so: it is strange.*
>
> *(304–305, 312)*

d

"In a Balcony," a play included in the first edition of *Men and Women,* although a love story, belongs in a category by itself. It introduces metaphysical questions and exemplifies structural problems beyond those of the love poems proper. In some respects, "In a Balcony" is reminiscent of the earlier poem, "In a Gondola." Both assert the power of love to awaken within man and woman the most intense passion and to propel them toward self-realizing action. "In a Balcony" goes beyond "In a Gondola," however, to consider the often conflicting responsibilities of the love-awakened individual to himself and to society.

"In a Gondola" avoids social and moral questions. Browning handles his materials so that the reader's response to the poem is limited. He reacts emotionally to love's triumph, without, however, becoming involved in matters that raise intellectual and moral questions. The husband, clearly a symbol of soul-destroying conventions, is a villain incapable of evoking sympathetic response from the reader. Moreover, the lovers have no obligation to society save perhaps a destructive one. Their only concern is self-realization, a process that occurs in a world of romantic imagination as detached as possible from everyday reality.

In the play, the situation is more complicated. Norbert and Constance too are concerned about self-realization. Their course of action, however, is less clear. They live among flesh-and-blood people in a world that makes real demands upon them. The Queen is a pathetic character with whom the reader becomes emotionally involved. Norbert and Constance cannot realize their love for each other without hurting her. Moreover, society in the play is worth man's sacrificial service, as Norbert declares. There seems no way, however, by which he can claim his love for Constance—a certain good—and at the same time govern the country—also a good, we assume. The lovers, in short, are placed in an ambiguous situation in which no course of action is open by which they can meet their responsibilities at once to themselves and to their Queen and realm.

The problem is not merely ideological but also aesthetic. Browning presents both the Queen and the idea of service too sympathetically for the reader to accept them as mere obstacles to be overcome at any cost by the lovers in their search for fulfillment in each other. The play raises questions and awakens expectations that are never resolved. It remains both structurally and thematically incomplete.

Perhaps Browning did not know how the play should end; that is, what constituted a "right" action for the lovers. An earlier writer would certainly have subordinated the lesser to the greater claim, the lovers to the moral and social responsibility imposed upon them. In "In a Gondola," Browning gave pre-eminence to the lovers by recognizing only their obligation to themselves. By 1845, however, he had lost faith in an externally imposed system of values and was unable to accept the solution that would have been obvious to a preromantic writer. To sacrifice the lovers would violate their individuality, negate the source of their potential moral life. It was inevitable, however, that Browning, with his complex, inquiring mind, should come to feel dissatisfied with his treatment of the problem in the earlier poem. By 1855, he felt the need to place his characters in a larger context and to confront them with the conflicting demands to which his new sense of reality gave rise. In the absence of clear, external directions and with an obligation for self-realization and assertion, Browning's lovers in "In a Balcony" face what appears an unsolvable paradox. Browning himself is equivocal.

"In a Gondola" ends with the death of the lovers, a triumphant if sentimental consummation to what we accept as a great love. The play, on the other hand, ends inconclusively. After her humiliation, the Queen leaves the room, and a moment later the music stops. The lovers hear the "measured heavy tread" of the guards approaching. What their mission is we never learn. We do not discover whether the lovers are punished or rewarded. It is clear that Norbert and Constance have achieved a personal good through their love for each other. It is equally clear, also, that they have claimed salvation at the expense of the Queen and the people. What are we to say, what does Browning say, of the conflict between that self-realization and the violation of social and moral values which he has so obviously built into the structure of his play? Browning equivocates. He withholds answer in the play itself. His later tentative explanation evades the real issue: "The queen had a large and passionate temperament, which had only once been touched and brought into intense life. She would have died, as by a knife in her heart. The guard would have come to carry away her dead body." [7]

In "In a Balcony" Browning acknowledges one of the human predicaments which his subjective morality creates: the paradoxical demands made upon man by his conflicting personal and social vision. This potentially tragic dilemma was to become a central concern in *The Ring and the Book*. Constance and Norbert stand somewhere between the lovers in "In a Gondola" and Caponsacchi and Pompilia in *The Ring and the Book*. "In a Balcony" signals a maturation in Browning's thinking. It emphasizes a theme that was increasingly to contribute a tragic motif to his poetry.

To the literary critic, Browning's increasing preoccupation with this human paradox has as much aesthetic as philosophical significance. The breakdown in the dramatic structure of "In a Balcony" signals his need for a new literary mode capable of realizing structurally his grasp of man's complex and often frustrating search for values in the modern world.

V ❦ *Dramatis Personae*

Dramatis Personae, though in many ways a continuation of *Men and Women*, exhibits striking differences. In the interval between publication of the two works, Mrs. Browning died and Browning departed Italy for England, leaving behind him, he tells us, his heart and also, we infer, much of the physical and emotional exuberance that distinguishes his earlier work. As Dowden observes, "Italy is no longer the background of the human figures. There is perhaps less opulence of color; less of the manifold 'joy of liv-ing.' " [8]

An even greater, although related, difference lies in Browning's increased preoccupation with ideas. Even in the best poems he subtly shifts emphasis from character development to thought, from unified experience to impassioned argument. This shift of emphasis has been observed often and lamented as a sign of Browning's waning poetic powers. It disturbs particularly those who see all Browning's poetry declining in value after *The Ring and the Book*. Such is not necessarily the case, however. Behind the shift, I suggest, lies Browning's growing concern—which we have already observed in "In a Balcony"—to discover some means of bringing his isolated men and women together in a relation that will transform their private visions into universal truths and provide some basis upon which meaning and values may be grounded. This effort is given heightened dramatic tension by the fact that Browning experienced a deepening loss of faith in all the conventional modes of organizing human experience into meaningful patterns. He increasingly lamented the limits of romantic love, of art, and of the Christian religion to provide for man a full and satisfying experience. Clearly, the noticeable shift of emphasis in *Dramatis Personae* anticipates a new stage in Browning's career that was to become clearly apparent in *The Ring and the Book*.

a

The love poems in this volume display a growing disillusionment and frustration. None of them expresses the passionate affirmation of the man-woman relation that characterized earlier poems like "In a Gondola," "Love Among the Ruins," or "In a Balcony." None celebrates immediately the joys of physical love like "Meeting at Night." The mood of these poems, rather, is nostalgic, embittered, sometimes skeptical. More often than not, the love relationship is never satisfactorily consummated and the disappointed lovers are left feeling incomplete and frustrated. Even love, the noblest of passions, Browning seems to say, is capable only rarely, and then momentarily, of giving man the experience of meaning and value.

The initial poem in the volume, "James Lee" (later called "James Lee's Wife"), is a sequence of nine lyrics in which a woman relates the progressive disintegration of her marriage. The lyrics are linked by theme and mood rather than by sequential events. Each depicts a new insight that reorders the past and projects the speaker into another stage of her development. We see James Lee only through his wife's eyes, and we see her partly through what she tells us and partly through what she unwittingly betrays. She laments his incapacity and unwillingness to love her wholly and exclusively; he, we suspect, is frightened by her feminine possessiveness and repelled by her doubts and hysteria. At the end of the poem, we are uncertain whether the two were separated by the real or the imagined. At any rate, a union which began in mutual love and trust deteriorates successively through initial alienation to final physical parting. Browning emphasizes less the causes than the inevitability of the separation. Neither James Lee nor his wife can prevent the tragedy which neither desires. Theirs is, essentially, the paradox of the two lovers in the campagna. The subject of the poem is the effect of the action upon the woman rather than the action itself. The poem is a subtle treatment of feminine psychology and suffering.

In "The Worst of It," a poem less subtly conceived and less skillfully executed, Browning reverses the situation and permits a man to lament the unfaithfulness of his wife. In "Dîs Aliter Visum," "Too Late," and "Youth and Art" Browning gives the subject another twist. In these, love is unfulfilled because the lovers failed to grasp it when they had the opportunity. The result is unfulfillment and frustration, as the speaker in "Youth and Art" reveals:

> *Each life's unfulfilled, you see;*
> *It hangs still, patchy and scrappy:*
> *We have not sighed deep, laughed free,*
> *Starved, feasted, despaired,—been happy.*
>
> *And nobody calls you dunce,*
> *And people suppose me clever:*
> *This could but have happened once,*
> *And we missed it, lost it forever.*
>
> (*Stanzas 16–17*)

"A Likeness" treats love as an illusion, not only incapable of being realized but highly subjective and inexpressible. Each of three pictures represents to its owner alone a dream of love. Two stand in sharp contrast to the reality: a wife in one case and a chance acquaintance in the other. The speaker himself possesses a mezzotint which has

> *. . . more than a hint*
> *Of a certain face, I never*
> *Saw elsewhere touch or trace of*
> *In women I've seen the face of:*
> *Just an etching, and, so far, clever.*
>
> (*37–41*)

He alone, however, is capable of seeing the illusion behind the object. Obviously its beauty resides within his mind and is without counterpart in the world. In all three cases art functions to achieve the illusion of an ideal that life cannot actually provide. Love may be experienced as a subjective illusion but rarely attained as a reality.

Three poems deal with love and death. "Confessions" relates the memories of a dying man who, in spite of direful admonition from his priest, finds comfort in an earlier love long since dead for some unstated reason. The poem ends in an affirmation that defies conventional religious strictures:

> *Alas,*
> *We loved, sir—used to meet:*
> *How sad and bad and mad it was—*
> *But then, how it was sweet!*
> *(Stanza 9)*

"May and Death" recounts the grief of a woman whose heart died with her lover. "Prospice," too, tells of lovers being separated by death, and it, alone among the love poems in this volume, anticipates a reunion of the lovers in an afterlife. Its affirmation, however, is insufficient to counterbalance the sense of loss and frustration which the other poems so forcefully assert. For the men and women of this volume, love provides limited incentive toward self-realization and values.

b

"Abt Vogler" is one of Browning's most satisfying poems about art. Its conception is dramatic, although its form is appropriately lyrical. Its concerns are psychological rather than philosophical; its solution to the problems of human existence is tentative rather than dogmatic. The poem depicts an experience in the life of a great musician as he moves through three psychological stages: the ecstasy of creation, the impassioned affirmation of life's meaning, the return to ordinary everyday existence. The poem is the embodiment of a developing experience rather than the statement of an argument. Certain attitudes about art and

its service to man do emerge, however. Abt Vogler declares
the supremacy of music over literature and painting, not
because he himself is a musician but because of the nature
of music and the kind of meaning that all art tries to
achieve. It is a purer, more faithful expression of the inner
life, of the naked will, of the creator than either literature
or painting; it is hindered by neither the static form of
painting nor the rational structure of language. It has
power to reconcile opposites (Abt Vogler's creation unites
the depths of hell with the heights of heaven) and to impose a unified, meaningful structure upon the outer world.
In the seventh stanza the musician achieves a unity of vision, a sense of meaning which few of Browning's characters, even his other artists, experience:

> *But here is the finger of God, a flash of the will*
> > *that can,*
> > *Existent behind all laws, that made them and,*
> > *lo, they are!*
> *And I know not if, save in this, such gift be*
> > *allowed to man,*
> > *That out of three sounds he frame, not a fourth*
> > *sound, but a star.*
> *Consider it well: each tone of our scale in itself*
> > *is naught;*
> > *It is everywhere in the world—loud, soft, and*
> > *all is said:*
> *Give it to me to use! I mix it with two in my*
> > *thought;*
> > *And, there! Ye have heard and seen: consider*
> > *and bow the head!*

From these lines it is clear that the order which Abt Vogler
momentarily calls into being is a subjective projection, not
a quality inherent in external matter.

In the next stanza, the inevitable occurs; the dream vision dissipates and the momentary illusion of meaning and self-fulfillment vanishes. Abt Vogler is left with a frustrating emptiness. The following three stanzas record his attempt to repair his loss. Unable to surrender the transitory vision and to face the meaninglessness of life, he projects, out of his need, a new vision of an existence beyond this one that will expand the fragment into a whole, transform the broken arch into the perfect round. It is important to observe the grounds upon which this hope is based and the ends it is capable of producing. The affirmation is not rational, not analogical. It does not follow inevitably from the experience he has undergone. It is "willed" just as surely and just as irrationally as his earlier creation. Both are extemporizations. The latter, the necessary answer to a psychological need, makes it possible for him to return to "The C Major of this life" without despairing. The poem records one man's encounter with and his ordering of reality through the creative imagination.

c

It is characteristic that Browning's poems on art and religion become almost indistinguishable in his middle and later works. The manner in which his use of the concept of Incarnation changes suggests the subtle alteration that was taking place in his thinking. In 1850, in *Christmas-Eve and Easter-Day,* he affirmed the Incarnation in theological language that encouraged his readers to interpret his thoughts quite traditionally. By 1864, when he published *Dramatis Personae,* particularly in "A Death in the Desert," he tried to divorce the meaning of Incarnation from historical fact and to discover for it some other ground of meaning. Browning continued to talk about Incarnation—

particularly in *The Ring and the Book*—as embodying a concept psychologically necessary to man, but he increasingly described it in aesthetic rather than theological terms. By the time he came to write *Parleyings* the concept had lost all of its theological meaning and had assumed a radically new significance in Browning's work.

Obviously, he was already moving farther from traditional Christianity in 1864, although in many cases he continued to use its terminology. He was beginning to invest old language with new meaning. Browning concludes *Dramatis Personae* with a very significant "Epilogue" in which three speakers, David, Renan, and "I," ostensibly the poet, express differing views. David celebrates in language reminiscent of the Psalms the glory of the transcendent Jehovah; Renan laments the disappearance of Christ, of that "Face," from the modern world, and the sad state of man "lone and left/ Silent through centuries." The "I," rejecting both the transcendental hope of David and the despair of Renan, attempts to retain in new form the essence of the Christian faith:

> *When you acknowledge that one world could do*
> *All the diverse work, old yet ever new,*
> *Divide us, each from other, me from you,—*
>
> *Why, where's the need of Temple, when the walls*
> *O' the world are that? What use of swells and falls*
> *From Levites' choir, Priests' cries, and trumpet-*
> *   calls?*
>
> *That one Face, far from vanish, rather grows,*
> *Or decomposes but to recompose,*
> *Becomes my universe that feels and knows!*
> *   (93–101)*

The problem becomes one of discovering what Browning was discarding and how he was reshaping what remained to make it relevant to the needs of contemporary man. Clearly, on one very practical level, the Face of Christ has become a symbol that enables man to encounter the external world and to impose upon it some semblance of order out of which values may be derived.

Three poems, particularly, in this collection deal significantly with religious problems: "Mr. Sludge, 'The Medium,'" "Caliban upon Setebos," and "A Death in the Desert." All three are concerned with contemporary efforts to reassert the presence of a spiritual dimension in life. The first treats the popular spiritualist movement; the second, both the current notion of a spiritual evolution which paralleled physical development and the Deistic attempt to find in nature a revelation of God; the third, the so-called higher criticism which was undermining fundamentalist faith in the historicity of Christianity and in the infallibility of Scripture. Browning's attitude, extremely complex, ranges from utter contempt to sympathetic understanding. His purpose, as I shall show, was not simply that of a popular controversialist; he was availing himself of popular concerns to explore the problem of reality upon which his career as a poet was grounded.

"Mr. Sludge, 'The Medium'" is a contemptuous dismissal of a crude spiritualism. The poem is perhaps an overlong, overingenious monologue spoken by a medium whose cheating has been detected by his gullible patron. In what follows both medium and patron are treated with equal scorn. In self-defense, Mr. Sludge argues, first, that he was conned into imposture by his gullible patrons (a charge not entirely untrue), and, second, shifting grounds, that perhaps he was not after all an imposter (a claim possibly true in a manner that the superficial Sludge could not understand). Perhaps, he suggests, his efforts, which on the surface appeared deceptive, were in reality a crude but effective testimony to a spiritual dimension in human experience. In his first defense he displays unwittingly his own capacity to be deceived. The second part of his argument is certainly not a serious defense of spiritualism; it is, however, an acknowledgment that even a Sludge can be ambivalent. There are moments, no doubt, when the grand deceiver is himself his own victim.

Throughout his discourse, Sludge displays less a villainous than a mean, petty spirit. He lacks the stature to be really evil. We are repelled primarily by his smallness and his crude vulgarity. In this poem, Browning avoids human complexities. We sympathize neither with Sludge nor his victim. The presence of the patron, obviously the fool if not the "brute-beast and blackguard" Sludge depicts him, fails to arouse our emotional response. The poem does have a certain intellectual subtlety, however. Sludge is something of a humorist who ironically makes himself the butt of his own jokes, turning mankind into a passel of fools of whom, unwittingly, he is chief. His last line is amusingly revealing: "Besides, is he the only fool in the world?"

That Browning's purpose in "Caliban upon Setebos; or, Natural Theology in the Island" was twofold is suggested by the title. His first aim, implied by the first half of the title, was to create a primitive character and to permit him to develop dramatically his necessarily childish and crude concept of God. The poem is a genuine triumph in the dramatic method.[9] If we judge Caliban's theology rationally and out of context we are repelled by it. Browning, however, makes it difficult for us to dissociate thought from emotion and sensation by presenting not an ordered argument but a character in the throes of self-realization. We respond sympathetically to this monstrous creature who not only endures the hardships of primitive existence but also the capricious spite of his Setebos. We share his struggle for self-understanding and, indeed, occasionally exult in what seems the glimmering of a deeper, more civilized insight into spiritual reality. Browning has considerably more sympathy for Caliban than for Mr. Sludge.

The poem has another level of meaning, however. Caliban's natural theology may appear a virtue on his primitive island, but on the English island and among Browning's contemporaries it seems crude indeed. That Browning intended to satirize natural theologians of the late eighteenth and early nineteenth century seems apparent.[10] The subtitle of the poem, "Thou thoughtest that I was altogether such an one as thyself," suggests that a man who today reduces God to his own image unwittingly reduces himself to the level of Caliban.

Read exclusively either as a character study or a satire upon contemporary theologians the poem appears one-dimensional. Read, however, as a character study and a commentary, the one reinforcing the other, it becomes richly and ironically complex. That the commentary is subdued and controlled, communicated more by implication than by direct statement, makes "Caliban" one of Browning's most effective poems in this volume. He also succeeds in embodying thought in character and action, giving it emotional and sensuous dimensions that are missing in the more pretentious poem, "A Death in the Desert."

"A Death in the Desert" demands attention, however, beyond its aesthetic merits for the light it throws on Browning's poetic vision and method. In this poem Browning realizes clearly and precisely an interpretation of the Incarnation that apparently he himself had come to accept. The stance from which St. John views man's search for reality suggests the intuitive insight that informs Browning's best work. The poem is an imaginative account of the death of the Beloved Disciple. Dying, St. John constructs a Christian apologetic for a coming age when skeptical men will question the validity of the historical account of the life of Christ. Obviously, the poem is a reply to Browning's contemporaries who questioned the rational and historical validity of Christianity; less obvious, however, are the terms of Browning's counterattack. He does not question their logic or their scholarship but argues that their conclusion—the discrediting of Christianity—is a *non sequitur.* He grants, at least for the sake of argument, their strictures against Christianity; he discards, also, traditional defenses based upon revelation and miracle. Mrs. Orr reports a statement by Browning which throws light upon the poem: "I know all that may be said against it [Christianity], on the grounds of history, of reason or even moral sense. I grant even that it may be a fiction." [11] It might seem that here Browning concedes his case, and on certain grounds he does. The dying John foresees just such an age as Browning's when not only his report but his existence itself will be questioned. In such a time, John, obviously Browning's spokesman, suggests that Christianity must be defended on other grounds. The new skepticism, he asserts, is necessary to man's spiritual development.

St. John develops his apology in essentially non-Christian language and thought patterns, carefully dissociating the essence of the Gospel from the mythical forms through which it is conveyed. In the "Epilogue," already referred to, even the Face itself is in a process of continual decomposition and recomposition. Mythical forms of Christianity can and must change if the truth they communicate is to remain viable. Man is in the position of a climber on a ladder, the rungs of which crumble beneath him as he ascends. The old myths dissolve as man pushes from one form of expression to another.

In his statement to Mrs. Orr, a portion of which I have already quoted, Browning continued: "But I am none the less convinced that the life and death of Christ, as Christians apprehend them, supply something which their humanity requires, and that it is true for them." The key phrases, "as Christians apprehend them" and "is true for them" provide the clues to Browning's own thought, throwing light on St. John's argument. They also confirm a truth discovered through another mode by the musician Abt Vogler. John defends the Revelation on a subjective rather than a historical or dogmatic basis. His concerns are more epistemological than ontological, more pragmatic than idealistic. His apology, neither mystical, dogmatic, rational, nor pietistic, breaks with tradition. It is essentially modern, at once pragmatic and existential. Christianity is valid, he asserts, because of all world views it best meets man's innate needs. For the individual, it may be at first a hypothesis to which he tentatively commits himself as a necessary precondition to self-realization. The experience that follows and the good it produces validates, if not the objective Truth itself, the experience which belief in that Truth makes possible. From these effects, man deduces the "fact." That which cannot be arrived at by reason proves reasonable. Contrary to Henry Jones and his numerous followers, Browning does not negate reason but assigns to it a new, active, though subordinate role.[12] The Pope in *The Ring and the Book* summarizes, saying:

> *There is, beside the works, a tale of Thee*
> *In the world's mouth which I find credible:*
> *I love it with my heart: unsatisfied,*
> *I try it with my reason, nor discept*
> *From any point I probe and pronounce sound.*
>
> (X, *1347–1351*)

The "works" come before the "Tale." Man loves and then reasons. He reasons not about the love itself but about its ends. These man finds consistent with his deepest needs.

Whether Browning himself believed the historical fact is uncertain; his position is at best equivocal. With this matter, however, we are not primarily concerned. What is important is that Browning's handling of this problem goes a long way toward defining the values and techniques that inform and structure his best poetry. In this poem, he reveals explicitly his concern to discover some viable ground for meaning and values. It is a concern that was to preoccupy him for the rest of his life.

❦ ❦ ❦ CHAPTER IV

Immortal Nakedness:
The Ring and the Book

Into another state, under new rule
I knew myself was passing swift and sure;
Whereof the initiatory pang approached,
Felicitous annoy, as bitter-sweet
As when the virgin-band, the victors chaste,
Feel at the end the earthly garments drop,
And rise with something of a rosy shame
Into immortal nakedness: so I
Lay, and let come the proper throe would thrill
Into the ecstasy and outthrob pain.

(VI, 964–973)

❦ On a June day in 1860, Robert Browning, browsing through items on a vender's stall in the Square of San Lorenzo in Florence, discovered the vellum-covered volume now known as The Old Yellow Book, source of *The Ring and the Book*. It attracted him immediately. One glance, he tells us, and " 'Stall!' cried I: a *lira* made it mine." He said later, ". . . a Hand, always above my shoulder, pushed me. . . ."

Returning to Casa Guidi, he read as he walked: "A Setting-forth of the entire Criminal Cause against Guido Franceschini, Nobleman of Arezzo, and his Bravoes, who were put to death in Rome, February 22, 1698. The first by beheading, the other four by gallows. Roman Murder-Case. In which it is disputed whether and when a Husband may kill his Adulterous Wife without incurring the ordinary penalty." [1] Beginning with that title page he became so engrossed in the sensational murder trial that he found himself in front of his house without knowing how he arrived there. During that fateful walk, he assures us, he penetrated beneath the lurid facts to discover there the dormant truth awaiting resuscitation.

Perhaps indeed Browning did on that day decide that Guido was guilty and Pompilia innocent. He was given to impulsive judgments. It was four years, however, before he set to work in earnest to write his poem and eight years before he published it, eight years of personal grief and disappointment. Mrs. Browning died in 1862; Browning's father, in 1866; Mrs. Browning's sister Arabel, in early 1868. During these years Browning watched with increasing apprehension and disappointment as his son Pen approached young manhood. By the time Browning finished the poem, it was clear that Pen would not be admitted to Balliol and that Browning would have to accept less from him than he had hoped.

It seems fitting that, during this period of sadness and disillusionment, the Greek dramatist Euripides became Browning's frequent companion. Both his personal losses and the tragic vision of the aged poet helped sharpen the sense of reality which informs *The Ring and the Book*. The materials for the poem fell into his hands at precisely the time in his life when he was capable of giving them his most penetrating and comprehensive interpretation. *The Ring and the Book* comes nearest of all his works to embodying his fullest vision.

In late 1862, Browning announced definite plans for beginning the poem. Writing to Miss Isa Blagden on November 19, he says, "Early in Spring, I print new poems, a number; then, a new edition of my old things, corrected: then begin on my murder-case." [2] By summer, 1864, he reports, "the whole thing is pretty well in my head," [3] and by autumn he had begun writing. Once under way, he worked rapidly, and on November 21, 1868, the first of the four volumes comprising the first edition appeared. The others followed shortly, the last two in early 1869.

I

The story as Browning found it in The Old Yellow Book is briefly as follows: Pompilia, daughter of Pietro and Violante Comparini of Rome, was married at the age of thirteen to the middle-aged and impoverished nobleman of Arezzo, Count Guido Franceschini, the Comparini coveting a title for their daughter, and the count, a dowry. Both, however, soon felt cheated. The Comparini, discovering the poverty of the palace and repelled by the count's cruelty, returned to Rome after a few months, leaving Pompilia behind. There they revealed that Pompilia was actually the daughter of a prostitute, purchased by Violante and passed off as her child in order to secure an inheritance that would come to her and Pietro only if they had children. With his new humiliation, Guido intensified his cruelties against Pompilia. Finally, realizing that she was with child and unable to bear Guido's torture any longer,

Pompilia persuaded the priest Caponsacchi to conduct her to Rome. Their journey proceeded without interruption until, shortly before they arrived, Pompilia became too exhausted to travel any longer. While she slept at an inn, Guido arrived, and both priest and wife were arrested and brought to trial. Pompilia was sent to a convent and Caponsacchi exiled to a monastery. After the birth of Pompilia's child, Guido, with four ruffians, killed her and her parents. He charged Pompilia with adultery and proclaimed the child illegitimate. He was tried in secular court and sentenced to death, a judgment upheld by the Pope. He and his four assistants were executed.

The Ring and the Book, however, is more than a retelling of this story. In fact, the narrative is relatively unimporant, although it appears in some form at least seven times. No single account is complete, some are contradictory, and all would fail as reconstructions acceptable to a modern historian. Browning's purpose was not reconstruction, however, but, to use his language, "resuscitation." What he meant by this he hoped to convey through his symbolic title, but his effectiveness in doing so has been debated. George R. Wasserman offers what seems to me a sound interpretation.[4]

The Book in Browning's title represents the historical record or, as Browning calls it, raw gold. Once the facts of the case were alive and meaningful, but in the transition from lived experience to written record they were severed from the life they represented. They needed reshaping so that "something dead may get to live again." The poet gives the raw gold new form, after rendering it malleable by mixing it with the alloy of imagination. The result is a ring, no less "fact" than before. Dead symbol is again made organic with experience. Browning's purpose, then, is not to describe the gold in its inert state but to present it in a new structure that will reveal its human significance. The troublesome part of the symbol comes when Browning asserts that, once the ring was shaped, he applied to it an acid which removed the alloy and left only the fact. He himself, he says, disappeared from the poem.

As Wasserman suggests, Browning distinguishes between the "I," the poet himself, and the imagination, that other half of the poet's soul, which "pilgrims o'er old unwandered waste ways of the world," fusing itself with and resuscitating the raw materials. It is the poet himself, not his imagination, that is finally removed from the poem. The imagination, the perceiving, shaping faculty, is as much a part of the materials, the facts, as the raw gold. Obviously, Browning had in mind the depersonalization which permitted him to work as shaper and re-creator without projecting upon the poem his own personality. In theory, if not always in practice, Browning held that his dramatis personae spoke for themselves; here he claims that his facts do also.

What do the facts say? Man once found self-definition and moral direction in the institutions and codes outside himself, but, finding them no longer credible, man today is driven within himself. The purpose of *The Ring and the Book* is neither to present the ideal society nor to delineate laws by which such a society should be formed and governed. Browning assumes an ideal order but regards its apprehension and assertion as beyond man's capacities. He attempts rather to depict the possible—the process by which man, in the absence of the ideal and of creedal and institutional guidance, may achieve a moral existence. Recognizing no charted course and no defined ends, Browning emphasizes the motives of a character's action, the intensity of his commitment, and the energy and persistence of his pursuit.

Judgment is central in *The Ring and the Book,* not because Browning hopes to communicate a final truth but because the act of judging may force a character into self-defining confrontation and saving action. The goodness of a judgment relates to the manner in which it is made more than to the end that it achieves. Both the Pope and Other Half-Rome, for example, pronounce Pompilia innocent and Guido guilty, but not with the same results. For the Pope alone is it an act of stewardship and a means of salvation. Browning is less concerned with truth as an abstraction than as a defining, motivating, saving force in the lives of his characters. Throughout, he concentrates on the internal process by which they attempt to achieve a moral life, and upon those things outside them that make this difficult or impossible.

The implications are comprehensive. *The Ring and the Book* is a penetrating comment on Browning's own times. His awareness of the limits of human reason and his distrust of those values codified in social customs and institutions, codes and courts of law, theological systems and religious institutions reflect more nearly the skeptical mood of the nineteenth than of the seventeeth century.

Browning's probings are at once an indictment of traditional values and an exploratory effort to establish a new basis for a spiritual and moral life. His attitude is ambivalent. On the one hand, *The Ring and the Book* is one of the most pessimistic documents of the century. Browning sweepingly dismisses as decadent and incapable of resuscitation those repositories of traditional culture: the classical ideal (contra Arnold); the feudal order (contra Carlyle); traditional religion and law (contra Newman); and both eighteenth-century rationalism and nineteenth-century amelioration (contra Mill).

On the other hand, Browning's faith in action based upon subjective apprehension of truth has been interpreted as naïvely optimistic. It must be said, however, that Browning never asserts that man could solve his problems through primitive intuition (that Pompilia, for example, represents the sum total of wisdom about human experience), as I shall show later. What he does suggest is offered in near desperation after everything else has failed. His approach has the virtue of being tentative, exploratory, capable of change and development. It seems relevant to contemporary experience.

Browning does not claim to possess absolute truth or to delineate unalterable laws. The Pope, for example, admits that his judgment may be wrong, and Fra Celestino asserts that one cannot expect good always to triumph over evil. Quite the contrary. Browning shifts emphasis from abstract universals to concrete problems, asking not what is absolutely right but what is right for a character in a given situation.

More deadly in Browning's ethics than a wrong action is inaction, because the latter is a denial of the self and a rejection of the potential moral life. It is conceivable that even a "wrong" action, on the other hand, can have salutary results. This position accounts for the intensity of his attack upon traditions. Traditional culture, law, and religion not only fail to provide direction, but, more seriously, they impose upon man a frame of mind, a code of behavior, a set of goals that have no relevance to the man within. They separate man from himself, preventing the confrontation that might result in spiritual awakening and development. A first step toward manhood is often a rejection of the institution and the code.

II 🌱

The Ring and the Book is essentially the story of two kinds of characters, those who achieve self-realization and those who do not. Those who do are made capable of choosing salvation or damnation. Even those who choose damnation achieve a higher morality than those who remain unaware, for damnation consciously chosen is a kind of victory.

Browning presents his characters in the order that best advances his action. He begins with the three representatives from Roman society, characters without self-awareness who are incapable of judgment and moral action. He turns next to Count Guido Franceschini, a character who ultimately achieves self-realization but who first appears as count rather than man. Browning's initial presentation of Franceschini is incomplete precisely because its continuation is the record of his transformation, an achievement that is psychologically impossible before the events recorded in Books VI through X have occurred. Browning next presents Caponsacchi and Pompilia and finally, to conclude the legal hearing, the two lawyers. Guido's appeal of his sentence from secular to Papal court introduces the Pope and motivates his speculations in Book X. The Pope's order to execution and Guido's approaching death provide the motive for Guido's second appearance and his eventual self-confrontation. Book XII offers a perspective from which we see the action completed. The books are arranged to constitute an organic work, about which Browning commented: "I honestly don't think, and cannot but hope, as an artist, that not a paragraph is extractable as an episode or piece complete in itself" (Hood, *Letters,* 128). I am in essential agreement.

For the sake of discussion, however, I shall initially consider the characters in a slightly altered sequence: the three representatives of Roman society, Guido, Caponsacchi, the Pope, Pompilia, the two lawyers, and, finally, the spokesman of Book XII.

a

Half-Rome, Other Half-Rome, and Tertium Quid, as their names suggest, are more social abstractions than individuals. They have just enough individuation to make them believable symbols. Not one of them grapples out of real conviction with significant issues but reacts rather to interests or pressures from without. Half-Rome and Other Half-Rome pass diverse judgments, and Tertium Quid passes no judgment at all. The first two might have spoken the same judgment or all might have refused to judge altogether, because none achieves through his judgment any personal involvement, a moral act. Half-Rome is motivated by the conduct of his wife to inveigh against all wives; Other Half-Rome is moved by sentimental idealism to defend any beautiful, young, unfortunate wife; Tertium Quid is prompted by self-interest to commit himself to no position.

Through these symbols of abstract man, Browning comments upon the illusiveness of truth and the improbability of social salvation. He does not argue that man should be clear-sighted, unselfish, and courageous but merely states that he is none of these. Once you get beyond the isolated facts, man en masse can say no more than that one should or should not kill his adulterous wife, or that the man who does should or should not be hanged. Such abstract truth is as inert as the facts of The Old Yellow Book. The Pope refers to

> *A thing existent only while it acts,*
> *Does as designed, else a nonentity,*
> *For what is an idea unrealized?*
> (X, *1500–1502*)

These three characters remain unrealized, nameless.

b

Beginning with Book V, Browning turns from abstractions to individuals who have reached or will reach some degree of self-realization: Guido, Caponsacchi, and the Pope. Each man achieves self-realization to a different end, and each illustrates a different aspect of the achievement. In Guido, we witness the process itself; in Caponsacchi, we see the transforming results of the process; and in the Pope, we are given a rationale for its ethical and spiritual implications. All three are organic parts of Browning's theme.

Browning emphatically rejected Julia Wedgwood's suggestion that Guido's "shame and pain and humiliation" be made endurable by the "irradiation of hope." [5] She obviously had something like a traditional conversion in mind. Browning felt that such an end to Guido's life of intrigue and cruelty would be unrealistic. There is, however, another level on which Guido changes. Like Caponsacchi, and the Pope, he undergoes a divestment by which at last he sees himself as a responsible human being. His last cry of terror, one of his first genuine acts, might be called a triumph. His story is a journey from counthood (Franceschinihood, he calls it) to manhood—a transformation that Browning suggests in the titles of Book V (Count Guido Franceschini) and Book XI (Guido). Even if Guido remains in wickedness, choosing to be damned rather than saved, he does so as a responsible man, not as a cultural manikin.

He first appears more the abstraction of a social institution than a man. He defends a decadent tradition, claiming that his murder of Pompilia wants "no more than right interpretation of the same" to prove itself an act to preserve old values, the organized society, the courts of law, the authoritarian church. When he speaks of himself as "all yet uncertain save the will/ To do right" (V, 1622–1623), we question his sincerity. Indeed, he later calls this statement a lie. It is a lie, however, from the new perspective which he achieves at the end of Book XI. The point is less that he first lied and then under pressure told the truth than that he came eventually to recognize truth from falsehood.

Guido begins with the traditional invocation "I' the name of the indivisible Trinity!" and proceeds to describe the enemies of order, the creators of chaos, whom he professes to find about him. There is just enough truth in his charge to make it somewhat believeable. The new democratic middle class with their materialistic values and bad manners are such villains. Once we permit their disdain for "honor of birth," he asserts,

> straight
> Your social fabric, pinnacle to base,
> Comes down a-clatter like a house of cards.
> (V, 443–445)

The religious liberal, particularly the heretical Molinist, those pietistic believers in private judgment, and those who challenge traditional law, common and codified, are others. Against these emissaries of disorder, he ostensibly sets himself. Exonerating him, he argues, the court would reaffirm the old values and restore Rome to her past greatness:

> Rome rife with honest women and strong men,
> Manners reformed, old habits back once more,
> Customs that recognize the standard worth . . .
> (V, 2039–2041)

Guido's uncomfortable awareness of decaying values and vanishing morals is real. Browning permits Guido, as he permits others of his villains, a modicum of insight. There is beneath the surface of his rationalization a sense of frustration and failure. For thirty years, he says, he sought advancement in the church, seeing "meanwhile many a denizen o' the dung/ Hop, skip, jump o'er my shoulder" (V, 293–294). He feels keenly his final humiliation by the inferior Comparini. With ambivalent hypocrisy and a real sense of grievance, he offers himself to the court as a suffering servant, a Christ-figure. Very early he refers to his "crucifixion"—"why, 't is wine,/ Velletri,—and not vinegar and gall" (V, 4–5)—and later to his "Gethsemane":

> *Yes, this next cup of bitterness, my lords,*
> *Had to begin go filling, drop by drop,*
> *Its measure up of full disgust for me,*
> *Filtered into by every noisome drain—*
> *Society's sink toward which all moisture runs.*
>   *(V, 879–883)*

The figures of suffering savior and losing gamester are related in that, as either, Guido is dispossessed, the outsider. We accept him more readily as losing gamester because as such he takes himself more seriously. We know that the terrified man who emerges from behind the trappings of the count is real. On another level, of course, the count, the cultural manikin, is real also in relation to the system that produced him. It is a reality without humanity, however. We condemn the count for inhumanity and the system for dehumanization. The system turns the man into count and the count reduces even Pompilia to an object.

The man Guido, submerged in Book V, extricates himself in Book XI. Count Guido Franceschini argues his case with logic and coherence; Guido ostensibly pleads his cause before Cardinal Acciaiuoli and Abate Panciatichi but talks as much to himself as to them. As the external world loosens its hold upon him, the surface order of Book V gives way to a near chaos that manifests itself in a new kind of coherence and syntax. Guido recounts once more his marriage to Pompilia and its tragic end, but he orders the facts differently, relating one to the other less by logic and chronology than by psychological association. In Book V, the materials are shaped by externally imposed pattern; in Book XI, they reflect the inner life. Book XI is an account of Guido's dialogue with himself, the record of his self-confrontation.

In Book XI we realize, perhaps as we cannot in Book V, that Guido is not the abstraction of absolute evil but a human figure, part of a historical and social milieu, subject to laws of probability, growth, and development, capable of salvation or damnation. He has an explainable, believable inner life, a common humanity that contrasts, for example, with Iago's consummate evil. This does not make Guido less despicable, but it does render him understandable as a character capable of change and thus an integral part, along with Caponsacchi and the Pope, of Browning's theme.

As count and cleric, Guido defends himself in Book V; as man, he discovers himself indefensible at the end of Book XI. As count and cleric, he argues his exoneration on the basis of law and custom emanating from society and the Church; as man, he undertakes a terrifying journey within, in search of self.

Depicting the journey from count to man presents both a metaphysical and an artistic problem. How can one so separated from self achieve self-recognition? How can that process be presented so that it is psychologically sound and artistically expressive? The Pope gives us a clue:

> *For the main criminal I have no hope*
> *Except in such a suddenness of fate.*

I stood at Naples once, a night so dark
I could have scarce conjectured there was earth
Anywhere, sky or sea or world at all:
But the night's black was burst through by a blaze—
Thunder struck blow on blow, earth groaned and bore,
Through her whole length of mountain visible:
There lay the city thick and plain with spires,
And, like a ghost disshrouded, white the sea.
So may the truth be flashed out by one blow,
And Guido see, one instant, and be saved.

$$(X, 2116\text{--}2127)$$

This image of organic growth is appropriate. Back of Guido's seemingly spontaneous self-discovery, which comes as a lightning bolt, there is careful motivation analogous to the development of the storm of which the lightning is culmination. Browning propels Guido toward self-recognition partly by bringing him to face death not as an event at some remote point in the future but as a present reality, grasped concretely and existentially. He says:

You never know what life means till you die:
Even throughout life, 't is death that makes life live,
Gives it whatever the significance.

$$(XI, 2373\text{--}2375)$$

Browning early establishes the reality of death as the focal point of Book XI through the symbol of the guillotine, "that red thing," which Guido describes with ambivalent attraction and revulsion. He circles around it, drawing constantly closer, until, at last, all illusion gone, the symbol becomes a reality, and the count discovers himself the man forced into a humanly significant act. The guillotine thus is simultaneously the symbol of death and life.

Guido is further motivated by fear and frustration. This

awareness, anticipated in the gamester figure, emerges with increasing clarity. "For unsuccess, explain it how you will,/ Disqualifies you, makes you doubt yourself" (XI, 1839– 1840), Guido remarks. He recognizes his failure as count and cleric but, even more bitterly, as man and lover.

As book XI opens, the Cardinal and the Abate stand before him, symbols of his assumed betrayal by the Church. They represent, indeed, as Park Honan says, the grace of God that is always available to Guido (*Browning's Characters,* 306). They represent, on another level, the role that he has played unsuccessfully for thirty years. Castigating them, he castigates himself; rejecting them, he rejects himself. Concluding his diatribe against them (unjust though it be) with the cry of "Enough of the hypocrites" (XI, 764), he reaches a turning point in his own development. He may revert partly to his former life, but having grasped a partial truth he can never go back completely. His attack upon the churchmen is both venomous abuse and self-castigation, simultaneous rejection of old and new, of the count and the grace of God.

Guido hates the Comparini less because they are ignorant, vulgar, grasping, and dishonest than because they too remind him of failure. It is galling to be surpassed by equals but intolerable to be defeated by inferiors. When they make him the laughingstock of Rome, he turns upon them with a violence near madness.

Guido hates Pompilia because she is good and he is evil and also because she reminds him of his bitterest failure. In Book V he remarks: ". . . I was near my seventh climacteric,/ Hard upon, if not over, the middle life" (345–346). In Book XI:

> *But myself am old,*
> *O' the wane at least, in all things: what do you say*

To her who frankly thus confirms my doubt?
I am past the prime, I scare the woman-world,
Done-with that way.

(*XI, 997–1001*)

Refusing at first to consummate the marriage, Pompilia finally, upon instruction, yields passively to her husband. Guido sees her aloofness as confirmation of his failure and hates her for it. Browning intensifies the situation by making Guido, contrary to history, the elder son and giving him responsibility for perpetuating the Franceschini name. Guido blames Pompilia and claims the right to punish her:

All women cannot give men love, forsooth!
No, nor all pullets lay the henwife eggs—
Whereat she bids them remedy the fault,
Brood on a chalk-ball: soon the nest is stocked—
Otherwise, to the plucking and the spit!

(*XI, 1422–1426*)

The violence of the imagery witnesses Guido's tension. With little regard for consistency, he charges Pompilia alternately with frigidity and unfaithfulness. He sees Caponsacchi as the man-lover he would like to be and hates him. Occasionally, there is a mitigating passage which reminds us that somewhere beneath the Count there is a tortured human being:

But why am I to miss the daisied mile
The course begins with, why obtain the dust
Of the end precisely at the starting-point?
Why quaff life's cup blown free of all the beads,
The bright red froth wherein our beard should steep
Before our mouth essay the black o' the wine?

Foolish, the love-fit? Let me prove it such
Like you, before like you I puff things clear!
                                    (XI, 1076–1083)

Guido's fears render plausible to his disturbed mind his accusation against Pompilia and Caponsacchi. He dwells upon their imagined relation with ambivalent torture and pleasure. He would rather believe Pompilia's disinterest in him to come from her love for another than from his inability. His fears illuminate the violent seizures and shameless violations of which she complains. His fears also explain his attitude toward the child. His birth moves Guido to greater violence than any other incident. He is torn between desire for an heir and doubt of his son's legitimacy. The latter triumphs and the baby becomes the focus of his hate.

The Cardinal and the Abate, Pietro and Violante, Pompilia and Caponsacchi symbolically represent partly what Guido is or, more often, what he wants to be, thus creating tension within him. This internal action is communicated largely through symbol. Guido becomes increasingly conscious of himself as losing gamester. He undergoes transformation as suffering savior-shepherd emerging first unconsciously and then consciously as wolf. Between the images, suffering savior-shepherd-wolf and losing gamester, there is a connection which incorporates the notion of the pursuer-pursued, the protector-destroyer.

Guido forestalls confrontation, blaming "luck," "Fate," and Pompilia, but the unconscious is continually becoming conscious. The image of himself as suffering savior gives way to his awareness of himself as destroyer. The subtlety with which Browning transforms one image into another follows the complex pattern of Guido's inner life. In line 405, Guido complains that the Pope unjustly considers him a wolf. In a passage beginning with line 433, as Park

Honan points out, he falls victim to his own rhetoric and, calling the Pope a shepherd thief, unwittingly brands himself a wolf (*Browning's Characters*, 308). This subconscious identification of himself becomes conscious as the poem continues. Despairing of protection from society and Church, he swaggers momentarily before he comes at last to face himself in the shadow of "the red thing":

> *The strong become a wolf for evermore!*
> *Change that Pompilia to a puny stream*
> *Fit to reflect the daisies on its bank!*
> *Let me turn wolf, be whole, and sate, for once,—*
> *Wallow in what is now a wolfishness*
> *Coerced too much by the humanity*
> *That's half of me as well!*
>
> (*XI, 2051–2057*)

This vicious image of destruction brings to a fitting climax those earlier figures through which he expressed his consuming hate for Pompilia. Under illusion of wolf strength, he scorns all weak "good" things:

> *I use up my last strength to strike once more*
> *Old Pietro in the wine-house-gossip-face,*
> *To trample underfoot the whine and wile*
> *Of that Violante,—and I grow one gorge*
> *To loathingly reject Pompilia's pale*
> *Poison my hasty hunger took for food.*
>
> (*XI, 2399–2404*)

It seems that here Guido fully unmasks. But there is more. He is to shift perspective so that what now appears strength is revealed as weakness. He is to see himself in a radically different relation with Pompilia. His boast, "I lived and died a man, and take man's chance,/ Honest and bold: right will be done to such" (XI, 2410–2411), takes on an ironic new meaning. Even though he has not lived as a man, he shall die as a man, and that death will reveal to him a new concept of right.

In the lines immediately following this declaration, death becomes real, concretely and symbolically, the great leveler capable of reducing even a count to manhood. We scarcely know how to interpret Guido's last recorded act. His final outcry:

> *Hold me from them! I am yours,*
> *I am the Granduke's—no, I am the Pope's!*
> *Abate,— Cardinal,— Christ,— Maria,— God, . . .*
> *Pompilia, will you let them murder me?*
>
> (*XI, 2422–2425*)

might signal either a conversion or mere terror. Which it is does not make a great deal of difference, since *The Ring and the Book* is not a traditional religious document. Browning's interests are psychological. Guido comes to discover manhood rather than sainthood. His cry is the culmination of a process that has been underway from the beginning. The great subterranean current that has steadily gained pressure breaks through, sweeping Guido out of Franceschinihood into manhood, making him for the first time in his life aware of himself as a responsible, choosing, acting human being. The last cry signals the ambivalent triumph and terror of newly achieved manhood. Whether it leads to salvation or damnation in the usual sense is relatively unimportant.

c

In Guido we witness the process of self-discovery, and in Caponsacchi we see its transforming power. Caponsacchi, unlike Guido, is not actively evil, but before he meets Pompilia he is spiritually dead, a clerical manikin. Browning changed the date of the flight to fall on St. George's Day, making *The Ring and the Book* another exploration of the myth that first captured his adolescent imagination. On one level, the poem is the account of a knight who rescues a distressed maiden; on another, it is less the story of the maiden's rescue than of the knight's or, better, less of Caponsacchi as rescuer than as rescued, as savior than as saved.

Although his transformation has occurred when he addresses the court, Caponsacchi views it anew in the sober light of Pompilia's death. For the first time he shapes it into a comprehensible, expressible whole. His account, therefore, appears as an immediate experience. Overwhelmed by the sobering mysteries of life and death, he is at once confident and groping, assured and dazed, triumphant and tentative. That he lives, a transformed man, is at once an ironic comment upon and the justification for Pompilia's death.

We see Caponsacchi and Guido at different stages. Drawing upon the same materials, each chooses those details given significance by his sense of reality. Guido dwells upon family, rights and privileges of nobility, decay of old values, personal abuses. He remains always the center of his story, the hero.

Caponsacchi subordinates himself to Pompilia who, transcending ordinary discourse, can be rendered intelligible only through a description of her transforming power over him. He talks about himself but his story extols a heroine rather than a hero.

Having come to terms with himself, Caponsacchi seeks rather than avoids truth. There is in his selection of materials, in his diction, syntax, and imagery, a directness missing in Guido's. Guido dwells upon Pompilia's adultery and the Pope upon her motherhood. Caponsacchi denies the former and ignores the latter. He can see Pompilia as mother only in an idealized setting, cradling some other woman's child in her arms, but is repelled by the thought of carnality in connection with her. Guido's "outrage" horrifies him, not because he is abnormally ascetic but because he regards Pompilia as inviolable.

She appears first as a vision transcending discourse:

> When I saw enter, stand, and seat herself
> A lady, young, tall, beautiful, strange and sad.
> It was as when, in our cathedral once,
> As I got yawningly through matin-song,
> I saw facchini bear a burden up,
> Base it on the high-altar, break away
> A board or two, and leave the thing inside
> Lofty and lone: and lo, when next I looked,
> There was the Rafael!
>
> (VI, 398–406)

Pompilia remains his Madonna, giving significance to his altar, drawing him with a power he has not before experienced. He sees her later standing in her window, "Our Lady of all Sorrows." And when he leaves her, she does not withdraw but is "withdrawn." What he reports as her plea to him is less her actual speech than what he willed to hear and chose to remember. It reveals as much about him as about her. We accept less the literalness of the report than the authenticity of the reporter. We believe Pompilia pure and accept her as a symbol of goodness and grace precisely because we know that she transformed the "coxcomb, fribble and fool" (VI, 98) of a priest into a "soldier-saint" (VII, 1786). "She has done the good to me," he says. He illuminates her transforming role by associating her with that other mystery, the Body of Christ on the altar:

> *I never touched her with my finger-tip*
> *Except to carry her to the couch, that eve,*
> *Against my heart, beneath my head, bowed low,*
> *As we priests carry the paten.*
>
> (*VI, 1617–1620*)

Browning has told us that Pompilia is innocent, and Caponsacchi convinces us. The "fact" has been given emotional and sensuous reality, has been resuscitated, by him.

Caponsacchi gives concreteness to his struggle by juxtaposing the way of the institution with that of the spirit, of the system with that of the heart. A renewed man, he looks back upon his Church which first made him into a "coxcomb, fribble and fool" with mixed feelings. Before he met Pompilia, he says, "I was good enough for that," the old worldly Church. Afterwards:

> *I'll no more of these good things:*
> *There's a crack somewhere, something that's unsound*
> *I' the rattle!*
>
> (*VI, 1878–1880*)

After visiting Pompilia, he sees the Church in a new dawn light:

> *I' the grey of dawn it was I found myself*
> *Facing the pillared front o' the Pieve—mine,*
> *My church: it seemed to say for the first time*
> *"But am not I the Bride, the mystic love*
> *"O' the Lamb, who took thy plighted troth, my priest,*
> *"To fold thy warm heart on my heart of stone*
> *"And freeze thee nor unfasten any more?*
> *"This is a fleshly woman,—let the free*
> *"Bestow their life-blood, thou art pulseless now!"*
>
> (*VI, 974–982*)

A new set of antitheses emerges: Church and Pompilia, system and grace, death and life:

> *Now, from the stone lungs sighed the scrannel voice*
> *"Leave that live passion, come be dead with me!"* . . .
>
> *Sirs, I obeyed. Obedience was too strange,—*
> *This new thing that had been struck into me*
> *By the look o' the lady,—to dare disobey*
> *The first authoritative word. 'T was God's.*
> $\qquad\qquad$ (*VI, 1000–1001, 1010–1013*)

Caponsacchi further focuses these tensions by opposing
two theological systems: the Thomist and the Molinist.
Miguel Molinos, a Spaniard, published in 1675 his *Guida
Spirituale*, outlining a pietistic faith which emphasized
private judgment and direct, intuitive apprehension of
God.[6] His teaching, countering the Thomistic view of the
Church, was generally regarded as heretical. Caponsacchi
identifies the Church with Thomism and Pompilia broadly
with Molinism. His patron, observing his new seriousness
after he met Pompilia, asks half in jest, "Are you turning
Molinist?" Caponsacchi answers, "Sir, what if I turned
Christian?" From this point the contrast is explicit.
Thomas Aquinas' *Summa Theologica* is associated with
darkness and depression (VI, 483–485) and Pompilia with
light and life (VI, 935–963). The *Summa* represents the
letter that kills; Pompilia, the spirit that enlivens; the
Summa, an intellectual, formalistic system outwardly imposed; Pompilia, an inward apprehension of God. The
struggle is thus finally concluded:

> *Then I retraced my steps, was found once more*
> *In my own house for the last time: there lay*
> *The broad pale opened Summa. "Shut his book,*

"*There's other showing! 'T was a Thomas too*
"*Obtained,—more favored than his namesake*
  here,—
"*A gift, tied faith fast, foiled the tug of doubt,—*
"*Our Lady's girdle; down he saw it drop*
"*As she ascended into heaven, they say:*
"*He kept that safe and bade all doubt adieu.*
"*I too have seen a lady and hold a grace.*"
                                    (*VI, 1096–1105*)

Over against the rationalistic Thomas he places the doubting Thomas with whom he identifies. He equates Pompilia with the Blessed Virgin. His spiritual journey takes him from Church to Pompilia, from *Summa* to Molinism, from rationalistic certainty to creative doubt, from ritual to grace, from priest to man. It is a divestation. His salvation is to stand at last in "immortal nakedness," a man before God:

Into another state, under new rule
I knew myself was passing swift and sure;
Whereof the initiatory pang approached,
Felicitous annoy, as bitter-sweet
As when the virgin-band, the victors chaste,
Feel at the end the earthly garments drop,
And rise with something of a rosy shame
Into immortal nakedness: so I
Lay, and let come the proper throe would thrill
Into the ecstasy and outthrob pain.
                                    (*VI, 964–973*)

Browning does not permit Caponsacchi's ecstasy to go unchallenged. The new man, forgetting for a moment that he is also priest and that Pompilia is dead, imagines what life lived with her might be. But not for long. The present returns with the sobering realization that salvation is ambivalent, that being man one must live at once with the vision of glory and the consciousness of limitations: "O great, just, good God! Miserable me!" (VI, 2105).

d

Pope Innocent, called upon to pronounce sentence upon another is himself under sentence. He is an old man confronting death and facing a final symbolic act, a microcosm of his past and future. Judging Guido forces him to examine the possible basis for moral action and serves as his personal Armageddon. His judgment is rendered before he speaks, and what he says is only incidentally concerned with judgment. The action of the book occurs within him. His speech is an internal dialogue, an argument with himself, rather than a pronouncement ex cathedra. Its movement is dialectical; its purpose, to confirm the rightness of the act of judging and to provide a rationale for it.

The structure of his monologue, following the movement of the evolving argument, falls into five sections: in lines 1–161 he examines the dogma of Papal Infallibility; in lines 162–476 he ponders his obligation to judge; in lines 477–1237 he repeats his judgment; in lines 1238–2097 he develops a rationale for moral action in a world where traditional values are no longer valid; in lines 2098–2134 he orders Guido's execution and speculates about his possible salvation.

The monologue opens in the middle of an action. The Pope, having determined Guido's execution, becomes inwardly involved in an argument with himself. The man demurs when the ecclesiastic justifies the judgment as an infallible act of Christ's Vicar. The Pope, yielding to the man, reviews the history of his predecessors, finding in their abuses of power argument to undercut the confidence of the staunchest churchman. Innocent's predecessors argued about the rightful occupant of the papal office, but Innocent challenges the office itself. "Which of the judgments was infallible?" he asks (X, 150), and his answer, in light of history, must be that none was.

The old Pope takes his staff with "uncertain hands," judging with "winter in my soul beyond the world's" as man, not as cleric:

> *Wherefore, Antonio Pignatelli, thou*
> *My ancient self, who wast no Pope so long*
> *But studied God and man, the many years*
> *I' the school, i' the cloister, in the diocese*
> *Domestic, legate-rule in foreign lands,—*
> *Thou other force in those old busy days*
> *Than this grey ultimate decrepitude,—*
> *Yet sensible of fires that more and more*
> *Visit a soul, in passage to the sky,*
> *Left nakeder than when flesh-robe was new—*
> *Thou, not Pope but the mere old man o' the world,*
> *Supposed inquisitive and dispassionate,*
> *Wilt thou, the one whose speech I somewhat trust,*
> *Question the after-me, this self now Pope,*
> *Hear his procedure, criticize his work?*
>
> (X, 382–396)

The monologue which follows details an argument among the Pope's several selves. Although uncertain of the rightness of any particular judgment, the Pope is convinced of the rightness of judging, because only by such commitment can man achieve maturity. He is resolute, even though he may err, because "it is the seed of act,/ God holds appraising in His hollow palm . . ." (X, 271–272). In this confidence, he condemns the count and exonerates Caponsacchi and Pompilia. His grounds for justifying them throw light upon his position. Pompilia, he affirms, acted "according to the light allotted her." Simple, innocent, unspoiled by the world, she did not question the voice that came to her: "It was authentic to the experienced ear/ O' the good and faithful servant" (X, 1090–1091).

Caponsacchi, however, having passed from innocence to knowledge, was incapable of Pompilia's spontaneity. He had to follow a more sophisticated path, first putting off the role of priest. Although the Pope can scarcely admire Caponsacchi as "coxcomb, the fribble," he does realize that by straying from the way Caponsacchi stumbled upon The Way. Browning's seventeenth-century Pope talks much like a modern theologian who advocates Christianity without religion. A man must escape, the Pope realizes, from abstractness to concreteness before he can make the choice and commitment that defines him as a moral being: "Life's business being just the terrible choice" (X, 1237).

If judgment were the Pope's only function, he would end his monologue once he had pronounced sentence. Instead, he continues for some eight hundred lines to talk about what on the surface appears mere theology. Clearly, however, as Browning develops it, it is less argument than meditation, less substantive than dramatic. It is organic to the Pope's self-realization and to the thematic development of the poem. Section four with its often tedious exploration counterpoints the preceding section in which the Pope impulsively and confidently pronounces judgment and the following section in which he orders the execution. It is the natural voice of reason and compromise.

Recognizing that he has merely an "inch of inkling" (X, 1282) and that the light by which he walks (as man and as priest) is at best a mere candle (X, 1263), he understandably wonders if perhaps his assumption of a divine being and a moral order is merely a projection of his need. Although he cannot solve this problem, he is convinced that disbelief takes from man all motive for action and renders him morally and spiritually impotent. Man must, he knows, for reasons psychological and moral, retain a basis from which action is possible. The Pope constructs such a base upon non-Thomistic premises. Indeed, he argues that man may apprehend a portion of truth through human reason and natural revelation, but this concession is only a prelude to his essential apology. There is, to be sure, the "tale," the Revelation—whether literal or symbolic the Pope seems uncertain ("A Death in the Desert"). But even this he must defend on new nondogmatic grounds. He believes it not upon authority of the Church but by the love he feels for it in his heart, and by the fact that it explains better than anything else a creation which he has experienced as love as well as knowledge and power. Such a position rests partly upon intellectualization but primarily upon subjective faith: "Beyond the tale, I reach into the dark,/ Feel what I cannot see, and still faith stands" (X, 1372–1373).

The old Pope is disturbed less by the loss of absolutes than by the moral failure of his institution. Caponsacchi found his way outside, not within, the Church. Euripides, one of the many voices from within the Pope, proposes disturbingly that even he, a Greek pagan, came closer to the Christian ideal than have most seventeenth-century churchmen. Can it be, Innocent asks, that the Church has lost touch with reality and is relevant now only through its heretics (Molinists) and its erring (Caponsacchi)? Must the existing structures of the Church be demolished?

> *As we broke up that old faith of the world,*
> *Have we, next age, to break up this the new—*

> *Faith, in the thing, grown faith in the report—*
> *Whence need to bravely disbelieve report*
> *Through increased faith in thing report belie?*
> (X, *1863–1867*)

The old Church, having belied the "thing," must perhaps be divested too. The Pope speaks with ambivalent sympathy of Luther, Calvin, and Molinos.

He is, nevertheless, no irresponsible revolutionary. Through the persona of an educated contemporary, echo of one of his own voices, he expresses reluctance to make drastic changes:

> *". . . in this case the spirit of culture speaks,*
> *"Civilization is imperative. . . .*
>   *"—nor the time*
> *"Admits we shift—a pillar? nay, a stake*
> *"Out of its place i' the tenement, one touch*
> *"Whereto may send a shudder through the heap*
> *"And bring it toppling on our heads perchance."*
> (X, *2016–2017, 2045–2049*)

This is the same argument that Guido offered earlier. The Pope is obviously torn between his desire for the ordered stability of the old world and his realization that such an order now exists only as a cruel parody of itself. This Guido failed to grasp. Orthodoxy and heresy, tradition and revolution, the charted and the chartless all struggle for supremacy within him. Ultimately the imperative to discover a new basis for meaningful moral action wins.

The Pope is brought back finally to the point from which he started: the consciousness of death and the necessity to perform this last symbolic act. In the role of man, rather than Pope, he accepts the challenge to choose (*"Quo pro Domino?"* "Life's business being just the terrible choice") and to act:

> *A thing existent only while it acts,*
> *Does as designed, else a nonentity,*
> *For what is an idea unrealized?*
> (*X, 1500–1502*)

It is precisely to exist, to realize himself, that he must pronounce judgment. His monologue is at once the record of his self-confrontation and an intellectual justification for action in a world where absolute certainty is no longer possible.

e

Pompilia, in contrast to Guido, Caponsacchi, and the Pope, is an innocent who does not need to achieve self-realization, salvation. She is "just seventeen years and five months old." On one level she is a naïve little girl and, on another, a woman, matured by four trying years, the birth of her son, and the approach of death.

Pompilia's monologue is both a psalm of thanksgiving, a magnificat for the birth of her son, and a defense of her "soldier-saint." Her story contains ambiguities, but if she recognizes them she is not diverted by them. With little time and no inclination to rationalize, she looks beyond surface contradictions to Truth itself, achieving by a different process a position much like the Pope's. If her monologue stood alone as a summation of Browning's wisdom, *The Ring and the Book* would be sentimental. But it does not stand alone. Pompilia is individual and partial, intentionally nonrepresentative. She is partly flesh and blood and partly symbol of pre-fall innocence. She retains the capacity to act instinctively and decisively even in the face of conflicting claims. Caponsacchi and the Pope, having passed beyond her level of innocence and having become fully aware of the ambiguities, must achieve truth by a more sophisticated route.

The Pope laboriously rationalizes what Pompilia intuits. He reaches for light beyond the dark, fully conscious of the dark. Pompilia, blinded by the light, is scarcely aware of the dark. For her, evil is subsumed in her new vision of ultimate goodness; for the Pope it remains vividly real, one pole in a dialectical moral system. Pompilia's affirmation is an instinctive response to good; the Pope's, a willed, rationalized response to man's need for good.

Pompilia's insight might be equated with knowledge. It comes, however, through experience rather than rationalization. She does not philosophize beyond her capacities. In fact, she doesn't philosophize. She talks about "truths" and "proofs," but these terms prove misleading. "I am held up, amid the nothingness,/ By one or two truths only," she says (VII, 603-604) and, a little later, explains that those "truths" are her "friend" and her son, not abstract concepts at all. "I had proof the archbishop was just man," she says (VII, 848), meaning that she discovered his advice to her was "wrong."

Motivated by her good experience in the Church of San Lorenzo, she submits to the Archbishop's guidance only to discover that he has misdirected her. In light of her new experience, but without new intellectual insight, she reacts instinctively against the organized Church:

> . . . henceforth I looked to God
> Only, nor cared my desecrated soul
> Should have fair walls, gay windows for the world.
> God's glimmer, that came through the ruin-top,

> *Was witness why all lights were quenched inside:*
> *Henceforth I asked God counsel, not mankind.*
> > *(VII, 854–859)*

This quietism, radical as Caponsacchi's or the Pope's, comes independently of reason and theology. The Pope accepted the witness of his heart, too, but in contrast to Pompilia subjected it also to the test of reason: "I love it with my heart: unsatisfied,/ I try it with my reason" (X, 1349–1350). Pompilia's position, intuitively arrived at, would be impossible for him.

Because of her innocence, Pompilia achieves in the confrontation at Castelnuovo what neither Caponsacchi nor Guido are capable of performing, a moral act. Both Guido and Caponsacchi hesitate. Guido later regrets that he did not claim his rights as husband and slay the seducer. Caponsacchi laments: "I could have killed him ere he killed his wife,/ And did not" (VI, 1894–1895). Pompilia follows impulse:

> *—then*
> *Came all the strength back in a sudden swell,*
> *I did for once see right, do right, give tongue*
> *The adequate protest: for a worm must turn*
> *If it would have its wrong observed by God.*
> *I did spring up, attempt to thrust aside*
> *That ice-block 'twixt the sun and me, lay low*
> *The neutralizer of all good and truth.*
> > *(VII, 1589–1596)*

Along with external forms of religion, Pompilia rejects the world and the flesh. At first she refuses to consummate her marriage and later yields passively to a relation from which she withholds her soul. Looking back upon this terrible experience she identifies herself with her prostitute mother, romantically claiming for both of them a purity which even a brothel could not stain.

Pompilia even denies Guido a share in her son: "My babe nor was, nor is, nor yet shall be/ Count Guido Franceschini's child at all—" (VII, 1762–1763). Insisting that only love begets life, Pompilia ignores biological realities, claiming in effect for her son an immaculate conception. She happily recalls Caponsacchi's name is Joseph. She associates her flight to Rome with that earlier trip to Bethlehem through repeated star imagery. Her son is born at Christmas; he is hidden from Guido (Herod), no longer father but destroyer. Were it not for Pompilia's obvious innocence this identification of herself with the Blessed Virgin would be blasphemous. But because of her innocence and inviolability she is precisely the Virgin.

It is obvious that Pompilia could not enter into a physical relation that did not involve spiritual union; it is less obvious that she could enter into such a relation under any conditions. She would perhaps have rejected the body of any man. The notion of her "soldier-saint" as human lover is incredible to her:

> He is a priest;
> He cannot marry therefore, which is right:
> I think he would not marry if he could.
> (VII, 1821–1823)

As Caponsacchi asserts, Pompilia is inviolable purity and, for him, a means of grace. She is at least potentially the same for Guido. Only a thin line separates Guido's hate and Caponsacchi's love. The Pompilia upon whom he calls in his extremity is the externalization of the subconscious image which he has held all along. His last appeal is motivated by a continuing, rejected, sense of guilt and frustration. For the old Pope, Pompilia is one compensation for his life of frustrating labor, his "one prize," "My rose, I gather for the breast of God" (X, 1046). Upon him too she casts a grace: "stoop thou down, my child,/ Give one good moment to the poor old Pope" (X, 1005–1006).

By the conclusion of the poem, Pompilia is so detached from the world and the flesh, both through her own speech and through the idealization of Caponsacchi, the Pope, and Guido, that we are ready perhaps to take with greater literalness than Browning intends her anticipated assumption, "And I rise" (VII, 1845). She is, I must repeat, however, individual and partial, a symbol of pre-fall innocence of an uncomplicated and instinctive goodness beyond the grasp of Caponsacchi and the Pope. Her presence in the story highlights the pathos of the ordinary human condition.

f

Between Pompilia's speech and the Pope's, Browning introduces his two lawyers, not merely as comic relief, as so often is said, but as necessary parts of the theme and action of the poem. Their speeches, overlong and often tedious, are, nevertheless, functional. They represent on the personal level a failure to achieve selfhood, making themselves part of that crowd of nondescripts: the Comparini, the nameless clerics, government officials, and social figures. They serve also to extend the scope of Browning's indictment of traditional values and institutions—in this case, of the law.

Arcangeli and Bottini actually fall somewhere between Half-Rome, Other Half-Rome, and Tertium Quid, on the one hand, and Guido, Caponsacchi, and the Pope, on the other. More individualized than the former (they do merit names), they fail, nevertheless, to achieve the self-realization of the latter. The man within each remains to the last obscured beneath his legal robes. Neither transcends "lawyerhood." They represent different degrees of failure. Arcangeli's affection for his fat wife and young son suggests that beneath the façade there is a potential man. His ridiculous pedantry, his legalistic hair-splitting, his unawareness of issues, his pointless argument, his unconcern for Pompilia (highlighted by his absurd interest in good food, good drink, good fellowship) ironically counterpoint his capacity for human affection. Bottini, however, has little to redeem him. Beneath his lawyer façade there is, so far as we can see, only vacuity. He remains the arid bachelor, incapable of self-awareness and affection.

Both lawyers mistake issues, Arcangeli trying to free Guido and Bottini to convict him, when neither Guido's exoneration nor conviction is the real issue. Both are occupied in achieving a legal victory when they should, for their own salvation, be concerned with human values. Unlike Caponsacchi, Guido, and Pope Innocent they never divest themselves of their official robes, remaining mere manikins.

Browning's contempt, however, is greater for the system which they embody than for the men they are. They are victims not of self-interest, as were the representatives of Roman society, but of institutionalism. Their grotesqueness results from the distortion which occurs when truth and goodness become codified and institutionalized. That the Court renders in this case a right verdict is beside the point. The end of its action is right, but its motives are wrong. Its operation, like that of society and of the Church, conforms to assumptions external to man and irrelevant to his soul needs. Law, faithful to the system, may as readily render a verdict superficially right but essentially wrong. The legal code by which society is governed is not Truth itself; it is not inevitably an instrument for achieving truth. Instead, like traditional social and religious institutions, it alienates men from themselves, rendering them incapable of self-realization and salvation. With this denunciation of legal institutions, Browning rounds out his gloomy assessment of Western culture.

III ❧

Although Book XI terminates the action on one level, it leaves important questions unanswered. What is the precise meaning of Guido's appeal to Pompilia, and how does his story relate to those of the other characters? What has Browning said about man's search for truth in a world of dissolving external values and decadent institutions? What are we to infer about the triumph of good over evil?

In Book XII, Browning remains the detached observer, approaching his subject through dramatis personae. Indeed the "I" who introduces Book XII is in some manner of speaking Browning himself, but he is also more. He is equally the dramatis persona in the seventeenth-century drama and the nineteenth-century poet in his London study. Browning telescopes time and identifies past with present to assert the continuity of human experience and to help locate the infinite in the finite. Literally, he introduces or reintroduces four characters whose "factual" statements place the action in the perspective best suited for its final interpretation: a Venetian gentleman, visitor in Rome and witness of the execution; the lawyers, Arcangeli and Bottini; and Fra Celestino, Pompilia's confessor. All help bring the poem into focus.

Three of the speakers refer to Guido's conversion and exemplary death, but with such motives or toward such ends as to undermine the validity of their report. Significantly Fra Celestino, whose judgment we respect, says nothing about Guido's conversion. Could this mean that he does not take it seriously? Browning apparently wished to leave the matter ambiguous.

Actually, Guido's gesture at the end of Book XI is as indeterminate as Childe Roland's at the end of "Childe Roland to the Dark Tower Came" and less capable of single interpretation. It might signal a transformation of which his submission to the Church is only an outward and non-essential manifestation. In that case, he would achieve the status of a Caponsacchi or a Pope. On the other hand, it might represent his final self-confrontation and deliberate choice of damnation. This would make his gesture to the Church hypocritical bravado. There is some evidence to support this interpretation. If this were the case, however, it would still constitute on one important level a human triumph. Even if he is damned, he, unlike Arcangeli and Bottini, has willed his damnation and in that act of choice and commitment achieves a manhood that gives him a privileged place among the lost.

If his final appeal to Pompilia is no more than animal terror and his "conversion" an attempt to achieve a conventional salvation within the system, most of Book XI is irrelevant. This I cannot accept. It seems clear, on the contrary, from the perspective of Book XII that Guido completes the journey from counthood to manhood, providing a vivid description of the process by which man achieves the humanity to save or damn himself. Browning remains ambiguous, shifting emphasis from external act to internal action in order to avoid having his work interpreted from a traditional religious point of view.

Fra Celestino's sermon places Arcangeli and Bottini in relation to the theme and action of the poem. After excoriating Bottini for his duplicity in assuming the cause of the convent against Pompilia, he summarizes what must be Browning's view of the Court:

> *"The inadequacy and inaptitude*
> *"Of that self-same machine, that very law*
> *"Man vaunts, devised to dissipate the gloom,*
> *"Rescue the drowning orb from calumny,*
> *"—Hear law, appointed to defend the just,*
> *"Submit, for best defence, that wickedness*
> *"Was bred of flesh and innate with the bone*
> *"Borne by Pompilia's spirit for a space,*
> *"And no mere chance fault, passionate and brief: . . .*
>
> (XII, 576–584)

By this time we realize that social, legal, and religious systems and institutions are at best instrumental and, more often, stumbling blocks to man in his search for truth. Man's approach to the infinite is an emanation from within rather than an imposition from without; it is the apprehension of the infinite within man through his finite choice and commitment. By such action, as tentative and subject to error as it is, man achieves self-realization, the moral life.

Finally there is the problem of the triumph of good over evil. "Because Pompilia's purity prevails,/ Conclude you, all truth triumphs in the end?" Fra Celestino asks (XII, 472–473), and answers his own question:

> *"Methinks I hear the Patriarch's warning voice—*
> *" 'Though this one breast, by miracle, return,*
> *" 'No wave rolls by, in all the waste, but bears*
> *" 'Within it some dead dove-like thing as dear,*
> *" 'Beauty made blank and harmlessness destroyed!'*
> *"How many chaste and noble sister-fames*
> *"Wanted the extricating hand, and lie*

"Strangled, for one Pompilia proud above
"The welter, plucked from the world's calumny,
"Stupidity, simplicity,—who cares?

(*XII, 482–491*)

Man is adrift in a world that is indifferent, perhaps antagonistic. More often than not, virtue goes unrevealed, guilt
unapprehended. Man, confounded by ignorance and evil,
may sometimes "by miracle" be saved. There is an occasional Pompilia, Caponsacchi, or Pope. There is even more
occasionally a Guido who may extricate himself from the
debris of outworn creeds and codes to achieve manhood.
There is little cause for optimism in *The Ring and the
Book,* however, if we ask more than the outside chance.

The *Ring and the Book* represents the culmination of
one stage in Browning's development. In his early works,
Pauline's poet, Paracelsus, and Sordello attempt to grasp
the infinite directly and fail, discovering over against God's
infinitude man's finiteness. In the plays, the leading figures
learn that man in his pursuit of truth is destined to work
within the confines of human limitations. In the great
monologues of the middle period, Browning himself accepts these terms and seeks the whole through the part,
God in the miniscule. The monologues are brilliant fragments of one sweeping work that remains always just beyond man's powers to realize. Each is related to each, and
all to some infinite Truth that defies apprehension. *The
Ring and the Book* represents Browning's most sustained
effort to relate the fragments by a common theme and action in a huge symbolic poem that expresses as nearly as art
can the wholeness of his vision. It is the fulfillment of that
adolescent dream which inspired *Pauline* but which at the
time was beyond Browning's power to realize.

✤ ✤ ✤ CHAPTER V

The Dialogue
of the Soul

What those who are familiar only with the
great monuments of early Greek genius
suppose to be its exclusive characteristics,
have disappeared; the calm, the
cheerfulness, the disinterested objectivity
have disappeared; the dialogue of the mind
with itself has commenced; modern
problems have presented themselves; we
hear already the doubts, we witness the
discouragements, of Hamlet and of Faust.
(Matthew Arnold, Preface, *Poems*, 1853.)

✤ Publication of *The Ring and the Book*
brought one stage of Browning's career to a climax. In the
decade which followed, he remained interested in the development of the soul, but became increasingly skeptical.
In the earlier poems, he had asked, with some assurance of
receiving an answer, how shall I act to prove what I am? In
the poems of the seventies, however, he is less certain and
more often is moved to question whether or not he has a
consistent, coherent being to prove. At the same time, he

appears more intensely aware of the gulf between private vision and universal values, and of the difficulties which the artist experiences when he tries to speak authoritatively on any subject outside his own immediate consciousness.

There are four long dramatic-narrative poems during this period: *Prince Hohenstiel-Schwangau* (1871), *Fifine at the Fair* (1872), *Red Cotton Night–Cap Country* (1873), and *The Inn Album* (1875). There are three works either translated or derived from the Greek: *Balaustion's Adventure* (1871), *Aristophanes' Apology* (1875), and *Agamemnon* (1877). Two works fall into neither of these groupings but are related thematically to them: *Pacchiarotto and How He Worked in Distemper* (1876) and *La Saisiaz and the Two Poets of Croisic* (1878).

I ❧ *Prince Hohenstiel-Schwangau*

Neither *Prince Hohenstiel-Schwangau* nor *Fifine at the Fair* should be judged by standards ordinarily applied to dramatic monologues. The speaker in each is less sharply defined, and the auditor is less functional than in the earlier monologues. Sensuous details and emotional elements are subordinate to intellectual subtlety and argument. Browning remains interested in the "soul," but, increasingly impatient with external manifestations of character, he seems determined to seize directly the inner life. He moves, consequently, toward a poetry of abstraction—dialectical, complex, subtle. When he fails in these poems it is less because he violates the monologue form, as many of his critics have assumed, than because he does not always achieve a new structure capable of expressing his poetic intention.

Prince Hohenstiel-Schwangau is not a defense of Louis

Napoleon as most of Browning's contemporaries believed. We might say of Napoleon and this poem what André Gide said of Wordsworth and "The Lost Leader": he "served Browning only as a pretext, his falling away only as a starting point, for a poem; one more opportunity for Browning to depersonalize himself in order to put himself momentarily into someone else." [1]

Browning's interests here are neither historical nor political, but metaphysical. His treatment of character in *Prince Hohenstiel-Schwangau* differs from that in the short monologues. Here he is more interested in the subjective reality of the character than in his relation to the external world. Browning's earlier characters ask how they can prove their souls through action in the external world; the Prince asks if he has a soul to prove. We assume a potential Sordello, a Caponsacchi, even a Guido, but is there behind the diverse manifestations of Prince Hohenstiel a single man? [2]

If so, who and what is he? There are contradictory possibilities. Initially, he appears a French exile taking tea with a young lady in Leicester Square. This seemingly substantial character quickly disappears, however, and is replaced by others less apparently corporeal. At first he is the Prince defending pragmatically his twenty-year rule of France. Later, however, he seems to become one Thiers-Hugo, an imaginary idealist who challenges the Prince, and in an argument with a shadowy character, Sagacity, attempts to demonstrate the course of action which Hohenstiel should have followed. We soon discover that Thiers-Hugo is merely one aspect of the multiple Prince, his long submerged idealistic youth, and that Sagacity is another, his disillusioned maturity. The quarrel between the two is internal. The action is subjective, abstract rather than concrete, intellectual rather than emotional, speculative rather than dramatic. The Prince rightly characterizes it as a "ghostly dialogue." He engages in what Matthew Arnold calls "the dialogue of the mind with itself." The conclusion of the poem compounds rather than clarifies the confusion. Suddenly we discover that the entire poem is a dream and that the historical figure—man or manikin—is still in France.

Several interesting issues emerge. The Prince cannot be certain that he has a single existence, one soul. He looks within himself, into his semirationalized, semiverbalized consciousness ("instinct, guess, again/ With dubious knowledge, half-experience" [2093–2094]) in search of selfhood. His groping and his uncertain achievement are reflected in the distorted syntax, asyntactical elements, broken rhythms, and incomplete sentences. In this quest lies the clue to the structure of the poem, both the dialectical arrangement of the larger parts and the unconventional handling of the smaller elements. The Prince cannot be sure that he himself exists, a consistent, responsible, choosing, acting individual: " 'Who's who?' was aptly asked,/ Since certainly I am not I!" (2078–2079).

Perhaps on some deeply subjective level, he has reality; nothing outside him, however, seems adequate to give structure to his chaos. The bridge between inner and outer is destroyed:

> Somehow the motives, that did well enough
> I' the darkness, when you bring them into light
> Are found, like those famed cave-fish, to lack eye
> And organ for the upper magnitudes.
>
> (2106–2109)

The Prince remains uncommitted, an opportunist by necessity. Browning does not defend the morality of opportunism, but he shows how under certain conditions a man has no course other than to be an opportunist. The Prince points to the chasm between aspiration and worldly achievement. Recalling his youthful idealism, he says:

> *This, with much beside,*
> *I spoke when I was voice and nothing more,*
> *But altogether such an one as you*
> *My censors.*
>
> (873–876)

But once a prince, things changed: "Once pedestalled on earth,/ To act not speak, I found earth was not air" (902–903).

The subtitle of the poem, "The Saviour of Society," is ironical. Each of the voices within the poem uses the word *savior* differently. The Prince and Sagacity are concerned to preserve the cultural frame, what they call "King, caste, cultus"; Idealism, to protect the abstract "rights of Man." No one is concerned primarily to save the individual.

Obviously, we can take no part of the argument at face value, precisely because the Prince does not. There are too many voices, each of which throws doubt upon all others: the Exile, the Prince, Idealism, Sagacity, the Dreamer, the old man in Paris. This cacophony of voices reveals the conflicts within Hohenstiel and emphasizes the breach between his inner and outer world. We emerge from the dream section of the poem aware that both Sagacity and Idealism are insubstantial dream figures. We come finally to discover the unreality of the dreamer himself, who failing to achieve identity finds no emphatic voice of his own. In this poem we witness not the development but the dissipation of a soul. Here Browning pushes his skepticism further than in any previous poem to question the reality not merely of the act but of the actor.

II ❧ *Fifine at the Fair*

Prince Hohenstiel-Schwangau disappointed many of Browning's friends; *Fifine at the Fair* embarrassed them. In the former, Browning seemed to defend political expediency; in the latter, conjugal infidelity. Dr. Furnivall assured a disturbed Browning Society, ostensibly on authority of the poet, that the purpose of the poem "was to show merely how a Don Juan might justify himself, partly by truth, somewhat by sophistry." [3]

Browning seems to have intended more, however. Alfred Domett records in his diary, "Browning tells me he has just finished a poem, 'the most metaphysical and boldest' he has written since Sordello, and was very doubtful as to its reception by the public." [4] This emphasis on the bold speculativeness of the poem encourages us to look for more in *Fifine at the Fair* than subtle analysis of a slippery character.

In subject, *Fifine* is a continuation of *Prince Hohenstiel-Schwangau*, a further exploration of the problem of *being*. It depicts universal change, a process at once good and bad, both the antithesis of and the means by which man achieves eternity. The poem seeks some abiding truth amid the dissolving fragments of the external world; specifically, the speaker gropes for reality of self and, by extension, for the reality of a changeless order beyond time. Eventually the speaker asserts for himself an identity in which the Prince could never believe:

> . . . *'t is they*
> *Convince,—if little, much, no matter!—one degree*
> *The more, at least, convince unreasonable me*
> *That I am, anyhow, a truth, though all else seem*
> *And be not: if I dream, at least I know I dream.*
>
> *(80)* [5]

> *Alack, our life is lent,*
> *From first to last, the whole, for this experiment*
> *Of proving what I say—that we ourselves are true!*
>   *(82)*

Browning's association of his character with the notorious libertine, Don Juan, encourages misunderstanding. Obviously, he is attempting a reconstruction not only of a character but of a metaphysics. He uses key words, *soul*, *true*, and *false*, in an untraditional manner. In *Fifine*, he gives *soul*, a term that he used throughout his career, its fullest amplification. Here it means both realization of the fullest, deepest level of one's being and, also, the recognition of affinities with and participation in something outside and beyond man himself—Eternity, God. The developed soul is conscious of itself and of its participation in the eternal.

The dissolving external world of *The Ring and the Book* becomes in *Fifine* a kaleidoscope of shifting perspectives in which nothing seems permanent. Even man himself seems *false*—that is, transitory, unreal. In such a world, he asks, is there permanence, *truth?* Can we prove "that we ourselves are true"? If so, how? Clearly we do not postulate *self* on an a priori notion of God; to the contrary, the knowledge of self proceeds and makes possible our assumption of God. The fear of nonbeing, always just beneath surface consciousness, rises occasionally to create moments of real terror, as, for example, when the speaker sees among the imaginary beings on the streets of Venice:

> *Age reduced to simple greed and guile,*
> *Worn apathetic else as some smooth slab, erewhile*
> *A clear-cut man-at-arms i' the pavement, till foot's*
> *tread*

Effaced the sculpture, left the stone you saw instead,—
Was not that terrible beyond the mere uncouth?

(95)

Man's lethargy or traditional social and moral restraints may produce nonbeing. In the recurring figures of the pennon the speaker provides an image of an awakened, aspiring man:

> . . . *how the pennon from its dome,*
> *Frenetic to be free, makes one red stretch for home!*
>
> (5)

> *Frenetic to be free! And, do you know, there beats*
> *Something within my breast, as sensitive?—repeats*
> *The fever of the flag? My heart makes just the same*
> *Passionate stretch, fires up for lawlessness, lays claim*
> *To share the life they lead.*
>
> (6)

The pennon making its "one red stretch for home," even though it is securely anchored (and will never achieve its objective), attains its "frenetic" life precisely because it is anchored (an unsecured pennon is less, not more, a pennon). It becomes an appropriate image for the speaker, who realizes in the process of his meditation that what he wants is the experience of being, caught between earth and sky, quivering with life, frenetically stretching for home while he remains firmly anchored to earth. His failure to achieve complete freedom is paradoxically his victory. Such experience, consciousness of being, is the only "truth" in a "false" world, confirming not only the self but that "other" to whom he responds, and without whom response, life, would be impossible.

Browning never intended *Fifine* to be a traditional monologue. The speaker is more an abstracted soul than a complete character. The auditor is not important as character. The action is internalized, relying little upon symbolic external scene and situation. Andrea's four walls and Lippo's street are concrete objects, essential to the poems in which they appear. A succession of places and things in *Fifine* denies rather than affirms their own substantiality. The gypsy caravan, the waving pennons, the dancing girls, the ocean foam, the dissolving clouds, the visionary streets, the Druid monuments, and, even, that final door behind which lies respectability, have the same insubstantiality as the violin, the donkey, the fish in a Chagall painting. Each is a part in that process of change which proves that in itself it is nothing. Space and time are scarcely the setting for this poem. The internal action, too, lacks its clear symbolic equivalent in the external world. The speaker's final return to Fifine seems less a summation than Andrea's concessions to Lucrezia or Lippo's return to his cell. In *Fifine,* Browning again records the dialogue of a soul with itself. The structure sprawls: the poem is overlong. In defense of the poet, we may say that he requires room for the organic development of his theme, and that the journey inward must of necessity follow an exploratory path. For logical progression, Browning substitutes a complex dialectical interplay of ideas and emotions. The poem grows.

Tone and action are equally important. Let us begin with the more difficult of the two, tone. It emerges primarily through Browning's implied attitude toward his characters and by the speaker's attitude toward himself and the two women, Elvire and Fifine.

It is not easy to disentangle Browning's own attitude toward his materials. It is obviously ambivalent. The speaker is not a simple libertine, although Browning suggests that we identify him partially with Don Juan. In the poem, he remains unnamed, partly to keep that association tentative and partly to suggest that he has not yet achieved identity.

Clearly Browning is neither shocked nor indignant but rather, over all, sympathetic. Emphasizing the metaphysical rather than the physical, the psychological rather than the moral, the poet circumvents traditional judgments. The speaker is perhaps guilty of infidelity and of dishonesty, but even these defects, although not entirely excused, are transformed into virtues. Molière's character deliberately chooses evil, but Browning's character pursues what at first seems evil as part of an over all scheme for good.

The speaker's motives are complex, defying simple schematization. He does not always speak truthfully when he refers to Elvire and sophistically when he refers to Fifine (as some critics have maintained). Rather, he hankers simultaneously for both, remaining incomplete with either alone. It oversimplifies the poem to associate Fifine with bad flesh and Elvire with good spirit.

W. O. Raymond observes that Fifine is a gypsy, of a group whom Browning customarily represents favorably.[6] In the early poem "The Flight of the Duchess," he used gypsies to represent freedom in contrast to institutions, good in contrast to bad. Although in *Fifine* his attitude is more complex, he remains ambivalent toward the gypsy girl. She is at once an attractive body and a symbol of spiritual freedom, an incentive to self-realization. She appeals to the speaker's elemental desire to be himself, untrammeled by conventions. He is drawn to her more by spiritual curiosity than by sexual passion. He returns to her less to enjoy her body than to escape the symbolic four walls of his home.

Browning's presentation of Elvire is equally complex. Our problem arises because of the traditional identification of Elvire with Elizabeth Barrett, to whom Browning addressed the prologue and epilogue. But if she is Elizabeth Barrett, Browning must be Don Juan. It would seem, indeed, that the poem reflects to some extent Browning's guilt, as W. O. Raymond persuasively argues, without insisting, however, that Elvire *is* Elizabeth or that Don Juan is Browning.[7] The evidence of the poem, as I shall show, is against such an identification. Browning's presentation of Elvire is decidedly ambiguous. The speaker's attitude toward her reveals itself consciously and unconsciously, in what he says and in what he implies. Perhaps in some ways he does prize Elvire above all women. At the same time he clearly resents her, his "sulky diamond" in contrast to Fifine, "Its sherd which, sun-smit, shines, shoots arrowy fire" (30). He chides Elvire for what appears dishonesty: "Come, come, that's what you say, or would, were thoughts but free" (31). Perhaps that is the key. He sees Fifine and Elvire as representing opposites: freedom, restrictions; lawlessness, law; change, fixity; dynamism, stasis; spirit, form; fertility, sterility; life, death. Ultimately, his subconscious impulses triumph, revealing his sympathies with Fifine's qualities. He finally concludes that Elvire is incapable of understanding him. For her, all paths lead back to the door behind which lie the safe, the conventional, the stultifying:

> *But wise, we want no more*
> *O' the fickle element. Enough of foam and roar!*
> *Land-locked, we live and die henceforth: for here's the*
> *villa-door.*
>
> (*129*)

This is negation, not affirmation; spiritual death, not moral achievement. In front of that door, Elvire emerges as what subconsciously he has known her to be all along:

> *How pallidly you pause o' the threshold! Hardly night,*
> *Which drapes you, ought to make real flesh and blood*
> *so white!*

Touch me, and so appear alive to all intents!
Will the saint vanish from the sinner that repents?
Suppose you are a ghost! A memory, a hope,
A fear, a conscience! Quick! Give back the hand I
*   grope*
I' the dusk for!

(*130*)

*   Elvire is land not sea—*
The solid land, the safe.
(*131*)

This new perspective conjures up a momentary vision of life, detailed in stanza 131, which contradicts every honest impulse of his nature: "Enter for good and all! then fate bolt fast the door,/ Shut you and me inside, never to wander more!" He cannot. He is less drawn to Fifine than repelled by Elvire. We begin to understand the two women as necessary polarities, capable together of stimulating that consciousness of self which is symbolized by the pennon. Neither is completely satisfying alone.

With the subject thus identified and tone suggested, we can turn now for a fuller discussion of the action. The movement is toward a state of consciousness rather than a system of thought or morals. It is psychological rather than logical; symbolic rather than rational. The poem falls into three parts, each representing stages in the speaker's development. The poem neither progresses nor ends, in an Aristotelian sense. The three stages are not strictly sequential but overlapping and repetitious. Each of the first two sections moves simultaneously toward a synthesis and its immediate dissolution; the final section achieves not the stasis of a final vision but momentary perspective, from which the speaker may move on to ever-renewing visions. Browning achieves in the structure of the poem a symbol of its significant action.

Part One (stanzas 1–87) is an apologia which deepens from casuistry to metaphysical speculation. The sight of the pennon sets the speaker speculating upon the paradoxes of human existence: the tension between man's infinite aspiration and his finite means, between his desire for freedom and his need for structure. He explores means of achieving identity, a process that places Fifine and Elvire in a counterpart relation. He feels but does not understand his paradoxical attitude toward them. His attempt to rationalize it leads to distortion because his reason, intolerant of ambiguity, forces him to prefer one to the exclusion of the other. This falsifies the experience as he instinctively knows it to be. He is forced into reducing Fifine to mere flesh and of elevating Elvire to a status which she does not in reality occupy. Elvire, contradicting what he tries to say for her, emerges both a lonely woman and a voracious female. He speaks for her:

> " 'Now, what's a smile to you? Poor candle that lights up
> 'The decent household gloom which sends you out to sup.
> 'A tear? worse! warns that health requires you keep aloof
> 'From nuptial chamber, since rain penetrates the roof! . . .
> 'What do I say? at least a meteor's half in heaven;
> 'Provided filth but shine, my husband hankers even
> 'After putridity that's phosphorescent, cribs
> 'The rustic's tallow-rush, makes spoil of urchins' squibs,
> 'In short prefers to me—chaste, temperate, serene—

'*What sputters green and blue, this fizgig called
Fifine!*'"

(33)

Elvire detects all the spuriousness and none of the genuineness of his argument: "Who is it you deceive—/ Yourself or me or God, with all this make-believe?" (60) He
reveals a seriousness, however, even when apparently he is
most casuistic. She says he prefers sense; he answers that
sense activates spirit and proves to himself that "I am I."
She calls him a profligate; he professes to be a seeker. A
woman, he maintains, makes a man conscious of himself by
separating the "I," the permanent, from the changing. She
reminds him that he is unfaithful; he explains that he requires constant reassurance and renewal. There is a place
in his life for the Fifines:

> . . . *some beauty, fate reserved*
> *To give me once again the electric snap and spark*   *1*
> *That prove, when finger finds out finger in the dark*
> *O' the world, there's fire and life and truth there, link*
>   *but hands*
> *And pass the secret on! till, link by link, expands*
> *The circle, lengthens out the chain, and one embrace*
> *Of high with low is found uniting the whole race,*
> *Not simply you and me and our Fifine, but all*
> *The world.*

(91)

Part One achieves a temporary synthesis based upon the
speaker's rationalization, his inseparable tangle of sincere
argument and clever casuistry.

Part Two (stanzas 88–123) shifts the exploration to another plane. The speaker finds his argument unsatisfactory less because it is false (as Elvire claims) than because it is rational and partial. Reason and words, he contends, cannot discover and fix truth. Symbol may perhaps suggest it, however. Like most of his contemporaries, at a time when the forms of painting and literature were less fluid than they are today, Browning regarded music as the best means of communicating an ultimate vision because "change is there/ The law, and not the lapse" (92). Music, eschewing human thought and language, transforms the changing, the false, into the permanent, the true, by shifting the scene from time to eternity (witness the musician Abt Vogler). Music of all the arts is most evocative of eternity.

In Part Two, Browning's character turns to music, to Schumann's "Carnival." Lifted out of time and place, he watches from a perspective above Venice the carnival in St. Mark's Square, seeing disgusting figures, either faceless or grotesquely masked. He is repelled until, as he plunges into their midst, his judgment turns to sympathy. On closer view, he discovers a discrepancy between what they apparently mean and what they say and do:

> *I saw the mouths at play,*
> *The gesture that enforced, the eye that strove to say*
> *The same thing as the voice, and seldom gained its*
> * point*
> *—That this was so, I saw; but all seemed out of joint*
> *I' the vocal medium 'twixt the world and me. I gained*
> *Knowledge by notice, not by giving ear,—attained*
> *To truth by what men seemed, not said: to me one*
> * glance*
> *Was worth whole histories of noisy utterance,*
> *—At least, to me in dream.*
>
> (*100*)

When he comes to see the distorted figures sympathetically from within, he moves in his speculations to a new synthesis:

> *Just so I glut*
> *My hunger, both to be and know the thing I am,*
> *By contrast with the thing I am not; so, through sham*
> *And outside, I arrive at inmost real, probe*
> *And prove how the nude form obtained the chequered*
>   *robe.*
>
> *(103)*

St. Mark's expands to become the world; the carnival, life; the masquerade, all men; the Feast Day, the past and present and future. The vision takes on a kaleidoscopic animation in which objects form only to dissolve and to reform in an attempt to suggest an inexpressible permanence. Browning's techniques here remind us of Strindberg's in *The Dream Play* and *The Ghost Sonata*. All things, evil included, become parts of man's continuing effort to apprehend and fix the eternal. Such a vision contradicts traditional good and evil and defies fixed metaphysical systems. It assumes a world, neither immoral nor amoral, in which emphasis shifts from the end of action to action itself, from achievement to striving:

> *And—consequent upon the learning how from*
>   *strife*
> *Grew peace—from evil, good—came knowledge that,*
>   *to get*
> *Acquaintance with the way o' the world, we must nor*
>   *fret*
> *Nor fume, on altitudes of self-sufficiency,*
> *But bid a frank farewell to what—we think—should*
>   *be,*

And, with as good a grace, welcome what is—we find.
(*109*)

This is also the world of Goethe's Faust, who follows an untraditional path to an untraditional heaven, described by the carrier angels:

> 'For he whose strivings never cease
> Is ours for his redeeming!
> If touched by the celestial love,
> His soul has sacred leaven,
> There comes to greet him, from above,
> The company of heaven.' [8]

Such striving can end only when the striver is transplanted from a temporal to an eternal scene. This may happen momentarily when he is caught up by music; it may happen permanently when time is dissolved into eternity. The latter happens to Faust but not to Browning's character, as we shall see.

From this generalization, the speaker turns to his own times to pronounce the temporality of existing forms, proudly and arrogantly established by religion, philosophy, and science. At best such forms are instrumental; at worst, and most often, they are impediments.

The vision ends with the fall of night, which reduces all objects to objectlessness and leaves the speaker speculating about the possible forms that objects assume in darkness, attempting to impose upon the unreal material an imaginative reality. Elvire still cannot understand. She responds to music no more than to reason. The speaker manipulates his walk so that they arrive at this point at the site of two Druid monuments, one still standing and the other now lying on its side (having been toppled by order of the curé). They become final and synthesizing symbols. They express both the temporal-permanent and the sense-spirit dialectic, bringing into one image most of the diverse themes of the poem.

In spite of time, the stones of the standing monument

> . . . *gleam unground away*
> *By twilight's hungry jaw, which champs fine all beside*
> *I' the solitary waste . . .*
>
> (*122*)

The standing tower is dedicated to death and associated with the Cross and the Christian emphasis on negation and suffering. The other, fallen by order of the priest,

> [. . . '*bides*
> *Its time to rise again!' (so somebody derides,*
> *That's pert from Paris)*]
>
> (*123*)

was originally a phallic symbol associated with fertility rites, remains of an earlier life-affirming paganism. Together the two represent the necessary tension between spirit and sense, law and lawlessness, restraint and freedom, death and life—Elvire and Fifine. They are parts of that eternal growth and development toward which the speaker aspires:

> *For as some imperial chord subsists,*
> *Steadily underlies the accidental mists*
> *Of music springing thence, that run their mazy race*
> *Around, and sink, absorbed, back to the triad base,—*
> *So, out of that one word, each variant rose and fell*
> *And left the same "All's change, but permanence as*
> *well."*
>
> (*124*)

Such "salvation" as this new vision suggests involves self-consciousness and a desire for wholeness, less a state than a condition, since it can be known only as a striving: "Let only soul look up, not down, not hate but love." We are reminded once more of *Faust:* "For man must strive, and striving err." [9] Browning's character continues:

> ". . . *so tempts, till we attain to read*
> *The signs aright, and learn, by failure, truth is forced*
> *To manifest itself through falsehood . . ."*
>
> (*124*)

That truth

> ". . . *sets aside speech, act, time, place, indeed,*
> *but brings*
> *Nakedly forward now the principle of things*
> *Highest and least."*
>
> (*124*)

Browning's speaker, beginning with clever self-justification, has by deepening seriousness penetrated the mystery of existence and for the moment stilled the voice of negation that would nullify both the outside world and the self, making aspiration and striving impossible. But this vision, like Abt Vogler's, cannot last: "poetry turns prose. . . . I dwindle at the close/ Down to mere commonplace which everybody knows" (126).

At the beginning of Part Three (stanza 126) he returns to his pre-vision skepticism with perhaps even deeper bitterness and despair. "We end where we began . . . wherever we were nursed/ To life, we bosom us on death" (127). In the stanzas that follow, we trace a natural reaction to the ecstasy of vision. The vision gone, he is tempted to deny its authenticity, a psychological if not logical consistency. He rejects what he has said and seen in Part Two and once more declares that Elvire is sufficient to his needs and that he wants only a quiet, undisturbed life within his villa:

> But wise, we want no more
> O' the fickle element. Enough of foam and roar!
> Land-locked, we live and die henceforth: for here's the
> villa-door.
>
> (*129*)

Such a state, were it to become permanent, would be more dangerous than his first. But the statement implies its own contradiction. "Land-locked" . . . "die" . . . "door": these images, surfacing from the depth of his subconscious, are evidence of a tension, a spiritual restlessness, that can never abide the restrictions he affects to accept. In a final flash of insight, he looks beyond Elvire to the life she invites him to share:

> In Pornic, say,
> The Mayor shall catalogue me duly domiciled,
> Contributable, good-companion of the guild
> And mystery of marriage. I stickle for the town,
> And not this tower apart. . . .
>
> (*131*)

This is too much. No amount of disillusionment over the dissipated vision can justify this new death. The speaker is reminiscent of Fra Lippo Lippi, who also refused to be immured. What he does—and that is not entirely clear—need not be defended as a good in itself. It is, however, an expression of will to life rather than to death, of continued striving rather than stagnation. The speaker has not chosen and acted once and for all; he has achieved no lasting vision. He is yet alive, however. There will be other moments of insight.

The last line of the poem must be read in light of stanza 130, where he also calls Elvire a ghost, an abstraction, a cypher for conventional social and moral restraints, it would seem, and not a flesh-and-blood woman. Here he says that if he does not return as he promises, she has his permission to invoke all the strictures of her ghostly conventions. She is a "good" woman. I find nothing in the line which suggests that she will soon die.

We are pained less by the speaker's rejection of Elvire than by Norbert's of the Queen because Browning has endowed Elvire with fewer sympathetic qualities. Nor does the speaker here so clearly have an obligation to his society. In fact, his final act affirms rather than negates his humanity. In *Fifine at the Fair,* Browning comes close to realizing the full implications of his vision by placing the external forms of society in a perspective which makes it impossible for us even momentarily to associate the form itself with eternity. Browning's vision of meaning and values has come clearly to focus upon the inner life of man rather than upon an ordered external structure. At the same time, however, the external world is no longer merely villain. It is part of a dialectical process by which man achieves fulfillment and participates in an imagined eternity of which the world is an integral part without being the end.

Finally, the troublesome prologue and epilogue must be accounted for. It is not at all clear that they are thematically and structurally related to the poem itself. Several of Browning's later poems contain dedicatory passages that are quite independent of the volume to which they are appended. It would seem that here prologue and epilogue are either unrelated or tangentially related as a result of the unhappy circumstance in Browning's life which is detailed in the article by Professor Raymond to which I have referred.

They perhaps serve a function, however. Detached from the main body of the poem, they provide another perspective from which we may see what happened. They confirm the necessity for striving, the difficulty of a single devotion, the mixed pattern of this life. They also suggest, in a less exalted spirit than Goethe's, that man's devotion can never become single and all-satisfying until he is transplanted from time into eternity. For Browning this event remains a hopeful possibility but, in this poem, nothing more.

III ❧ Red Cotton Night–Cap County

Browning's next poem, Red Cotton Night–Cap Country, is his version of an actual case reported in the Journal de Caen during July, 1873. It relates the apparent suicide of one Monsieur Léonce Miranda, and the subsequent court battle in which his relatives attempt to set aside his will. The events occurred near St. Aubin, where Browning spent the summer following the trial. Browning altered the story only by changing proper names and by giving Miranda motives which he could only imagine.

Miranda was killed when he fell from a tower on his estate where he lived with his mistress, Clara. His death terminated years of conflict within him and between him and his family. His will, leaving his estate to the Ravissante, the Virgin, patron of a nearby monastery, and, at the same time, providing for the maintenance of his mistress, was contested by his Paris cousins, who insisted that Miranda's fall was a successful third attempt at suicide (once before he had thrown himself into the Seine and, again, had in a fit of remorse plunged his arms into a fire which consumed his hands before he was dragged to safety). These macabre acts, along with others almost as bizzare, they maintained, proved Miranda insane and therefore incompetent at the time he made his will. The court, however, ruled that Miranda was competent but left the question of the possible suicide unanswered.

Browning, after hearing the merest sketch of the story, concluded that "there was no intention of committing suicide, and I said at once that I would myself treat the subject *just so*" (Hood, *Letters*, 309).

The poem is not entirely successful imaginatively and structurally. Browning seems uncertain of his intentions: He wishes to commemorate his friendship with Miss Annie Thackeray, to whom he addresses the poem; he is attracted by the grotesque irony of the subject, a study in abnormal psychology; he is also incensed by the superstitious nature of a religion which in the name of saints destroys human beings. He develops neither of these latter possibilities, however, into a single, unifying theme.

Browning's interpretation of the death gave him opportunity to concentrate on Miranda's inner conflict. If this were his main purpose, events should serve as symbols of Miranda's inner life. The most obvious symbols are the Ravissante and Clara, Miranda's heavenly and earthly ravishers. These are reinforced by a series of supporting images: turf-tower, Paris-country, Boulevard-Belvedere, flesh-spirit, mud-rock, red-white. These antithetical images do not mirror a clear dichotomy between obvious bad and good. Many of them are intentionally ambiguous. Just before Miranda plunges to his death he explores his conflict. He can surrender neither the Ravissante nor Clara. Indeed, he argues, if the Virgin really possesses the powers attributed to her, he should have to give up neither. She could suspend natural laws and purify the illegal bond be-

tween him and Clara and, by conducting him safely through
the air to her shrine, unify his earthly and heavenly aspirations. Browning summarizes:

> *Here's our case.*
> *Monsieur Léonce Miranda asks of God,*
> *—May a man, living in illicit tie,*
> *Continue, by connivance of the Church,*
> *No matter what amends he please to make*
> *Short of forthwith relinquishing the sin?*
>
> (*III, 876–881*)

Partly as an act of faith, partly as a challenge (his Spanish piety and his French skepticism), and partly to satisfy
his need to know, he throws himself from the tower: "A
flash in middle air, and stone-dead lay/ Monsieur Léonce
Miranda on the turf" (IV, 341–342).

As a psychological study the poem is marred, however,
by the fact that Miranda's conflict, although tense, is abnormal. He is victim of perverse religion and perverse sensuality, not of a healthy tension between body and spirit.
We can imagine no reconciliation, and watch with horror
as he is swept toward final self-destruction. The poem, at
best, is a study in abnormality, with power to fascinate and
repel but not to involve the reader.

The poet-narrator, on the other hand, seems most concerned to denounce superstitious religion: he presents the
priests and nuns as scheming, dishonest, materialistic, ignorant, superstitious. His attitude toward the Ravissante,
for example, is suggested by the name he gives her. Of the
two, the heavenly and the earthly mistress, the former is
more vicious and destructive. He compares Clara with a
grub (in the process of becoming a butterfly) but likens the
ministrants of the Ravissante to the scarabaeus, a dung
beetle. Moreover, Browning cannot restrain his contempt

for the Church's abuse of its pretended miraculous powers.

The climaxing scene in which Miranda throws himself from the tower is an obvious parody of the second temptation of Christ. Miranda, with the Church as guide, does precisely what Christ refuses to do. By implication, then, Browning associates the Church with the devil, the instrument of human destruction rather than of light.

Miranda is destroyed as much by forces without as by forces within, and among those external ones none is more vicious than the Church, which actually encouraged Miranda's perversions:

> . . . *sane, I say.*
> *Such being the conditions of his life,*
> *Such end of life was not irrational.*
> *Hold a belief, you only half-believe,*
> *With all-momentous issues either way,—*
> *And I advise you imitate this leap,*
> *Put faith to proof, be cured or killed at once!*
> *(IV, 351–357)*

Browning was never sympathetic with the Roman Church, but in no other poem does he denounce it so dogmatically. It should be said, however, that his criticism is pragmatic rather than theological. If he had been told that he did not understand Catholic doctrine, he would, no doubt, have retorted that he did nevertheless understand the practices and influence of the Church.

Browning's failure to focus his materials is reflected in the structure of the poem. He abandons the monologue form or perhaps, more accurately, becomes speaker himself in a monologue addressed to Miss Thackeray. The story is not his, however, but one he relates as an observer who, unlike the narrator in "The Flight of the Duchess," has no functional role in what seems the central concern of the poem. He carries on a parlor argument with Miss Thackeray, countering her more "idealistic" view with his more "realistic," insisting that red cotton night caps better depict the general human condition than do white ones. The bizarre effect on this polite game is established by the image of himself, an aging gentleman, engaged in a duel with a very proper Victorian spinster. The parryings carry all the conviction of a comic opera.

The earlier parts of the poem are marred by a careless colloquialism which brings into the poem irrelevant materials. The poem suffers particularly from inconsistency of tone. Browning's jocularity (a parody of his earlier self) and his kittenish humor are inconsistent with what we must consider the spirit of the poem. The sentence structure no longer follows the path of developing thought but ambles pointlessly. The poem is a series of loosely related incidents and thoughts, not a tightly structured, dialectically arranged development of conflict—either between Browning and Miss Thackeray, Browning and Miranda, Miranda and his family, Miranda and society, or within Miranda.

Browning does in the fourth part create two memorable scenes. First, dropping his little game with Miss Thackeray, he turns to Miranda, showing for the first time in this poem that concern with character which marks his best work. In a brilliantly conceived soliloquy, Miranda exposes the conflicts of his soul and develops the rationale leading to that perverse act of faith which destroys him.

Clara, too, comes to life a little later when she speaks to the cousins, giving what amounts to an apology for her part in Miranda's tragedy. She emerges an ambivalent figure, at once Miranda's savior and his destroyer, ironically achieving that union which eluded Miranda—identification with the Ravissante.

Beneath his jocularity, Browning displays here a disillusionment which sees life as more red than white, too often an irreconcilable struggle between turf and tower. His bitterness is directed against social and religious institutions which use their power to destroy rather than save human life. He comes closer in this poem perhaps than in any other to seeing man as a victim of his environment.

IV ❧ The Inn Album

Like *Red Cotton Night-Cap Country, The Inn Album* is based upon fact. For the central character and for the incident of the poem, Browning borrowed from the life story of the early nineteenth-century roué and gambler, Lord de Ros. Originally, he told Domett, he intended to write a play but changed his mind when he heard that Tennyson was working on a tragedy (*Queen Mary*). *The Inn Album* does give evidence of having been conceived as a drama. Browning remains outside the action, creating three characters (actually four, but one is insignificant) and permitting them to develop along with the plot. The action, advanced through dialogue, is single and moves rapidly toward the melodramatic climax characteristic of Browning's early dramas. By riveting attention upon the three characters, he minimizes the weakness of the improbable situation and its overwrought conclusion.

The situation may be summarized briefly. A young man and an older companion, a roué of fifty, arrive at the inn of a village where the young man's fiancée lives. He has come to arrange his marriage. While waiting for his meeting with the girl, he exchanges confidences with his companion. The younger man, four years earlier, had fallen in love with a country girl who rejected him because, she said, her heart belonged to another. The older man, too, had, at about the same time, seduced a girl, daughter of a country parson, who had assumed he would marry her. Not comprehending but impressed by her indignation when she learned of his deception, he offered to make her "amends by marriage" and was stunned by her scornful rejection. He heard later that she married a clergyman. Now both men look upon their past with regret. The young man laments the loss of youthful love; the older, his loss of a woman who might have given meaning to his empty life. While they talk, a third character arrives at the inn, a friend summoned by the young man's fiancée, who proves to be the woman both had loved. The three are brought together in a situation which forces each to expose his inner life and leads eventually to tragedy. The situation, although highly contrived, provides the setting for three penetrating character studies. If three such people were to find themselves in this situation, they would undoubtedly behave as Browning depicts them.

The older man is one of Browning's cleanest villains. He is essentially uncomplicated, and Browning makes no case for him. Sophisticated, self-centered, cynical, he appears less a deliberate sinner than a victim of a perverted view of human nature. He cannot imagine a virtuous or idealistic impulse, refusing to see the authenticity of any good act. He suspects the young man's generosity and mistakes his romantic idealism for either naïveté or knavery. He regards his own affair with the woman as a pleasant diversion, misconstruing her expectations of marriage and her indignation when she discovers she has been deceived.

Nevertheless, the woman's behavior made an unforgettable impression on him. He admires her without understanding her strength. Now four years later, feeling the approach of old age, he wonders if he should not have married her. He turns to her as to the youth, identifying with the one and seeking help from the other. It is consistent

that he seek reconciliation. Moved by his wounded pride
and by a feeling that youth is passing, he speaks with some
sincerity. He means precisely what he says, but no more.
Arthur Symons perceptively comments: "in the fact that
this passionate appeal should be only half sincere, or, if sincere, then only for the moment, that to her who hears it, it
should seem wholly insincere, lies the intensity of the situation." [10] The two talk at cross purposes, as the following
excerpts illustrate. She says:

> "But when,
> That self-display made absolute,—behold
> A new revealment!—round you pleased to veer,
> Proposed me what should prompt annul the past,
> Make me 'amends by marriage'—in your phrase,
> Incorporate me henceforth, body and soul,
> With soul and body which mere brushing past
> Brought leprosy upon me—'marry' these!"
>
> (IV, 194–201)

and he:

> "Well, I have been spell-bound, deluded like
> The witless negro by the Obeah-man
> Who bids him wither: so, his eye grows dim,
> His arm slack, arrow misses aim and spear
> Goes wandering wide,—and all the woe because
> He proved untrue to Fetish, who, he finds,
> Was just a feather-phantom! I wronged love,
> Am ruined,—and there was no love to wrong!"
>
> (IV, 482–489)

A few minutes later, his old cynicism returns and he urges
the young man to love the woman and leave her. Such misunderstanding is almost inconceivable, but he believes

what he says. That she, following her rejection of him, marries another man—a young rich clergyman, he wrongly supposed—confirms his convictions that her pretensions were hypocritical. She wants, he concludes, not virtue but respectability. He misconstrues her kindness to her old husband as mere deception and assumes she will give herself to the young man in exchange for his silence about her past. He proposes, therefore, that she spend a month in Paris with the young man, who, in turn, will accept this kindness as payment for the gambling debt which the older man owes him. This last act confirms his incapacity to understand a moral or idealistic thought or act. Had he lived he would have been as baffled by the young man's fury as he was earlier by the woman's indignation.

The young man is a contrast to the older one, although at the beginning of the poem he did not think himself so. After his love affair, he attempted to reshape himself in the older man's image. On the surface, he made progress. Initially, he arrives at the inn to arrange a marriage of convenience, one certainly no more idealistic than that proposed four years earlier by the older man. Moreover, we learn, he has become a competent gambler, having beaten the older man at cards. He has youth and money. His triumph, however, is illusion not yet challenged by reality. The inn parlor becomes the symbol of that reality, a stage upon which posturing actors become responsible human beings and social bravado becomes moral commitment.

Outside the ugly little room stretches the sleeping countryside: "Hail, calm acclivity, salubrious spot!" The country, no longer the symbol of natural innocence, provides a scene where men move unaware and imperceptive. In that idyllic atmosphere, the two men recreate their romantic past. Within the four walls of the inn parlor, however, they face reality.

The parlor in all its ugly details is a faithful replica of a real room, reminding us of the setting for an early-middle Ibsen play. Here the two men face themselves and each other. Browning seems to say that man must face realistically his existential situation if he is to achieve self-realization. In this stuffy little parlor, the young man comes to understand what the wiser woman knew all along. His initial love for her was superficial, a youthful illusion. He sees the older man for what he is. Ambiguously, he sees romance dissolve into reality and what he took for reality dissolve into romance. His transformation is marked by his discovery of real love and by his rejection of negation and cynicism. When he faces issues and makes a genuine choice and commitment, his acquired sophistication slips away and he acts impulsively out of the goodness of his being. He climaxes his affirmation by strangling his former master, an act symbolizing his rejection of that recent part of himself which was at counter purposes with his true being. The inn parlor, with all its ugly accessories and its enforced confrontations, provides the stage upon which this posturing actor becomes a real man.

The woman is more complex than either of the men. She is neither Puritan nor hypocrite. In one sense, her development counterpoints that of the young man. His is a progress of increasing idealism; hers, of the deepening knowledge that the ideal is unattainable in this world. He is challenged to life; she, to death.

Her first love experience provided her initial lesson in human frailty. She surrendered to lust in the guise of love and was debased when the offender proposed to make amends by marrying her. What he offered was no substitute for what he had taken. Looking back, she is repelled less by the physical act than by her betrayal of love itself:

> "My eyes were all too weak to probe
> This other's seeming, but that seeming loved

> *The soul in me, and lied—I know too late!"*
> *(V, 108–110)*

She rejected the young man's initial proposal, she now reveals, because she realized that he never loved her. His feelings, sincere within their limits, were superficial:

> *". . . and I knew at once*
> *My power was just my beauty. . . .*
> *. . . So much in me*
> *You loved, I know: the something that's beneath*
> *Heard not your call,—uncalled, no answer comes!"*
> *(V, 111–112,*
> *115–117)*

To have married the young man out of sympathy would have been as much a betrayal of love as to have married the older as compensation.

In contrast, however, she could enter into an agreement with the old clergyman. He did not ask, nor did she give love. Their relation was more pragmatic than romantic. An old friend of her father, he needed help:

> *"I saw this—knew the purblind honest drudge*
> *Was wearing out his simple blameless life,*
> *And wanted help beneath a burthen—borne*
> *To treasure-house or dust-heap, what cared I?*
> *Partner he needed: I proposed myself,*
> *Nor much surprised him—duty was so clear!"*
> *(IV, 275–280)*

Psychologically this action is sound. With the old clergyman, she futhered her education in the ways of the world:

> *"I teach the poor and learn, myself,*
> *That commonplace to such stupidity*

Is all-recondite. Being brutalized
Their true need is brute-language, cheery grunts
And kindly cluckings, no articulate
Nonsense that's elsewhere knowledge. Tend the sick,
Sickened myself at pig-perversity,
Cat-craft, dog-snarling,—maybe, snapping. . . ."

(*IV, 303–310*)

This is the voice of a woman, not of a naïve girl. We are impressed by her maturity, which far exceeds that of the more worldly older man. In contrast to her insight, his cynicism appears mere posing. She bears marks of the sickness which comes from eating "that root of bitterness called Man/ —Raw" (IV, 311–312). Part of her greater maturity, however, lies precisely in the fact that she rejects her former lover's negation and cynicism. Repelled by the ugly world around her and by her husband's unenlightened religion, she, nevertheless, finds in him and his parish an authenticity that the older man never achieves. He is all fake.

Hardened by her experience, she is as capable of hate as of love. Out of context, her scorn of her former lover appears unsympathetic, but in context it demonstrates her maturity, her simultaneous devotion to the ideal and her clearheaded awareness of the ways of the world. She is completely unsentimental. Capable of hardness, she still retains a tenderness, as her attitude toward the young man shows. She is one of Browning's most admirable women. Neither the otherworldly Pompilia nor the worldly Lucrezia, she is aware of self and understands what it means to be human. Death is indeed the price she pays for her clear grasp of and her devotion to the ideal. Her death, in contrast to Miranda's, is chosen and purposeful, her sacrifice being consistent with both her realism and her idealism.

Browning speaks in this poem only by indirection. His

meaning is clear, however. He demonstrates once again what it means to be man in a world which ironically challenges one to an unattainable ideal. He depicts that soul sickness which comes with knowledge, and the salvation that may result from man's engagement with reality.

V ❧ The Three "Greek" Poems

Of Browning's Greek poems only one, *Balaustion's Adventure*, enhanced his literary reputation. However, taken together, the three make a significant comment about the nature and function of poetry.

Several things from Browning's past unite to produce *Balaustion's Adventure*. The poem is certainly a tribute to Elizabeth Barrett and an expression of their mutual admiration for Euripides. It is also the first tangible evidence of Browning's decision following *The Ring and the Book* to speak out in defense of his art against those critics who had harassed him from the beginning of his career. It was, additionally, as DeVane notes (*Handbook*, 349–353, 376–384, 415–419), partly Browning's protest against the nineteenth-century praise of Aeschylus and Sophocles at the expense of Euripides—a movement initiated by A. W. Schlegel in Germany, promoted in England by Matthew Arnold, among others, and brought to a flourishing climax in the rhetorical pyrotechnics of Friedrich Nietzsche. *The Birth of Tragedy* appeared in 1871, so it is unlikely that Browning had read it before he wrote *Balaustion's Adventure* (also published in 1871); indeed, it is unlikely that he ever read it. Nietzsche's theory, however, echoes the almost universal judgment of his immediate predecessors and summarizes a critical position that Browning emphatically rejected.

Encouraged by the warm reception of *The Ring and the Book* and with the image of Pompilia (and of Elizabeth Barrett) before him, Browning approached *Balaustion's Adventure* in a mellow mood, emphasizing admiration over acrimony, tribute over attack. Four years later, irritated by abuse of his two most recent poems and angered by new attacks upon Euripides, he took up the cudgel once more, this time with considerable vehemence.

Balaustion's Adventure, however, containing as much sweet reasonableness as anything Browning wrote, became an immediate favorite with his contemporaries, achieving an elevated position among his works, which it still retains.

The poem, a transcription of Euripides' *Alcestis,* is given contemporary relevance by the dramatic frame within which Browning places it. Following a clue from Plutarch, Browning has his imaginary Balaustion, a young girl from Rhodes sailing with companions to Athens, arrive at port in Syracuse only to be refused harbor until the natives learn that she can recite Euripides' poetry. Discovering this, the Sicilians welcome her ashore, and in exchange for their hospitality she describes a production of *Alcestis* that she had seen in Rhodes, reciting the play and embellishing it with her own interpretative comments. The greatest change from the original is the alteration of Admetus, who undergoes a gradual ennoblement so that by the end of the play he has become worthy of Alcestis' love.

Clearly Browning identifies himself with Euripides. "Men love him not," he has Balaustion say of the Greek, a statement which echoes a reference to himself in *The Ring and the Book:* "Such British People, ye who like me not." Euripides, in contrast to Sophocles, is antiestablishment, antitraditional, more loved abroad than at home. Interested in the internal development of men and women, he is a psychological realist. These descriptive terms Browning also applied to himself.

Betty Miller sees the poem as an expression of Browning's guilt for having betrayed Elizabeth Barrett in his proposal to Lady Ashburton,[11] an interpretation with which DeVane agrees (*Handbook*, 350). Perhaps Browning's alteration in Admetus' character expresses his own resolution to talk more worthily of his dead wife in the future.

Following her recital, Balaustion suggests an additional possibility. After quoting Elizabeth Barrett, she proceeds to tell the story as she thinks it might have happened or could have happened, justifying her boldness by pleading that the greatest compliment one can pay an artist is to become artist in turn. In her revision, Admetus reforms before the main action begins and becomes an ideal king. Thus the decision of the gods that he must die is arbitrary and unjust. When he receives the news, although saddened, he makes no attempt to save himself by sacrificing his wife. Instead, she takes the initiative and, extracting from the gods a promise that Admetus' life will be spared in exchange for her own, offers to die in his place, a sacrifice inspired both by her love for Admetus and by her desire to preserve the ideal kingdom. This double motive renders her action complex and makes possible the ironic conclusion that follows. Admetus learns of her intended sacrifice too late to prevent its execution. He protests, but she dies in his arms. Such love, however, is greater than death and she returns to life. This idealistic celebration of the powers of love takes place within a grim framework. Her hopes are only partly realized; her sacrifices, partly efficacious:

> *So, the two lived together long and well.*
> *But never could I learn, by word of scribe*
> *Or voice of poet, rumour wafts our way,*
> *That,—of the scheme of rule in righteousness,*
> *The bringing back again the Golden Age,*
> *Our couple, rather than renounce, would die—*

> *Ever one first faint particle came true,*
> *With both alive to bring it to effect:*
> *Such is the envy Gods still bear mankind!*
> $\qquad\qquad\qquad\qquad$ (2652–2660)

We have then three versions of Admetus' character, all in one way or another true. The first is that of the original, implied though not given; the second, that of the transcription; the third, that which Balaustion reconstructs. *Balaustion's Adventure* presents the Alcestis legend from the point of view of Euripides, Browning, and, I suggest, Elizabeth Barrett. This latter appears to me especially likely if we assume with Mrs. Miller and Professor DeVane that Browning engages in self-recrimination, using the poem to understand his motives for "unfaithfulness" to his wife. Balustion's reconstruction, introduced and concluded by a quotation from Elizabeth, represents the view which perhaps she might have taken, one considerably more charitable than either of the earlier ones. Certainly, the similarity between Balaustion and Pompilia and Browning's indebtedness to his wife for both are obvious.

At times, however, Balaustion must also speak for Browning. Her direct references to Elizabeth are his. Her pessimistic statement about the ineffectuality of love to transform the world also echoes a conviction that he often expressed during the last two decades of his life. Indeed, it would seem a universalization from his own bitter experience of love's failure to ennoble completely.

In this poem, "the most delightful of May-month amusements," Browning called it, the lighter elements predominate, but just beneath the surface the darker ones lie waiting to emerge as the dominant mood in *Aristophanes' Apology*, which Browning was to write four years later.

In *Aristophanes' Apology* Browning speaks angrily to Euripides' critics, Aristophanes particularly, and to certain of his contemporaries implicitly. The poem is a harsh, perhaps unfair, denunciation of current detractors of Euripides and also of his own critics, particularly Alfred Austin, who was destined to become poet laureate after the death of Alfred Tennyson.

Like *Balaustion's Adventure, Aristophanes' Apology* is partly a translation, in this case of *Herakles*. The translation, however, is subordinate to the commentary, a debate between Balaustion and Aristophanes. Although the debate is imaginary, Browning uses historical materials, his poem being a patchwork of scholarly information from several sources. His purpose transcends factual reconstruction, his interest focusing more on the present than on the past. As J. A. Symonds points out, "The point of view is modern. The situation is strained. Aristophanes becomes the scapegoat of Athenian sins, while Euripides shines forth a saint as well as a sage." [12]

Browning's characterization of Aristophanes is in the main true in spirit to the great Greek dramatist. Browning himself later urged, however, that his portrayal did not represent the whole of the real man. Balaustion is entirely fictional. Although the characters are dramatic, Browning by associating himself with Euripides makes Balaustion spokesman not only for the Greek poet but also for himself.

Aristophanes, on the other hand, represents conservative old Athens and parallels the critics who heckled Browning from the time one of them dismissed *Pauline* as "a piece of pure bewilderment." Aristophanes condemns in Euripides the qualities which Browning's contemporaries disliked in him. Euripides, he charges, is a recluse, devoting himself to art and refusing to become involved in social problems. He is more popular among foreigners than at home; he accepted temporary exile in Archelaus' court in Macedonia. Browning, particularly during his early career, was chided for apparent indifference to the "condition of England,"

and one of his volumes was dismissed angrily as "refuse from the sewers of Paris." Like Euripides, some of his warmest admirers were foreigners (*Paracelsus* was dedicated to Amédée de Ripert-Monclar and *Sordello* to J. Milsand). He too lived comfortably abroad.

Aristophanes' most serious charge is that Euripides is an atheist. He is devoted to innovations which hasten the destruction of Athens. Aristophanes is both the voice of the conservative past and the terrified present, driven by fear to attribute Athens' present precarious condition to foreign influence and the new Socratic philosophy (Nietzsche's villain), which Euripides embraces. The spirit of insularity and reaction, he summarizes his case against Euripides:

> *"Whereupon I betake me, since needs must,*
> *To a concluding 'Go and feed the crows!*
> *Do! Spoil your art as you renounce your life,*
> *Poetize your so precious system, do,*
> *Degrade the hero, nullify the god,*
> *Exhibit women, slaves and men as peers,—*
> *Your castigation follows prompt enough!*
> *When all's concocted upstairs, heels o'er-head,*
> *Down must submissive drop the masterpiece*
> *For public praise or blame: so, praise away,*
> *Friend Socrates, wife's-friend Kephisophon!*
> *Boast innovations, cramp phrase, uncouth song,*
> *Hard matter and harsh manner, gods, men, slaves*
> *And women jumbled to a laughing-stock*
> *Which Hellas shall hold sides at lest she split!*
> *Hellas, on these, shall have her word to say!'"*
>
> (2168–2183)

The conservative religious press had found Browning's early poetry shocking. Balaustion observes that in attacking

Euripides' atheism, Aristophanes has in mind less disbelief in gods than disbelief in particular gods, arguing for one form of theism, his own. If the old gods are dead, he asserts, the system to which they gave rise must pass and, with them, Athens too.

In contrast, Euripides is the voice of realism and progress. He distinguishes between the eternal substance of truth and its temporal expressions—customs, creeds, institutions of a time and a people. When formal expression becomes antiquated and no longer communicates the substance, replacing creative life with stultifying legalism, new modes of expression, even new gods, must be found. Balaustion charges that Aristophanes' adoration of worn-out forms, and not the new Socratic humanism, poses the real threat to Athens.

Indeed, the only hope for restoration lies in the bold, iconoclastic, evolutionary way proposed by Euripides. New creeds, new institutions, new gods must be discovered through which the eternal truth may once more be communicated. Balaustion ends her argument with the words: "There are no gods, no gods!/ Glory to God—who saves Euripides!" (626–627). Balaustion, like the Pope of *The Ring and the Book,* comes close to turning Euripides into a nineteenth-century liberal Christian.

The debate points up differences between Aeschylus and Euripides, and, without depreciating Aeschylus, Browning reveals his preference for Euripides. In a perceptive article, Donald Smalley discusses *Aristophanes' Apology* as a statement "of Browning's own faith and practice, a dramatic and individual 'parleyings' with Aristophanes." [13] Against Aristophanes' frontal assault on human foibles and erring behavior, Balaustion defends "a poetry of power" which awakens potential good in men and women, effecting by indirection what Aristophanes fails to achieve directly.

In 1877, Browning published his translation of *Aga-*

memnon. After his triumphal transcription of *Alcestis* and his interesting rendering of *Herakles,* we may wonder what he had in mind when he produced this almost unreadable version of *Agamemnon.* There is a plausible theory, supported by Mrs. Orr (*Life,* 294), Sir Frederick Kenyon, and Professor DeVane (*Handbook,* 415–418), that Browning's purpose was perhaps not to produce a satisfactory translation. Sir Frederick suspects other motives: "If he wanted to carry further the controversy as to the rival merits of Aeschylus and Euripides, it was hardly fair to weight the scales in this way." [14] That Browning did wish to push the quarrel seems apparent. He is determined, he says in his preface to the translation, to be absolutely literal in order to illustrate Matthew Arnold's assurance that

> "the Greeks are the highest models of expression, the unapproached masters of the grand style: their expression is so excellent because it is so admirably kept in its right degree of prominence, because it is so simple and so well subordinated, because it draws its force directly from the pregnancy of the matter which it conveys . . . not a word wasted, not a sentiment capriciously thrown in, stroke on stroke!"

"So may all happen!" Browning concludes, and proceeds to render the Agamemnon so as to illustrate—and perhaps refute—Arnold's contention that "the action of the piece" is the "all-in-all of Poetry" and that the Greeks provide the unsurpassable models for literary style. This location of ideal style in the past contradicts the evolutionary position which Browning through Balaustion had taken in *Aristophanes' Apology* and which he reiterates in numerous other places. Browning might also have hoped through this literal translation to place Aeschylus in unfavorable contrast with Euripides.

His efforts were scarcely successful. His unattractive

translation neither refutes Arnold (he might have argued more persuasively in some other manner) nor proves Aeschylus inferior to Euripides. It merely illustrates that Browning could produce a poor translation.

VI ❦ *Of Pacchiarotto*

Between *The Inn Album* and *Agamemnon,* Browning published *Of Pacchiarotto, and How He Worked in Distemper,* a work which begins with an attack on critics and ends with an assault on readers. In between is a collection of miscellaneous and for the most part undistinguished shorter poems. The volume is primarily interesting as an additional comment upon Browning's theory of poetry.

In the title poem Browning indirectly attacks his contemporary critics through the person of Giacomo Pacchiarotto, a minor and almost forgotten sixteenth-century Italian painter. In the first lines of the poem:

> QUERY: *was ever a quainter*
> *Crotchet than this of the painter*
> *Giacomo Pacchiarotto*
> *Who took "Reform" for his motto?*
> (*Stanza 1*)

he suggests that the villain of his piece is really Alfred Austin, an ardent Tory, who had recently engaged unsuccessfully in politics. Browning had satirized the conservatives in *Aristophanes' Apology* but was apparently unwilling to let the great Aristophanes represent the little Austin. A more appropriate likeness, he seems to say, is a figure of little wit and talent and of ludicrous pretentions. Browning's quarrel with Austin was, of course, literary as well as political. Austin had for years waged an attack on Browning's poetry, often resorting to unseemly invective. In *Pacchiarotto* Browning retorts in kind:

> *Troop, all of you—man or homunculus,*
> *Quick march! for Xanthippe, my housemaid,*
> *If once on your pates she a souse made*
> *With what, pan or pot, bowl or* skoramis
> *First comes to her hand—things were more amiss!*
> *I would not for worlds be your place in—*
> *Recipient of slops from the basin!*
>
> *(Stanza 27)*

Then turning to Austin, Browning identifies him unmistakably:

> *While as for Quilp-Hop-o'-my-thumb there,*
> *Banjo-Byron that twangs the strum-strum there—*
> *He'll think, as the pickle he curses,*
> *I've discharged on his pate his own verses!*
> *"Dwarfs are saucy," says Dickens: so, sauced in*
> *Your own sauce, . . .*
>
> *(Stanza 27)*

Austin was a mere five feet tall; he was the self-appointed champion of Byron in the late nineteenth century. It should be observed that Browning identifies Austin not with Byron but with a Banjo-Byron of Austin's own creation.

Browning, having smarted as much from neglect as from abuse, follows this attack upon critics with a blast at readers. Once more he defends modernity by challenging those who claim the superiority of Shakespeare and Milton over modern poets to demonstrate their love for the old through deeds as well as words, implying that many who profess to find contemporary poetry unreadable perhaps read no poetry at all.

In "At the 'Mermaid' " and "House," he reaffirms his dedication to dramatic poetry:

> *Which of you did I enable*
> *Once to slip inside my breast*
> *There to catalogue and label*
> *What I like least, what love best,*
> *Hope and fear, believe and doubt of,*
> *Seek and shun, respect—deride?*
> *Who has right to make a rout of*
> *Rarities he found inside?*
> *("At the 'Mermaid,' " Stanza 5)*

> *" 'With this same key*
> Shakespeare unlocked his heart,' *once more! "*
> *Did Shakespeare? If so, the less Shakespeare he!*
> *("House," Stanza 10)*

In "Shop" he insists that man, even the public figure, has the right of privacy. In all three he argues that a writer's merit resides in his poetry, independently of his life.

One other poem in the collection, "A Forgiveness," requires notice, since Browning chose it as one which might represent his narrative powers.[15] I find the choice difficult to defend. The action is contrived; the conclusion, the result of chance; the characters, lacking in psychological subtlety and coherence. The poem is a skillful melodrama but inferior to Browning's best work.

VII ❧ *La Saisiaz*[16] and *The Two Poets of Croisic*

In 1878, Browning published *La Saisiaz* and *The Two Poets of Croisic.* In the latter, he returns once more to speculations inspired by Austin's attempt to fix literary reputations and to render final judgments. Recounting the story of two forgotten poets who in their own day enjoyed popularity, he comments upon the fickleness of fame and the fallibility of critics.

La Saisiaz perhaps adds no more than *The Two Poets of Croisic* to Browning's literary stature. It is a more rewarding poem, however, because it does bring certain of his ideas into focus, providing a perspective from which we may more clearly view his broader achievements. The poem might be called an elegy, for like Milton's "Lycidas" and Shelley's "Adonais" it is a personal meditation on the subject of immortality evoked by the unexpected death of one of his friends. The vast differences between Browning's treatment of the subject and Milton's and Shelley's indicate how radically Browning had departed from conventional modes of religious thought.

In *La Saisiaz,* for example, nature is a significant element, but it does not function symbolically to support the death and rebirth cycle which provides the basic structure of the traditional elegy. Browning fails to find in external nature any mirroring of a divine order upon which he can rest his hope for immortality. Nor does he take any comfort in the rational formulations that have traditionally supported the doctrine. Instead, he is forced to look within himself and to evolve his own subjective vision. He seeks nothing so ambitious as universal truth; he attempts to speak for self alone, neither for God nor man:

> But, O world outspread beneath me! only for myself
> I speak,

*Nowise dare to play the spokesman for my brothers
strong and weak,
Full and empty, wise and foolish, good and bad, in
every age,
Every clime, I turn my eyes from, as in one or other
stage
Of a torture writhe they, Job-like couched on dung
and crazed with blains
—Wherefore? whereto? ask the whirlwind what the
dread voice thence explains!
I shall "vindicate no way of God's to man," nor stand
apart,
"Laugh, be candid," while I watch it traversing the
human heart!*

(349–356)

This problem, for Browning and for all men, is of necessity personal. The death of his friend is important primarily because it converted an abstract proposition into an existential reality and made him grapple with it on the only
level meaningful to man:

*I will ask and have an answer,—with no favor, with
no fear,—
From myself. How much, how little, do I inwardly
believe
True that controverted doctrine?*

(208–210)

Browning's poem is no more about Miss Anne Egerton-
Smith than Milton's is about King or Shelley's is about
Keats. His specific subject, the immortality of the soul, is
only one aspect of a broader concern, which is the problem
of meaning and values in life. How can life have meaning?
What are its values? Browning anticipates an answer to

these questions not from a divinely ordered nature but "From myself." He begins by asking what man may know and how he may know it. That which he may know, he concludes, is small indeed:

> *Question, answer presuppose*
> *Two points: that the thing itself which questions, an-*
> *swers,—is, it knows;*
> *As it also knows the thing perceived outside itself,—a*
> *force*
> *Actual ere its own beginning, operative through its*
> *course,*
> *Unaffected by its end,—that this thing likewise needs*
> *must be;*
> *Call this—God, then, call that—soul, and both—the*
> *only facts for me.*
>
> *(217–222)*

These two facts—the I and the Not-I—are not empirically provable but are rather products of man's consciousness: "my own experience—that is knowledge." "This sure, the rest—surmise."

Browning does not regard "surmise" lightly, however. Indeed, man, in order to remain alive, a growing, developing consciousness, must have some coherent view that postulates meaning and values. Man needs to believe in immortality, not for the bliss it promises in the future but for the meaning it gives the Now. Since man receives no coherent view from without and is severely limited in what he can know from experience, he must evolve through "surmise" some construct which potentially provides the meaning and values that life demands. The most important section in the poem is a dialogue between fancy and reason. Regarding neither as definitive, Browning permits the two to evolve together a construct that fills the void left by the departure of traditional systems of meaning, providing a new basis from which man may undertake self-realizing action. To ask if such a construct is "true" misses the point, if by *true* we mean that which is supported by historical or empirical evidence. Browning asks instead whether it works; that is, whether or not it provides a perspective from which action is possible. He interprets "facts" pragmatically rather than empirically. For man to ask more is to invite intellectual disillusionment and personal stagnation:

> *Break through this last superstructure, all is empty air*
> *—no sward*
> *Firm like my first fact to stand on "God there is, and*
> *soul there is,"*
> *And soul's earthly life-allotment: wherein, by hypoth-*
> *esis,*
> *Soul is bound to pass probation, prove its powers, and*
> *exercise*
> *Sense and thought on fact, and then, from fact educing*
> *fit surmise,*
> *Ask itself, and of itself have solely answer, "Does the*
> *scope*
> *Earth affords of fact to judge by warrant future fear*
> *or hope?"*
>
> (518–524)

In *La Saisiaz* Browning begins with the two facts deduced from experience and, through reason and imagination, fashions a possible, workable system which he can defend not historically or empirically but pragmatically and psychologically. He embraces—the act is too personal to be called a defense—the doctrine of immortality and of eternal rewards and punishments (although he rejects the latter in other poems) because such a faith validates itself, proves itself "true" in the sense that it gives man a reason for living. Browning is careful to claim no more than he can defend on the basis of experience aided by reason and imagination. His conclusion has the support of neither empirical evidence nor irrefutable logic: "So, I hope—no more than hope, but hope—no less than hope."

It is significant, I think, that in this poem on immortality, Browning does not mention the Incarnation, a subject that received so much of his attention during the fifties and sixties. In *La Saisiaz* he goes beyond his position in "A Death in the Desert." In that poem he dispensed with historicity. In *La Saisiaz* he projects a construct in which the Incarnation has no part either as a historical, mythical, or imagined fact. He has come, it would seem, to place all possible constructs which man may devise on precisely the same level and to judge them on the basis of their pragmatic potential. Professor DeVane explains Browning's silence on the Incarnation in this poem by saying that he wrote according to the rules set down for the series of articles on the subject of the future life running at the time in *Nineteenth Century* (*Handbook,* 422). This conjecture is plausible but not entirely satisfactory. Willingly accepting the strictures against recourse to divine revelation, Browning admits at least the possibility that a satisfactory belief in immortality can be had without support of the Christian faith. Browning does quote approvingly from Dante. Whether, however, he sought to identify with Dante the Christian apologist, or Dante the lover, or Dante the Christian-lover is not clear.

Browning began the decade of the seventies by asking in *Prince Hohenstiel-Schwangau* whether the self—the only creative source of meaning and values left to modern man —actually existed or whether it too was an illusion. If the latter were the case, man would, indeed, face a black nothingness. That Browning considered this at least a possibility accounts for the undercurrent of pessimism present especially in the works of the last two decades of his life. By the time he came to write *La Saisiaz,* however, he had determined what of necessity his position was pragmatically: Man as a dynamic, creating being exists in a dialectical relationship with a Not-Self, God, that makes values possible within the narrow range of man's subjective experience.

By insisting that each man can speak only for himself, Browning rejects the possibility ever of converting the private vision into the universal social system. His position is saved from irresponsible solipsism and despair, however, by the emphasis he places on love. In his mature poems, Browning's awakened individual becomes a sensitive human being, part of a brotherhood of all such individuals. Within the limits permitted, man and men may discover meaning and value in human existence.

In the poems of the last decade of his life, Browning was to take up once again and develop more elaborately a subject that had troubled him from the beginning of his career: man's limitations in formulating and communicating even the little which he appears to know.

CHAPTER VI

The Language of Our Ignorance

"So shalt thou do man's utmost—man to
  man:
For as our liege the Shah's sublime estate
Merely enhaloes, leaves him man the same,
So must I count that orb I call a fire
(Keep to the language of our ignorance)
Something that's fire and more beside . . ."
                    ("The Sun," 82–87)

☙ During the last decade of his life, Browning, embarking upon still another stage in his long career, returned to the shorter poem, not merely to repeat his earlier accomplishments but further to explore in new structures and from new points of view his continuing interest in the problems of meaning and self-realization in a world from which traditional values had departed. He came increasingly to concentrate upon the discrepancy between vision and reality, intuition and knowledge, meaning and language, and man's need and his capacity. Repeatedly he turned his attention to the necessity for man to believe in and to act upon more than he could rationally apprehend or logically express. He moved even further toward a non-rational, a-logical ground of being from which he could posit subjective values and realize selfhood. The image and the symbol, products of man's ignorance, of his incapacity completely to grasp and communicate the meaning which his needs demanded, became his common mode of expression.

I ❧ *Dramatic Idyls*

In 1879 he published *Dramatic Idyls* and in 1880 *Dramatic Idyls, Second Series.* These titles link his new work with his old, reasserting his wish to speak through imaginary characters and to express ideas not necessarily his own. The new experimental element is suggested by the word *idyls,* the meaning of which he explained in a letter to Wilfred Meynell:

> An idyl, as you know, is a succinct little story complete in itself; not necessarily concerning pastoral matters, by any means, though from the prevalency of such topics in the idyls of Theocritus, such is the general notion. These of mine are called "Dramatic" because the story is told by some actor in it, not by the poet himself. The subjects are sombre enough, with the exception of the Greek one; and are all in rhymed verse; this last in a metre of my own.[1]

These poems differ from the earlier monologues in their greater reliance upon story as a means of revealing character and also in their more speculative nature. Browning has become more obviously interested in exploring the nature and source of meaning and in understanding those irrational, subterranean forces which contribute so much to the formation of character. In short, he shifts from a dramatic to a speculative position, intent less upon character as an act of positive will than as a response to irrational inner forces. Many of the poems are somber studies in remorse and frustration. A character suffers from something which he either has or has not done; baffled by his lack of self-understanding, he often feels himself the victim of uncontrollable forces.

The first series, clearly superior to the second, contains four outstanding poems: "Ivàn Ivànovitch," "Martin Relph," "Halbert and Hob," and "Ned Bratts." Only one in the second series, "Clive," is of equal significance.

In some respects, "Ivàn Ivànovitch" is among Browning's best works. Its setting is symbolic. The little village, an oasis of semicivilization, is surrounded by the wolf-infested forest, a forbidding wilderness that threatens continually to engulf the little clearing. In that forest a woman is forced to make a choice which means her salvation or damnation. The poem is concerned with describing that choice and discovering its source and its consequence, discerning between the apparently real and the genuinely real.

We see the action from two points of view, the woman's and Ivàn's. Both, motivated by the irrational subconscious, act impulsively and violently. She, in uncontrollable terror, throws her children to the wolves. He, in wrathful indignation, kills her. Both acts are in some respects inscrutable.

In spite of her horrible deed, she has not in the past seemed an evil woman. From all evidence, she is a good mother. She does, as she insists, try to save her children and is terrified by their death. Recovering consciousness after reaching the village, she tries to explain what happened in the forest to convince both herself and the villagers that she acted only as she had to.

Perhaps she did. We feel—something she cannot fully

understand—that she is terrified less by her action than by a half-realized awareness of her real motive for acting. It becomes clear to us—and, on some level and to some extent, to her—that she did not sacrifice her first child to save the other two. Indeed, she sacrificed all three to save herself. It is this terrible self-realization that she struggles to avoid. In her hysteria, she unwittingly becomes her own accuser:

> No fear, this time, your mother flings . . .
> Flings? I flung? Never! But think!—a woman, after all,
> Contending with a wolf!
>
> (168–170)

> Too hard
> To die this way, torn piecemeal? Move hence? Not I—
> one inch!
> Gnaw through me, through and through: flat thus I
> lie nor flinch!
> O God, the feel of the fang furrowing my shoulder!—
> see!
> It grinds—it grates the bone. O Kìrill under me,
> Could I do more?
>
> (222–227)

Her conflict is between the clearing and the wilderness, the rational and the irrational, the conscious and the unconscious. The poem is a vision of life as a woman contending with a wolf.

There was perhaps no way to save the children, but this is not the point. Her failure is more subtle and more devastating. In a real sense, she indeed "flung" (the word which she lets escape in a unguarded moment) the children to the wolves in order to save herself. It is the awareness of this animal potential within her that terrifies her.

She attempts in her monologue to rationalize her actions and to quiet the accusing voice within. She cannot. She sees herself from a new perspective which reveals the cruelty beneath the tenderness, the selfishness beneath the love, and reduces her precisely to the level of the wolves.

Ivàn, on the other hand, is her counterpart. He too acts instinctively, and, sensing what she really is, kills her. She was motivated by selfishness and cowardice; he, by decency and goodness. The mainspring of both actions, however, is shrouded in mystery. Hers can be justified by no rationalization; his requires none.

Unfortunately, Browning is unwilling to let the situation speak for itself. In the last part of the poem, he explores, through a dramatic character, the moral implications of the acts. A voice from the crowd gathered around Ivàn and the woman poses the conventional question of right and wrong. Is Ivàn not guilty of murder? The parish priest, Browning's "old Pope," answers. The mother he condemns for breaking a natural law and, by destroying her young, committing an act repugnant even to animals. Her act was a perversion which the sensitive Ivàn instinctively felt and impulsively righted: "I proclaim/Ivàn Ivànovitch God's servant!" Ivàn, by taking what the mother should have given, her life, restores human dignity and decency.

Browning is not saying, however, that any man may suspend a moral law when he finds it objectionable. Nor is he saying that the impulsive act is always good; obviously, the woman also acted impulsively. The poem treats a moral paradox, emphasizing the complexity of good and evil and the irrationality of human conduct. The woman is damned by her violence; Ivàn, saved by his. The difference lies not in the acts themselves but in the motives that prompted them. Morality is subjective rather than external. Why the impulsive action of two people should proceed from such diverse motives and produce such different ends remains inscrutable. The prefatory poem to the second series comments ironically upon man's tendency to oversimplify his internal life:

> *"You are sick, that's sure"—they say:*
> *"Sick of what?"—they disagree.*
> *" 'T is the brain"—thinks Doctor A.,*
> *" 'T is the heart"— holds Doctor B.,*
> *"The liver—my life I'd lay!"*
> *"The lungs!" "The lights!"*
> *Ah me!*
> *So ignorant of man's whole*
> *Of bodily organs plain to see—*
> *So sage and certain, frank and free,*
> *About what's under lock and key—*
> *Man's soul!*

Ivàn, who took a life and is nevertheless innocent, contrasts with Martin Relph, who did nothing but is guilty. "Martin Relph" is the study of a guilty conscience. In the poem, an old man recalls an event of his youth, less as it actually occurred perhaps than as he, tormented by remorse, remembers it. He might have saved two lives, he says, by speaking out, but he said nothing. The one moment allotted him in which to act passed and then it was too late. An innocent woman was executed as a spy. Why didn't he speak? He wants to believe that he was made incapable by fear. But he isn't sure. Perhaps, he muses, his motives were more sinister. Did he secretly love the girl? Did he hate the man whom he saw approaching with evidence that would have cleared her? Was he coward or murderer? Eager to clear himself of murder, he proclaims his cowardice as though it were an honor. His bizarre conduct, however, betrays a terror of almost unimaginable complexity.

"Ned Bratts" is a third study in remorse, but the subjects here, Ned and his wife Tab, are very different from Martin. Ignorant and unsophisticated, they are incapable of moral subtleties. When they are converted to evangelical Christianity by John Bunyan, they embrace a simple morality as wholeheartedly as they had previously reveled in crime. In the poem, they appear before the judge not only to confess their guilt but to prescribe their punishment. They ask to be hanged and are granted their request. The apparent simplicity of the moral problem is a reflection of their naïveté. They are incapable of the uncertainties of Martin. Only such an interpretation gives the poem psychological reality. Ned and Tab are totally "bad" before their conversion; they are afterwards capable of total "goodness." They have no inner depth in which the reader may become involved. The poem is appropriately enlivened by a comic spirit which renders the situation general rather than specific, intellectual rather than emotional.

In "Clive" Browning once more counterpoints appearance and reality, traditional morality and native goodness. The poem is an account of Clive's suicide told by one of his old friends who sees the death as an act of cowardice, which in the light of Clive's past bravery he cannot understand. He succeeds, however, through his muddling, to focus the issue and to suggest the right question: was the suicide an act of cowardice or of bravery, evil or good? The speaker listens to Clive's account of what he considers the single bravest act of his long brave career. When he was a young man, Clive relates, he caught an officer cheating at cards and challenged him to a duel. Nervous and perhaps frightened, he prematurely discharged his pistol, leaving himself at the mercy of the dishonest officer. With his adversary's weapon pressed against his temple, he maintained his charge that the officer had cheated, preferring to die rather than to live on the terms offered him—renunciation of his accusation. The officer, obviously overwhelmed by Clive's bravery, admitted his guilt and spared the young man's life.

Recalling the story, Clive, now an old man, a broken, unhappy victim of opium, learns anew the meaning of fear and courage. He realizes that if his antagonist, maintaining his innocence, had thrown away his weapon and said, "Go, and thank your own bad aim/Which permits me to forgive you!" (216–217) he would have picked up the discarded weapon and shot himself. There are conditions, he knows, under which a brave man will refuse to live. His auditor, the speaker of the poem, utterly fails to understand:

> *". . . for here's in rough*
> *Why, had mine been such a trial, fear had overcome disgrace.*
> *True, disgrace were hard to bear: but such a rush against God's face*
> *—None of that for me, Lord Plassy, since I go to church at times,*
> *Say the creed my mother taught me! Many years in foreign climes*
> *Rub some marks away—not all, though! We poor sinners reach life's brink,*
> *Overlook what rolls beneath it, recklessly enough, but think*
> *There's advantage in what's left us—ground to stand on, time to call*
> *'Lord, have mercy!' ere we topple over—do not leap, that's all!"*
>
> (226–234)

The relation between the suicide report by the speaker in the last stanza and the rest of the poem is clear. The old man, recalling this event from his past, has relearned the meaning of courage and come to see that continuing to live on the terms now available to him is as despicable as accepting those which he had earlier rejected. Once more he must prove his courage: "Yes—courage; only fools will call it fear."

In these four poems Browning probes deeply into the sources of man's actions, pondering the impact of the subconscious upon human behavior. In "Halbert and Hob," he provides an interesting comment upon the major poems in these volumes, summarizing in the last line what may be his own position: "That a reason out of nature must turn them soft, seems clear" (66). Appropriately, the action of "Halbert and Hob" occurs at Christmas. The poem relates a struggle between old Halbert and his son, young Hob. The two quarrel and Hob orders Halbert out of the house, enforcing his command by dragging the old man toward the door. Halbert offers no resistence until he reaches a spot one yard from the doorsill. Here he stands calmly, faces his son, and tells him that on a Christmas many years ago "for such a cause," he dragged his father thus far:

> "... but, softening here, I heard
> A voice in my heart, and stopped: you wait for an outer word.
>
> "For your own sake, not mine, soften you too! Untrod
> Leave this last step we reach, nor brave the finger of God!
> I dared not pass its lifting: I did well. I nor blame
> Nor praise you. I stopped here: Halbert,[2] do you the same!
>
> (47–52)

Hob stopped, and the violent encounter was over. That night the father died and the son was miraculously transformed into a broken, prematurely old man. Why did Hob stop? Why did the death of his father whom he hated so affect him? The action, on one level, is obviously a rite of initiation in which the son kills the father and assumes his place. There is no joy in this triumph, however. Browning gives an old myth a modern psychological turn. The reference to Shakespeare's *Lear* is also significant. Hob was prepared to overcome strength with strength, to meet violence with violence, but he was unprepared for his father's unsuspected submission and his appeal to filial piety, based though it was upon tribal custom rather than love. He found himself suddenly in an ethical world beyond his comprehension. The experience required a response of which he was incapable, and he was destroyed by it. Browning is equally interested in Halbert's seemingly benign behavior after years of violence and brutishness and by his revelation of how he in a similar situation had acted years earlier. Such transformations, he seems to say, defy rational expectations and can be explained only as a Christmas, a something out of nature.

II ❧ *Jocoseria*

Browning published three additional volumes during his last decade, *Jocoseria* (1883), *Ferishtah's Fancies* (1884), and his last (following the *Parleyings With Certain People of Importance in Their Day,* which will be discussed in the next chapter), *Asolando* (1889).

Jocoseria is perhaps Browning's most unrewarding performance. Although it continues the narrative mode of *Dramatic Idyls* and *Dramatic Idyls, Second Series,* it is concerned more with statement of idea than with story or character. Its style is often barren and harsh, qualities which, in these poems, are related neither to subject matter nor to an effort to write colloquially. Many of the poems are a paradoxical mixture of compression and verbosity expressed in what appears a willfully distorted syntax. The asyntactical elements, the appositives, the many subordinations, and the erratic punctuation which served in the monologues to reflect thought and passion in the process of developing are, for the most part, nonfunctional and thus obtrusive in these poems.

The longest, "Jochanan Hakkadosh," is an overelaborated tale based upon Jewish lore. Its point seems to be that the wise old Rabbi must return to a Pippa-like state of simplicity before he is able to act. The tortuous syntax and the harshness of the sound recall the infelicity of "Rabbi Ben Ezra" and make one wonder if Browning were attempting to communicate some perverted notion of colloquial Hebrew.

The best poem in *Jocoseria* is "Ixion." Browning returns to Greek legend for a subject, characteristically resuscitating rather than resurrecting his central character. Browning takes considerable liberty with his original. In his version, Ixion is a wronged man condemned by a harsh Zeus to eternal suffering because he has dared to love beyond the limits established for man. Actually, Browning seems less attracted to the story itself than to the image of the torture wheel. Ixion, at once victim and victor, is symbol of man's humiliation and triumph. The poem is more than a renunciation of the theological dogma of eternal punishment (a possibility which Browning seemed to entertain at least momentarily in *La Saisiaz*). Browning reinforced his real meaning by introducing a cluster of characters from Greek legend: Sisyphus, Tantalus, and the Titans. All share with Ixion the fact that they are unjustly punished; all, except the Titans, are men, not gods. All are placed in situations that emphasize their human limitations: Ixion to spin on the torture wheel, Sisyphus repeatedly to roll a stone to the crest of a hill only to have it fall back, Tantalus to suffer from thirst and hunger although he stands in water up to his neck and underneath fruit, which is, however, just beyond his reach. To be a man is in itself a hell that can be overcome only through suffering. Suffering is paradoxically man's punishment and his liberation.

The wheel upon which Ixion is bound has special symbolic meaning. It is both the cause of man's suffering and the means by which he is eventually "flung" forward to a new stage of spiritual awareness. Browning surmises that once the present dream is over and the dreamers Sisyphus and Tantalus awake, they will recognize their punishments as modes for projecting them forward rather than for holding them in subjection. Zeus is the villain. He appears initially as a tyrannical force, an objective reality outside man. As the poem develops, however, he appears less corporeal that illusory, the product of man's invention. He is at once the temporary expression of man's limited understanding and the means by which he projects himself forward. Browning introduces the Titans as a reminder that, as Zeus replaced his predecessors, so he himself shall eventually be replaced. Only God—"the Not-Thou beyond it,/ Fire elemental, free, frame unencumbered, the All" (103–104)—endures. Every human attempt to image him in human form—the Titans, Zeus,—in intellectual system or in institution is partial and temporary.

This poem alone is sufficient to contradict the charges that Browning was an easy optimist. Man the finite, indeed, moves toward the infinite, but slowly and painfully. The burden of manhood is hunger, thirst, frustration, pain. Man, individually and corporately is part of an eternal process of formation, dissolution, and re-formation—progress:

> *Out of the wreck I rise—past Zeus to the Potency*
> *o'er him!*
> *I—to have hailed him my friend! I—to have clasped*
> *her—my love!*
> *Pallid birth of my pain,—where light, where light is,*
> *aspiring*
> *Thither I rise, whilst thou—Zeus, keep the godship*
> *and sink!*
>
> *(121–124)*

This last line recalls the conclusion of *Aristophanes' Apology* "There are no gods, no gods!/ Glory to God. . . ."

III ❧ *Ferishtah's Fancies*

When Browning was young he wrote "In a Gondola," giving the highest value to the passionate experience of the moment. In *Ferishtah's Fancies,* he reaffirms as an old man, his youthful enthusiasm, attempting, however, to provide an intellectual framework for his intuitive affirmation. He is only partially successful.

Appearing in the readily recognized disguise of a Persian dervish, Browning moves through a series of loosely related episodes, using each as an excuse for imparting "wisdom." His "message" emerges more blatantly in this volume than in any of his others. The method of development in each of the episodes is catechetical: a young disciple asks a question and the wise old master answers. Browning may have intended a dialectical interplay of ideas characteristic of his monologues, but, if so, he failed to achieve his purpose.

The situations are obviously staged and the questions are planted not to develop character but to evoke pronouncement. The external situation fails to become symbolic of internal struggle, and the result is less thought in the process of forming than of thought formulated and fixed.

Browning continues, nevertheless, to experiment with form, attempting here to embody structurally the complex and sometimes contradictory facets of even simple experience. Each of the twelve sections is divided into two parts. Both parts treat the same theme but in different forms: the first as narrative, and the second as lyric. The result is unsatisfactory. The first is too often dogmatic prose; the second, in spite of its occasional genuine feeling, is one-dimensional. The effect is that of experience dichotomized, mind abstracted from emotion and emotion from mind.

There is in the arrangement of the parts no clear sequential pattern. Their arrangement could be altered without serious damage to the poem. We have a random collection of experiences which invite the dervish to pronounce upon problems of human existence. In one place or another Browning once more asks and answers most of the questions that troubled him throughout his career. *Ferishtah's Fancies* elaborates without significantly expanding his continuing intellectual interests.

In two of the sections, "Shah Abbas" and "A Pillar at Sebzevah," Browning establishes the heart and will rather than reason alone as the source of man's belief in God. His argument in these poems, as in *La Saisiaz,* proves, however, less a case against reason itself than an acknowledgment of its limits. Man may not grasp ultimate truth through reason, but he may use his rational faculties as a means of advancing himself spiritually. Reason becomes a handicap when it hardens into an inflexible and final system. Every body of knowledge, Browning's dervish argues, anticipates its superior and begins, as quickly as it is formed, to disintegrate for eventual regrouping into some new, more spiritually advanced combination. Each new system should carry man a little closer to the "unknown." In contrast to knowledge that is partial and temporary, Browning's character counterpoints love that is complete and final. Knowledge is an instrument; love is an end. Reaching this conclusion, Browning reiterates a position which he had fully developed as early as 1850 when he published *Easter-Day*.

In "The Sun" the dervish asserts that man can know God only inferentially. He has only the language of his ignorance and the limited faculties of his manhood to respond to the "unknowable." He must be satisfied with anthropomorphic symbols of God because they alone provide an object capable of being loved. Man cannot love abstractions. The act of loving and not the precise object of the love is man's salvation. It is unnecessary that man know his love is received and returned. It is enough that he love.

Prayers, he argues in "The Family," may not be heard and answered, but man must pray nevertheless, not because he expects to receive but in order to satisfy his need to merge his finitude with God's infinity. Prayer, unsatisfactory as it may be, is one of the modes available to man as a means of spiritual growth. In "Cherries" he defends religious practices for their pragmatic effect upon the worshiper. Although man cannot give adequate thanks to God, he must, nevertheless, offer his imperfect gratitude, again for the spiritual benefit which he derives from the act itself.

"A Camel-Driver" contains a definition of hell not as a place of torment but as a state of incompleteness. Anything that prevents man from merging with infinity is hellish. The unpardonable sin is the spurned act that might have advanced man spiritually:

> "However near I stand in his regard,
> So much the nearer had I stood by steps

> *Offered the feet which rashly spurned their help.*
> *That I call Hell; why further punishment?"*
>
> (*VII, 108–111*)

In "Two Camels" the dervish urges man to accept himself and his world, joyfully turning even the temporarily hellish to spiritual ends. Finally, in "A Bean-Stripe: Also, Apple-Eating," he affirms the meaningfulness and goodness of creation and argues that man fails to recognize its beneficence only because of his myopic human vision.

The epilogue contains the best poetry in the poem. Sometimes Browning's conclusions in *Ferishtah's Fancies* seem too easily achieved and too lightly held. Although he dwells upon man's limitations and recognizes the slowness and painfulness of his spiritual progress, he fails to realize the tension poetically or to make the pain felt. There remains a gap between idea and emotion. The epilogue, in a dramatic reversal, suddenly places the work in a new perspective, introducing into it an intellectual and emotional honesty which challenges the too-glib assurances of the dervish:

> *Only, at heart's utmost joy and triumph, terror*
> *Sudden turns the blood to ice: a chill wind disen-*
> *charms*
> *All the late enchantment! What if all be error—*
> *If the halo irised around my head were, Love, thine*
> *arms?*
>
> (*Epilogue, 25–28*)

It is important to observe in the poem, which on its surface seems so optimistic, how little cause for optimism Browning sustains. He acknowledges the partiality and tentativeness of divine revelation, and reduces commonly accepted acts of worship—prayer and thanksgiving—to pragmatic instruments that are perhaps without intrinsic meaning. He radically revises orthodox notions of good and evil, of heaven and hell. He is left finally with little more to bolster his faith than the conviction, derived from experience, that man is an incomplete being whose nature yearns for a wholeness that can come only through his re- union with God. Here, as in *La Saisiaz,* Browning places severe limitations upon man's faculty to know.

Generally Browning pushes his skepticism just so far. The gods are dying, but God lives; old codes and old insti- tutions are passing, but man continues to pursue the eter- nal of which these are imperfect symbols. Only occasion- ally, in such lines as those which conclude *Ferishtah's Fancies,* does he go so far as to question the existence of all truth and of all value. Browning perhaps could envision the demise of Christianity, but, unlike Nietzsche, he was unprepared to sustain the idea that God was dead. The fact that occasionally the possibility seized him, however, pre- served him from an easy and optimistic liberalism. Never- theless, he remained one of the pious free-thinkers, object of Nietzsche's scorn, who believed in an eternal Truth that lured man on to something higher and better than any- thing he has yet achieved. He continued to postulate reli- gious constructs for their pragmatic if not their absolute worth.

IV ❦ *Asolando*

Asolando, published the day Browning died, was first conceived as a continuation of *Jocoseria.* In fact, Browning intended originally to call it *A New Series of Jocoseria.* He changed the title shortly before publication to *Asolando,* a word of his own coinage which meant, he said, "to disport in the open air, amuse one's self at random." The volume is a collection, miscellaneous in subject and uneven in quality. DeVane divides the poems into three groups: love poems, narrative poems, reflective poems (*Handbook*, 526–527).

In spite of the surprising audaciousness of the love lyrics, there is a solemnity about the volume. Browning writes with a finality which suggests that he knew it would perhaps be his last work. The impression appears most obviously, of course, in the now famous "Epilogue," but it is present also in many of the other poems. "Development" is an old man's reminiscence containing a charming portrait of Browning's father instructing his young son in Greek myth.

In this volume, Browning once more repeats in summary fashion his preference for imaginative rather than for speculative poetry. Both "Reverie" and "Rephan" are eschatological. In the latter an erstwhile angel comforts the "world-weary earth-born ones" by telling them how he left a blissful heaven, "a neutral Best," to become an earth creature. He explains:

> *A voice said "So wouldst thou strive, not rest?*
>
> *"Burn and not smoulder, win by worth,*
> *Not rest content with a wealth that's dearth?*
> *Thou are past Rephan, thy place be Earth!"*
> *(105–108)*

Perhaps the best work in the volume is "Bad Dreams" I, II, III, IV. Browning uses for these poems a structure unified by an association of ideas and emotions, giving them a quality of the dreams which they recount. The somberness contrasts sharply with the gaiety of such lyrics as "Summum Bonum," "A Pearl," "Speculative," and the charming little narrative "Muckle-Mouth Meg." The precise prose meaning of "Bad Dreams" often eludes us. The series is made up of dialogues between a man and a woman, obviously lovers, who sense that beneath the placid surface of their conventional relation there are tumultuous depths only furtively glimpsed which contradict all that they ostensibly think and feel. The poems are a paradoxical admixture of love and hate, of trust and suspicion, of union and alienation. In them Browning displays a profound insight into the relation between dream and waking reality, an area which Freud was later to explore more fully. The poems are not whimsical excursions into the temporarily fantastic but insights into man's ambivalent depths:

> *"A mere dream"—never object!*
> *Sleep leaves a door on hinge*
>   *Whence soul, ere our flesh suspect,*
> *Is off and away: detect*
>
> *Her vagaries when loose, who can!*
>   *(II, 77–81)*

The series of disjointed, distorted dream images that constitute the movement of the poems is closer, we come to feel, to the "real" than are their waking counterparts. The poems produce both terror and pathos: terror of the savagery and violence which these fugitive glimpses reveal; pathos for the man and woman who are victims of such irrational, inescapable forces. Browning communicates the sense of terror through language reminiscent of "Childe Roland to the Dark Tower Came":

> *Ah, but the last sight was the hideous!*
> *A City, yes,—a Forest, true,—*

> But each devouring each. Perfidious
>   Snake-plants had strangled what I knew
> Was a pavilion once: each oak
> Held on his horns some spoil he broke
> By surreptitiously beneath
> Upthrusting: pavements as with teeth,
> Griped huge weed widening crack and split
>   In squares and circles stone-work erst.
> Oh, Nature—good! Oh, Art—no whit
>   Less worthy! Both in one—accurst!
>   (III, 25–36)

We are moved by the plight of a man and a woman whose attempts to form a satisfying relation are frustrated by their own partially understood, never fully grasped frailties. They are, unwillingly, responsible for the suspicion, hate, and pain which separate them. Their situation is especially poignant because their love continues even after their lives are severed. In the last of the series, the woman, dead beneath the churchyard slab, is shocked to discover at last that her husband is shedding tears over her grave.

The other outstanding poem in the collection is " 'Imperante Augusto Natus Est—'." A Roman senator, meditating upon the achievements of Augustus, speculates about change as a universal principle, a necessary part of man's growth and development. The poem is set in that period just prior to the birth of Christ and looks both backward and forward. In view of past and future, the seemingly Godlike present of Augustus seems to us less than eternal, an insight not fully grasped by the speaker. The poem in its details is a triumph of irony, an achievement comparable to "Cleon" and "Karshish." The discrepancy between the literal meaning and the universal implication of the speaker's word gives rise to one of Browning's most

brilliant poems. The concluding lines bring the poem into
focus and at the same time reiterate an idea about change
that Browning often expresses in his poetry:

Who stands secure? Are even Gods so safe?
Jupiter that just now is dominant—
Are not there ancient dismal tales how once
A predecessor reigned ere Saturn came,
And who can say if Jupiter be last?
Was it for nothing the grey Sibyl wrote
"Caesar Augustus regnant, shall be born
In blind Judaea"—one to master him,
Him and the universe? An old-wife's tale?

Bath-drudge! Here, slave! No cheating! Our turn next.
No loitering, or be sure you taste the lash!
Two strigils, two oil-drippers, each a sponge!

(152–163)

CHAPTER VII

The Focusing Artifice

Soon shall fade and fall
Myth after myth—the husk-like lies I call
New truth's corolla-safeguard: Autumn comes,
So much the better!

("*Avison,*" *378–381*)

Thus moaned
Man till Prometheus helped him,—as we learn,—
Offered an artifice whereby he drew
Sun's rays into a focus.

("*Mandeville,*" *300–303*)

I ask no more
Than smiling witness that I do my best
With doubtful doctrine.

("*Mandeville,*" *16–18*)

❦ In *Parleyings With Certain People of Importance in Their Day,* published in 1887, Browning drops the superficial disguise which he assumed in *Ferishtah's Fancies* and appears in his own person. Although he called this work *parleyings,* arguments between himself and other personages, it is really a soliloquy, a dialectical internal argument with himself or, perhaps, between diverse elements of himself. In spite of his own presence, *Parley-*

ings With Certain People seems less subjective than *Ferish-tah's Fancies.* The "self" here is obviously multifaceted, ambivalent, dialectical, each element asserting its claim in opposition to or in amplification of others. Neither is permitted final and exclusive authority. The poem is essentially dramatic, and the fact that the drama takes place within a single individual rather than between two individuals or between a single individual and some external force or fate in no way lessens the tension of the action.

Browning's purposes are obviously multiple. While he was working on the poem he wrote to a friend, expressing the hope that it "ought to be my best" (Hood, *Letters,* 254). Mrs. Orr affirms the seriousness with which Browning undertook this poem (*Life,* 347). Clearly he considered *Parleyings* a major work, projecting it as "the focusing artifice" of his career. It takes its place along with *Sordello, The Ring and the Book,* and *Fifine at the Fair* as a poem essential to an understanding of his work.

The poem is no autobiography in a literal sense. It is perhaps misleading even to call it the autobiography of a mind, if by that we suggest a chronological and sequential growth and development of Browning's inner life. The poem ignores chronology and sequence, positing its reality in the present and identifying its action as the dynamic flux, the dialectical ebb and flow, the paradoxical struggle of the infinite yearnings to realize themselves in finite forms. The poem is a serious treatment of the intellectual and spiritual crisis of the early modern period. It is concerned with both ontology and epistemology, that is, with the ultimate basis of reality and with man's mode of knowing. It marks a shift from objectivism to subjectivism, from idealism to skepticism, from moral absolutism to relativism.

The organization is a master stroke. Browning chooses to parley with seven men from the past. The choice of interlocutors may seem curious: Bernard de Mandeville, the early eighteenth-century philosopher, author of *The Fable of the Bees;* Daniel Bartoli, seventeenth-century Jesuit historian; Christopher Smart, eighteenth-century poet, author of "The Song of David"; George Bubb Dodington, politician during the reign of George II; Francis Furini, seventeenth-century Italian priest and painter of nudes; Gerard de Lairesse, late seventeenth-century Dutch painter and aesthetician, author of *The Art of Painting in All Its Branches;* and Charles Avison, eighteenth-century organist at Newcastle, composer of march music. Obviously Browning did not choose these figures because they were the crucial influences upon him (where are Dante, Shakespeare, Donne, and Flaubert?). His choice was not whimsical, however. He was writing a metaphysical rather than a psychoanalytic or strictly autobiographical poem, and he selected each of these men for a necessary and integral function in his over-all scheme.

Introduction of these figures from the past with the clear implication, in several cases, that each has his parallel among Browning's contemporaries gives the poem simultaneously a distance and an immediate relevance.[1] It also makes possible the subtle handling of time through which past is refashioned and future is reduced to present. Even Browning's concept of growth and development takes its meaning from the present (the degree of self-consciousness which it brings the soul) rather than from the future (some anticipated ultimate good). The cast of diverse characters also provides the scope necessary for a large-scale metaphysical poem in which Browning attempts to give artistic form to his profoundest sense of reality.

The implied names of the antagonists are legion. They are, indeed, Browning's predecessors, men who yet lived in his consciousness as catalyzing spiritual agents; they are his peers—Disraeli, Arnold, Tennyson, traditional moralists, free-thinking theologians, aesthetes—whom Browning must engage in debate; they are symbols of diverse contemporary efforts to understand and explain reality and values; they are objectifications of elemental forces at the matrix of man's being. Separately they are fragmentary, often irreconcilable. Together they compose a modern, nonrepresentational portrait of Browning's inner life, his sense of reality, as he intuits it—imperfectly and partially by virtue of its very immensity—at the moment he is writing.

The poem consists of a prologue, seven sections, and an epilogue. Together they make a whole action, less a horizontal movement of events through time and space than an enmeshment in dynamic relationship around a central consciousness of interacting fragments of intellectual, emotional, and sensuous perceptions and intuitions. The poem begins with Greek mythological figures and ends with modern man. The prologue takes place in a fanciful nether world and the epilogue in a printing office. In the beginning Apollo, "law flouter, use trampler . . . upstart," descends into darkness to plead for the life of a man, Admetus, but the scene of the poem is not in the nether world. Browning's poem, unlike Shelley's *Prometheus Unbound,* takes place on earth within the mind and heart of an ordinary human being.

There is a clear relation between the parts, although their organization is thematic, psychological, and associational rather than logical and sequential. The poem's structure is closer to that of music than to that of traditional poetry. The poem achieves two peaks of intensity. The first comes with the third section, which is devoted to the poet Christopher Smart, and the final and climaxing peak with the seventh section, which is devoted to the musician Charles Avison. The movement rises slowly to a height, then subsides, and finally achieves a crescendo in a magnificent vision of a celestial symphony.

There are other evidences of thoughtful structuring. There is a substantive as well as structural parallel between the parleying with Mandeville, which begins the first movement, and that with Dodington, which initiates the second. Both, in a relatively low key, are more speculative and argumentative than emotional or visionary; both introduce themes with which succeeding sections will be concerned. Appropriately, partly because of its material and treatment and partly because it comes after rather than before "Christopher Smart," "Dodington" is tauter than "Mandeville." Both provide a base from which a heightening movement is possible, and the contrast between them is a measure of the mounting action of the poem. A similar relation exists between "Bartoli" and "Furini" and between "Smart" and "Avison." "Gerard de Lairesse" has a special function which I shall explain later.

Smart and Avison serve to climax each movement less because of their actual achievements than for the significance which Browning attributes to their mode of working. Smart's one triumph illustrates the means of apprehension (intuitive, imaginative) and of communication (symbolic, artistic) by which man grapples with reality. Avison, too, thinks and speaks as an artist. His superior position in the poem reflects Browning's conviction that music, of all the arts, brings man into closest contact with the infinite: it best pierces surface appearances to reveal the ground of being; it best provides the "focusing artifice" of that "inferred immensity."

Each section of the poem, too, has its own internal movement, its rising action. It is a process by which disparate ideas, stated initially as debatable issues, are brought into a synthesis investing them with sensuous and emotional qualities that turn disparate into dialectical, disorder into order, argument into vision. Obviously the point of view for each section and for the poem as a whole is extremely complex. Browning achieves here a subtlety that evaded him even in *The Ring and the Book*. There are the various figures from the past, their modern equivalents, and Browning himself, a complex, ambivalent, often ironic "I." There are tensions within each section and tensions between sections. No poem in the English language is more multiform, more refractory.

The prologue, "Apollo and the Fates," establishes the metaphysical perspective, suggests the scene, and introduces the theme and action. It is a dramatic presentation of the apparently irreconcilable voices of Apollo and the Fates. Apollo is a symbol of light, not of easy optimism but of hopeful affirmation. He believes that there is meaningfulness in creation and that man has a desire for wholeness. He argues for Admetus on the grounds that life is worth living. The Fates, on the other hand, are symbols of darkness, representing nihilism. They refuse to extend Admetus' life, firmly convinced that to do so would be pointless and cruel. The issue is between these two positions, and Browning's concern is less to pronounce dogmatically upon them than to explore ways by which modern man, in the absence of traditional guides, can come to make a significant choice between them.

The problem is to distinguish the real from the apparent and to determine the relation between seemingly antagonistic forces of good and evil. That is, are good and evil exclusive, irreconcilable forces, or is their apparent diversity a necessary aspect of an ultimately beneficent but obscure purpose? Apollo asserts that darkness is an unreality which light dissipates; the Fates assert that light is an illusion which falsifies the dark reality. The poem suggests that these issues can perhaps be determined only relatively. Perhaps their "reality" is less objective than psychological. Apollo asserts that for the perceiving, enjoying consciousness the reality of light is not dependent upon any objective base. That man through his imagination can transform the "iceball" of earth into a "fire orb," he attempts to demonstrate with the aid of Bacchus (or Dionysus), god of poetic imagination. He plies the Fates with wine, fruit of man's cultivation, until the nether world rings with their frenetic affirmation. He seems to have won his point, until suddenly their orgy is ended by a protesting rumble from the earth. Terrified by what they consider a rebuke, they resume their old position, and Apollo is left to confront the equally real but antithetical transforming triumph and the negating rumble. He is forced into compromise. The Fates agree to spare Admetus if he can find someone to die in his place. The prologue ends in an antiphonal exchange between Apollo and the Fates:

Apollo. *On mine, griesly gammers! Admetus, I know*
 thee!
  Thou prizest the right these unwittingly give
 Thy subjects to rush, pay obedience they owe thee!
  Importunate one with another they strive
 For the glory to die that their king may survive.

 Friends rush: and who first in all Pherae appears
  But thy father to serve as thy substitute?
Clotho.   *Bah!*
Apollo. *Ye wince? Then his mother, well-stricken in*
 years
 Advances her claim—or his wife—
Lachesis.   *Tra-la-la!*

Apollo. *But he spurns the exchange, rather dies!*
Atropos.   *Ha, ha, ha!*
                                                        (256–265)

That mocking laughter is a prelude to the search for affirmation which follows. Its counterpointing echoes are heard throughout the poem.

The next three sections comprise a unit, one movement in the development of the poem. Sections one and two are complementary and both are a contrast to the third. The first is argumentative; the second, narrative; the third, visionary. The first and second are assertive and the third, symbolic. All treat a central problem.

In "Bernard de Mandeville" Browning takes up the challenge of the Fates and attempts to prove that life is not all darkness. He is especially concerned to relate good and evil as necessary parts of the divine whole, to assert man's psychological need to "realize" (not merely understand) God, and to substitute for eighteenth-century rationalism a new mode of apprehension.

Perhaps Browning did not understand Mandeville. Nevertheless he appropriately chose him as subject for this first parleying. Mandeville, like Browning, challenged the glib assumptions of his day, pointing out the inconsistency between commonly accepted private and public virtues. Mandeville was aware of the developing ethical crisis in Western culture and, in the role of satirist, exposed the widening chasm between metaphysics and conduct. Browning rightly makes him a critic of "Addison's tye-wig preachment." It is less certain, however, that Mandeville saw the entire problem from Browning's own perspective. Browning makes him prophet of a new morality in which so-called good and evil are necessary and complementary parts of an all-encompassing divine purpose. In contrast to the role assigned him by his contemporaries, Browning presents him as defender of meaningfulness and purpose against the nihilist:

> . . . *so did not say*
> *That other sort of theorists who held*
> *Mere unintelligence prepared the way*
> *For either seed's upsprouting: you repelled*
> *Their notion that both kinds could sow themselves.*
>
> *(114–118)*

It must be remembered, of course, that Browning is not recreating history but writing a poem in which a historical figure serves as a persona, actually as one of the voices in an argument which takes place in Browning himself. In such a role, Browning's recreated Mandeville is right.

Browning rebels against the nihilism of the Fates. He is convinced that man is an incomplete creature who compulsively aspires toward the All-complete: "I . . ./ When all-developed still am found a thing/ All-incomplete" (262–264). He is aware of a tumultuous inner force that propels him Godward, "Mind seeks to see,/ Touch, understand, by mind inside of me,/ The outside mind" (268–270). At the same time, he feels that his aspirations are futile. No way appears open by which he may approach that which he most wants to embrace. He cries out in frustration:

> *I solely crave that one of all the beams*
> *Which do Sun's work in darkness, at my will*
> *Should operate—myself for once have skill*
> *To realize the energy which streams*
> *Flooding the universe.*
>
> *(277–281)*

He possesses no such skill. Here then is his dilemma. The problem for him is more psychological than theological—

and so is his solution. In desperation, Browning once again postulates upon man's need a system of belief which may or may not have objective validity but is, nevertheless, necessary to him if he is to fulfill his nature. That it works is its justification.

He realizes that if he is to experience "Sun's earth-felt thrill" he must give up hope of apprehending God through reason. The close and sterile argument of the first portion of the poem proves only that argument is sterile:

> *Shall mind's eye strive*
> *Achingly to companion as it may*
> *The supersubtle effluence, and contrive*
> *To follow beam and beam upon their way*
> *Hand-breadth by hand-breadth, till sense faint—confessed*
> *Frustrate, eluded by unknown unguessed*
> *Infinitude of action? Idle quest!*
>
> (309–315)

Having with the aid of Mandeville established good and evil as necessary parts of a dynamic and purposeful creation, Browning now turns to Euripides (". . . it thus/ Must be Euripides not Aeschylus") for assistance in getting man out of the spiritual morass resulting from the breakdown in Enlightenment assumptions about reality and man's way of knowing. The old certainties are gone. Man must remain essentially estranged from God; he cannot hope to look into the sun itself. He has neither the scope to see nor the capacity to bear so great a light. The alternative to such immediate vision, however, is not the darkness of the Fate's cave. Browning recalls Euripides' Prometheus, an obvious parallel to Apollo in the prologue. Both teach man how through imagination to achieve a little light. Prometheus taught man the use of optics:

> *Thus moaned*
> *Man till Prometheus helped him,—as we learn,—*
> *Offered an artifice whereby he drew*
> *Sun's rays into a focus,—plain and true,*
> *The very Sun in little: made fire burn*
> *And henceforth do Man service—glass-conglobed*
> *Though to a pin-point circle—all the same*
> *Comprising the Sun's self. . . .*
>
> (300–307)

Thus man creates a focusing artifice which enables him to infer the immensity that he can never know. That such an inference falls short of absolute knowledge, Browning readily recognizes. That it leaves unanswered many questions, he knows. He defends it not because it is final and complete but because it is all that man can hope for, and, more importantly, because it gives meaning to an otherwise meaningless existence: "Little? In little, light, warmth, life are blessed—/ Which, in the large, who sees to bless? Not I" (318–319).

Although Browning's intent is less immediately clear in "Daniel Bartoli," his second parleying complements the first by pushing his speculations forward into still another area of thought. In "Bernard de Mandeville" he challenges eighteenth-century rationalism; in "Daniel Bartoli" he rejects medieval Christian supernaturalism. In the latter, his emphasis shifts, and we see clearly—a fact implicit in Apollo's descent into the cave in defense of Admetus—that Browning is less interested in creating a new image of God than of man. Even the "inferred immensity" of "Bernard de Mandeville" takes its significance from its human rather than from its heavenly implications. In "Bartoli" Browning attempts to form a new and essentially secular definition of sainthood. Bartoli, whom Browning once admired as a stylist and now scorns as a historian, serves as his point of departure. After a brief introduction in which Browning challenges the Jesuit's veracity as historian, he turns to a tale of his own that is intended to reveal the implausibility of Bartoli's method by contrasting chronicle with legend. His purpose is clearly to supplant the traditional fancy of the Church by the fancy of fact. His, in contrast to Bartoli's, is an earthly scene and his concern is with human deeds and human values.

His heroine is an ordinary woman, a druggist's daughter, who, unaided by the supernatural, achieves a human stature vividly contrasting with that of St. Scholastica, Bartoli's heroine. Her deeds require of us a different, more human, but no less noble reaction:

> *Saint, for this,*
> *Be yours the feet I stoop to—kneel and kiss!*
> *So human? Then the mouth too, if you will!*
> *Thanks to no legend but a chronicle.*
>
> (257–260)

Browning's saint calls us to life rather than to veneration. Even Charles, though weak and in some respects comtemptible, is not utterly lost: "up we'll patch/ Some sort of saintship for him" (261–262). Browning's treatment of him is at once realistic, sympathetic, and unsentimental. In the assertion here of a new humanism, Browning rejects supernaturalism as thoroughly as he earlier rejected rationalism. The full implication of his statement has not been generally recognized.

In the third parleying, that with Christopher Smart, the eighteenth-century poet whose poem "The Song of David" he greatly admired, Browning brings the first movement of his poem to a crescendo. It is at once an assertion and a demonstration, the focusing artifice, of the imaginative powers by which man infers the immensity. From its opening line, it provides a tonal contrast to the preceding two. Reason and disputation give way to wonderment and awe. The opening fragment, "It seems as if . . . ," suggests that what Browning has to say here overtaxes the resources of ordinary language. We pass from both the enlightenment and the supernatural to art; from reasonableness and dogma to madness. The "ground gave way" underneath Smart, we are told, and he caught a fleeting glance of a world beyond the reach of Mandeville and Bartoli. The awesomeness of such an experience is suggested by the disproportionate number of interrogative sentences. All of section VII, for example, is one twenty-five-line question. There are many others, some of them almost as long. We realize, however, that these questions are not real queries designed to elicit rational responses. They are rather symbolic structures, reflexes of a mind overwhelmed by a reality beyond its grasp. They are at once question and answer, expressions of bewilderment and affirmation. Their subject is one about which the human mind can formulate neither an adequate query nor a dogmatic assertion. The distorted syntax, the ellipsis, the rapidly shifting thought, the piling of metaphor on metaphor, the frequent bursts of lyricism, particularly in the first five sections, all reflect Browning's own pursuit of an artifice capable of inferring the inexpressible.

Smart is a particularly effective figure for the role he must play here. He is at once the product of the enlightenment ("the Golden Mean without a hint/ Of brave extravagance that breaks the rule" [22–23]) and the momentary possessor of the ecstatic vision. Browning is struck primarily by the fact that Smart only once in the middle of his long career wrote a supremely good poem, an artifice expressive of the immensity. The fact that a man who had previously written only ordinary verse could produce the magnificent "The Song of David" is exceeded in strangeness only by the fact that the creator could thereafter "resume the void and null,/ Subside to insignificance" (99–101).

Browning emphatically refuses to measure poetic achievement quantitatively. To have impinged upon the "all-unapproachable" even for one moment, he knows, is an inexplicable triumph. Smart, alone between Milton and Keats, "pierced the screen/ 'Twixt thing and word, lit language straight from soul" (113–114). Browning's description of the moment is one of the glories of the book:

> *Left no fine film-flake on the naked coal*
> *Live from the censer—shapely or uncouth,*
> *Fire-suffused through and through, one blaze of truth*
> *Undeadened by a lie,—(you have my mind)—*
> *For, think! this blaze outleapt with black behind*
> *And blank before, when Hayley and the rest . . .*
> *But let the dead successors worst and best*
> *Bury their dead: with life be my concern—*
> *Yours with the fire-flame. . . .*
>
> *(115–123)*

Smart presents the anomaly of a man who for once caught a vision of the Immensity. Such direct apprehension was not his ordinary way, however. He glimpsed naked truth once when the disguise fell from Nature, but such an experience can endure only one brief, maddening moment. "The Song of David," an inventory of the "lovelinesses infinite/ In little" (words which recall the conclusion of "Mandeville": "In little, light, warmth, life are blessed") is the prototype of man's normal quest for God. Even the poet cannot hope—save for the occasions so rare that their occurrence is utterly disorienting—to approach God directly. He must proceed rather by indirection, beginning where he is with the world itself—a world in which God is immanent—and, by seizing first one and then another of the fragments, move, as it were, toward the apprehension of the "all-complete," the transcendent God. There is for man no other than this slow, often painful, certainly frustrating way. It is a quest of ambivalent reward. Each of its stages is an end in itself, capable of turning the "ice-ball" into a "fire-orb." (This section of the poem is tied closely to the prologue by repetition of the "fire" and "light" language and imagery.) On the other hand, each is at best partial and momentary. Clearly, man can never possess all, be all, become God in all His immensity. Perhaps this is why, after the visionary reaches of the earlier sections, the poem ends on a prosaic note: "Live and learn,/ Not first learn and then live, is our concern" (264–265). True, perhaps, but no more elevating than the "mere grey argument" of Mandeville's most unexalted moments.

After the crescendo achieved in "Christopher Smart," the poem resumes on a lower, less intense level. The parleying with George Bubb Dodington, roughly paralleling that with Bernard de Mandeville, begins the long build toward the climaxing peak achieved in the parleying with Charles Avison.

In "George Bubb Dodington," Browning turns from speculation to conduct, from vision to politics. The shift produces a change in perspective. The character not only of the auditor but also of the speaker, the "I," alters radically. Our inclination perhaps is to dissociate the speaker in this section from those in the preceding sections and from Browning himself. DeVane says, for example, "Of all the *Parleyings* this one was most evidently written for the sake of an attack upon a contemporary" (*Handbook,* 508). The implication is that it is less closely related thematically and structurally than are the others to the rest of the poem. The issue is not simple, however.

In *In a Balcony, The Ring and the Book, Prince Hohen-*

stiel-Schwangau, and *La Saisiaz,* Browning had observed how difficult it is to realize the private vision in a social structure. Man's failure leads naturally, he seems to say, to cynical negation or to political charlatanry. The cynical Dodington represents not only an external enemy whom Browning wished to attack but also the potential for negation and quackery that exists in all men.

Dodington is the natural counterpart to Christopher Smart, his cynicism and negation calling into question the affirmations of the artists; his failures representing the incapability of the politician to realize the private vision in social structures. The relation between Smart and Dodington is thematic and psychological, involving both the development of an idea and its apprehension by the speaker.

This relation is not immediately clear, however. Browning's attitude emerges only gradually. The first clues are stylistic. The diction, syntax, rhythm, and tone of "Dodington" contrast with that of "Smart." The facile statement and crude dogmatism of the speaker in "Dodington" suggests the speaker's superficiality. There is also his attitude toward vocation. Browning had claimed for Smart, the poet, a beneficent spiritual power, which readily established him as teacher and leader. Browning knew, however, that such power is ambiguous. Dodington is a parody of Smart, an example of the perversion of power. The speaker's assertion that ordinary men want to be awed by their leaders seems almost a burlesque of Carlyle's doctrine of the Hero. Browning acknowledges the thin line separating the adept from the quack, the savior from the scoundrel. He is aware of the precarious balance between authentic "vision" and "mendacious intrepidity." Again and again he returns in his work to probe the inner life of a character who misuses his powers and becomes not a hero but a scoundrel. The persistence of this theme in his poetry illustrates his awareness of ambiguities inherent in power and of the temptation for all men to misconstrue it and to misuse it.

In "George Bubb Dodington" he contrasts the politician who regards his vocation as a "trade" with the artist who accepts his as a divine commission. The speaker confuses crude folk wisdom with scripture; he accepts unquestioningly a naturalistic morality which equates man with unthinking animals; he uses such words as *sham* and *quack* with cynical indifference. There is no other character like him in the entire poem. For this reason, he is indispensable, and his appearance at this juncture is calculated to produce precisely the thematic and psychological effect for which the poet strove.

Browning was generally contemptuous of politicians because he regarded them, like the lawyers in *The Ring and the Book,* as social manikins rather than individuals; for him, they represented the perversion of private "vision" into "mendacious intrepidity." He could scarcely imagine the operation of spiritual powers on other than individual levels. His distrust of tradition and institutions as inherently dehumanizing permeates all his thoughts and makes him more radical socially than is usually recognized.

Dodington represents the abstraction, the systematization, the dehumanization against which Browning protests in the prologue. Obviously on the side of the Fates, Dodington stands not only for Benjamin Disraeli but for others (the nineteenth-century Calibans) among Browning's contemporaries who promoted a society controlled by "natural morality." Dodington is in Browning's view the logical culmination of such a premise, the cynical manipulator who operates with disregard of the individual. He perverts spiritual powers to personal ends.

At the beginning of the section, Dodington, finally deserted by his constituents and retired by them to private life, speculates about his failure. The speaker chides him not for his ends but for his means: "Ah, George Bubb Dodington, Lord Melcombe,—no, / Yours was the wrong way!" Both accept a "natural" universe in which values involve less a choice between right and wrong than the discovery and employment of effective means toward personal power. Dodington, the speaker insists, failed because he pretended to sacrifice himself for his constituents, a fraud which they inevitably discovered. Such an appeal as his assumes motives inconsistent with a morality which values shrewdness over sacrifice. Had he a subtler understanding of psychology he would have known that

> *Who would use*
> *Man for his pleasure needs must introduce*
> *The element that awes Man. Once for all,*
> *His nature owns a Supernatural*
> *In fact as well as phrase—*
>
> (*188–192*)

He continues with great urbanity to dissociate himself from the old "mystery," the "chalked-ring, incantation-gibberish," asserting that contemporary man can be controlled only by a "new wizard-craft." The skillful "quack" brazenly displays his selfishness:

> *No use*
> *In men but to make sport for you, induce*
> *The puppets now to dance, now stand stock-still,*
> *Now knock their heads together, at your will*
> *For will's sake only—while each plays his part*
> *Submissive: why? through terror at the heart:*

"Can it be—this bold man, whose hand we saw
Openly pull the wires, obeys some law
Quite above Man's—nay, God's?" On face fall they.
                                                    (332–340)

In these lines, the impersonality and mechanism, implicit in the poem from the beginning, are made explicit, and man is reduced to an automaton.

By accepting Dodington's naturalistic premises and arguing the failure of his means rather than the evil of his ends, the speaker doubly exposes the inhumanity of a contemporary perspective against which Browning protested. This section of the poem is an ironic statement in highly stylized language and imagery that counterpoints the notion of man as a free, creative being which Browning attempts to evoke. The counterpointing of part one and part two of the poem, specifically of "Smart" and "Dodington," initiates a dialectical movement which is resolved finally at the conclusion of the seventh and last parleying.

The parleying with Francis Furini is on the surface a refutation of Baldinucci's report that Furini on his deathbed repudiated his earlier paintings of the feminine nude. It is also a slap at contemporary critics who blasted Robert Barrett Browning's paintings, also of the nude, as immoral. On a deeper level, however, Browning continues to explore themes already familiar in the poem: the nature of good and evil, the limits of man's knowledge, man's need to achieve spiritual wholeness through growth and development, the significance of the world and the flesh, and the role of the artist in apprehending and communicating truth. He further elaborates upon the tension between affirmation and negation by contrasting Furini's pictures, which celebrate the beauty of earthly things, particularly the feminine body, with medieval Christian paintings which depict ". . . some orthodox sad sickly saint/ —Grey

male emaciation, haply streaked/ Carmine by scourgings"
(552–554).

Browning's choice of Furini as an interlocutor serves his
purpose well. Although he distorts the historical figure,
Browning achieves for Furini an identity consistent with
itself and with the poem in which he appears. This section
is divided into clearly defined parts: Browning's appraisal
of Furini as a good painter with a skillful hand but a limited head; his attack upon Baldinucci (and upon contemporary critics) for subjecting art to moral rather than aesthetic standards; Furini's prayer addressed to " 'Bounteous
God,/ Deviser and dispenser of all gifts/ To soul through
sense' " (232–234); Furini's sermon in which he relates his
fleshy paintings to a metaphysical position; and, finally, a
section in which Browning himself speaks.

Browning's realistic appraisal of Furini clarifies issues
and establishes the painter's usefulness to his purpose.
Moreover, it elaborates an aesthetic position which Browning stated also in "Christopher Smart." Art has its beginnings in earthly things, and its end in a vision which joins
heaven and earth. Furini was limited in his scope. He
painted the feminine nude with remarkable skill:

> . . . *the dear*
> *Fleshly perfection of the human shape,—*
> *This was apportioned you whereby to praise*
> *Heaven and bless earth.*
>
> (55–58)

Unfortunately, however, he was unable to penetrate beyond to the mystery. His work fell short of the highest
achievement. The short section containing Furini's prayer
serves as a collect to introduce the sermon which follows.
The sermon is not irrelevant, as some critics have charged,
nor is the fact that he addresses it to a nineteenth-century

audience a flaw. Browning is not writing history. Furini must be given his opportunity to relate his fleshly painting to a metaphysical position and to defend himself against a narrow puritanical moral code.

Once again, through the painter, Browning speaks of soul as self-consciousness, in words which echo *Fifine at the Fair:*

> . . . *soul's first act*
> (*Call consciousness the soul—some name we need*)
> *Getting itself aware, through stuff decreed*
> *Thereto (so call the body)—who has stept*
> *So far, there let him stand, become adept*
> *In body ere he shift his station thence*
> *One single hair's breadth.*
>
> (*369–375*)

Self-consciousness is man's goal. He achieves such a state not through abstractions or systematized knowledge but through experience. Aliveness is being involved in a struggle for good against evil, a struggle which begins on earth and ends, we hope, in heaven. Furini's paintings mark the point of beginning. Like all good art, they give permanence to fugitive truth and become the artifice capable of inciting men toward growth and development. Browning returns once more to the problem of good and evil and, rejecting a narrow puritanical interpretation, insists that both type and antitype (good and evil) are necessary if man is to experience growth. Good and evil are psychological if not objective realities. They are also psychological necessities:

> *Though wrong were right,*
> *Could we but know—still wrong must needs seem*
> *wrong*

To do right's service, prove men weak or strong,
Choosers of evil or of good.

(*504–507*)

And again:

Ah, friends, you touch
Just here my solid standing-place amid
The wash and welter, whence all doubts are bid
Back to the ledge they break against in foam,
Futility: my soul, and my soul's home
This body,—how each operates on each,
And how things outside, fact or feigning, teach
What good is and what evil,—just the same,
Be feigning or be fact the teacher,—blame
Diffidence nowise if, from this I judge
My point of vantage, not an inch I budge.

(*508–518*)

The section ends with the sad reminder that Furini was prevented by his limitations from achieving the highest reaches of art. He has not, like Christopher Smart, even the single transcendent moment to his credit. This, nevertheless, does not nullify the good he did achieve—the beautiful depiction of the feminine nude. "Francis Furini" marks the initial recoil against the negativism of "George Bubb Dodington" and points toward the final triumph of cautious affirmation in "Charles Avison." As a work of art, this section of the poem is marred by the intrusion of Browning's personal feelings, which cause him to lose control of his materials and to prolong the poem beyond the bounds of good art.

As "Dodington" roughly parallels "Mandeville," "Furini" parallels "Bartoli." In the latter two Browning turns from the negativism implicit in medieval legend and art to an affirmation of man's capacities for spiritual development. "Gerard de Lairesse" has no precise parallel in the first part of the poem, but it is anticipated. It summarizes and focuses one of Browning's major themes. From the beginning of *Parleyings,* Browning's view has been implicitly modern. He has rejected the sterile rationalism of the Enlightenment, the religious orthodoxy of the Middle Ages, and the dehumanizing implications of the new science. He has consistently emphasized the present over the past and the value of personal experience over tradition and institution. In "Gerard de Lairesse" he turns specifically to defend this modern view particularly against Hellenizers who profess to find significant values only in the past. As DeVane has indicated, he certainly had Matthew Arnold in mind. Indirectly, he must certainly also have been thinking of Carlyle, who romanticized the Middle Ages, preferring past over present.

In many respects, this poem is an extension of Browning's earlier "Greek" poems, in which he argued the superiority of Euripides over Aeschylus, the modern over the antique. Here his adversary is Gerard de Lairesse, a late seventeenth-century Dutch painter, who in his aesthetic theories anticipated the nineteenth-century German and English romanticizers. The fact that Browning once felt respect for him gives to his denunciation an ambivalence and complexity that his attack in "Furini" upon contemporary art critics does not have. This makes for greater artistic control in "Gerard de Lairesse."

Browning challenges Lairesse's argument that art created from a modern point of view and on a contemporary subject is necessarily inferior to the ancient by proposing himself to describe a "walk," which will rival that which Lairesse has established as a touchstone (in Arnold's sense) of excellence. Not content to say merely that the present is the equal of the past, he argues that modern man possesses deeper insight and clearer vision than his predecessors.

Browning's walk begins just prior to dawn and ends at dusk, a progression that symbolizes the dawning and waning of Greek culture. It contains a small group of carefully selected vignettes of representative Greek heroes: Prometheus, Artemis, Lyda and the Satyr, and Alexander the Great. Browning's treatment of each is perceptively ambivalent. Like Lairesse he sees and admires the external grandeur of these old figures; unlike Lairesse, however, he discovers beneath their grandeur a human insensitivity and a spiritual void that culminates in despair and ultimately in disintegration. The portrait of Prometheus emphasizes the defiant spirit of the great rebel, but de-emphasizes the nineteenth-century stress on his love for mankind. Even more prominent than Prometheus is Jove, who reminds us that at the core of Greek thought and religion there was from the beginning an inseparable violence and brutality:

> *O thou, of scorn's unconquerable smile,*
> *Was it when this—Jove's feathered fury—slipped*
> *Gore-glutted from the heart's core whence he ripped—*
> *This eagle-hound—neither reproach nor prayer—*
> *Baffled, in one more fierce attempt to tear*
> *Fate's secret from thy safeguard,—was it then*
> *That all these thunders rent earth, ruined air*
> *To reach thee, pay thy patronage of men?*
>
> *(195–202)*

Prometheus represents the predawn of Greek civilization. Artemis, whom Browning introduces next, represents its morning. His choice of the goddess of hunting for this role is especially significant in light of Browning's intense hatred for the sport. Chastely beautiful but at the same time humanly insensitive, she is linked by her cruelty with

Jove. At its best Browning found Greek culture incomplete. He reveals his attitude toward the classical past in the following lines:

> *Let me glide unseen*
> *From thy proud presence: well may'st thou be queen*
> *Of all those strange and sudden deaths which damped*
> *So oft Love's torch and Hymen's taper lit*
> *For happy marriage till the maidens paled*
> *And perished on the temple-step, assailed*
> *By—what except to envy must man's wit*
> *Impute that sure implacable release*
> *Of life from warmth and joy?*
>
> (253–261)

Choosing Artemis (the archenemy of Aphrodite—Browning must have had Euripides in mind) as symbol of early Greece, he presented pre-Christian and medieval past alike as epochs which negated life. Surely the concluding statement is ironic: "But death means peace."

The noon of Greek culture is represented by Lyda and the Satyr, symbols of lust and ravage. Artemis' unnatural chastity and inhumanity inevitably produce its antithesis, so that at its meridian Greek culture is destroyed by its partiality. Browning ends his walk with the presentation of Alexander the Great, in whom the insensitivity, the lust and will for power, culminate to produce despair and chaos. The history of Greek civilization, according to Browning, is the record of progressive dehumanization. Certainly, he seems to say, it can provide no model for contemporary man. His summation is contained in the lines: "The dead Greek lore lies buried in the urn/ Where who seeks fire finds ashes" (392–393). The last figure that Browning sights at the close of his walk is appropriately a ghost who represents the lifeless remains of Greece after all beauty and grandeur have departed. Browning's interests were never in ghosts but in flesh-and-blood men and women, never in the past but in the present.

In this emphatic, unsentimental view of Greek civilization, Browning attempts to undermine the argument of the Hellenizers and—contra Arnold and Carlyle—to point to the present and future as containing man's hope:

> *Some fitter way express*
> *Heart's satisfaction that the Past indeed*
> *Is past, gives way before Life's best and last,*
> *The all-including Future!*
>
> (*364–367*)

"Gerard de Lairesse" contains some of Browning's best poetry. In it he achieves an intensity that prepares for the intellectual and emotional climax that he is to reach in his last parleying, "Charles Avison." Browning chooses to conclude his meditations with a commentary upon music. From the beginning he has opposed the artist to the philosopher-scientist-politician. He brought the first part of the poem to a peak in his discussion with a poet. He achieves a steadily mounting intensity in the second part when, after his initial bout with a politician, he engages in an exchange with a painter and a painter-aesthetician. Finally, he turns to a musician, as in *Fifine at the Fair*, to help him shape his last thought.

He chooses Avison, as he has chosen Furini, for reasons other than his greatness. Browning admits that the musician's perspective was neither broad nor deep and that his form of expression has little contemporary meaning. The spark of truth, the "march-motive," which informs his music, remains truth still, however, and "endures resetting." Browning prefaces his remarks about Avison by recreating an imaginative world which the old bandmaster's music once had power to create for him. Such a world no longer satisfies fully his mature mind, but so far as it goes it is honest and powerful. Its very immaturity is a virtue in that it leaves room for development. Browning uses this parleying to bring into focus and to give final form to those themes with which he has been most concerned throughout the poem; indeed, throughout his career. The multiple interests of the prior meditations are here reduced to two or three unifying considerations, chiefly with the reality of the soul and the power of art, especially music, to resolve man's discourse into a unity of thought and passion.

Once more he returns to comment upon that indefinable reality which throughout his poetry he has for want of a better name called *soul*. In this parleying he makes no further attempt to define the word, being satisfied rather to talk about it indirectly, through symbol, not as it may exist in any absolute sense but as it is felt to exist in relation to experience and values. He describes it as a tumultuous river of unknown origin and unforeseeable destination over which the world phenomenon, like a bridge, is built. Browning is dogmatic only in insisting that the bridge is not an independent and ultimate reality. The river that it spans is also real. The bridge is constantly swayed by the surges of the subterranean river, and, occasionally, the waves break over it to join momentarily the seen with the unseen. Such moments represent a vision as nearly ultimate as man can experience. That kind of vision came once to Christopher Smart.

Browning seems to associate the stream with passion and the phenomena with mind, but his dichotomy is not simple. To use the word *passion* in such a sense stretches it beyond its ordinary limits. The stream is not irrational but nonrational, not a counterpoint to but a complement of the bridge. It completes, not contradicts, the world of mind and sense. Man is most conscious of being a bridge, but he knows also that he is related to and is part of the stream. His insatiable impulse is to have the bridge submerged by and to be drawn into the swirling, onrushing stream.

Insisting that modern man is often one-dimensionally intellectual and needs to rediscover the nonrational, Browning reminds us of some twentieth-century writers, D. H. Lawrence, for example. He differs from Lawrence most, perhaps, in his refusal to analyze and castigate. Lawrence ironically spends a great deal of time intellectualizing modern man's overintellectualization. There is in Browning, in contrast, very little of the cultural historian. Moreover, Browning knew too much about the Christian tradition to permit him to indulge in facile generalizations about its destructive influence upon Western culture. His denunciation of Christianity is always specifically directed against the medieval perversion of the gospel of affirmation and joy.

Browning offers the arts, particularly music, as a means by which man may be made whole. Art reunites rational and nonrational not by creating something new but by structuring that which already exists. It is the object of art to "arrange,/ Dissociate, re-distribute, interchange/ Part with part, lengthen, broaden, high or deep/ Construct their bravest" (201–204). Santayana's famous attack upon Browning is at once a model of insight and oversight. He was right in saying that Browning praises the passionate experience of the moment; he was wrong in saying that Browning was unmindful of structure. Browning's ultimate defense of art is that it saves man precisely from those barbarous elements of "chance" and "change" which Santayana found so disturbing in modern society.

Browning does not rebel against the past, but he does refuse to become its prisoner. The past as historical event is relatively unimportant. As such it possesses no power to disturb our souls and to galvanize our lives. Browning's rebellion, to the extent that it is a rebellion, is not against the truths of the past but against outworn modes of communication. In *The Ring and the Book* he stated that his purpose was to "resuscitate" old fact and to make it live once more. He returns to Avison for the same purpose, seeing him not as an isolated case, but, along with "Brahms,/ Wagner, Dvorak, Liszt" (99–100), as part of man's continuing efforts to express the infinite through the finite, an endeavor in which no truth regardless of its size is insignificant:

> *I devote*
> *Rather my modicum of parts to use*
> *What power may yet avail to re-infuse*
> *(In fancy, please you!) sleep that looks like death*
> *With momentary liveliness, lend breath*
> *To make the torpor half inhale.*
>
> (276–281)

Art has power to capture the evanescent moods, the momentary glimpses of wholeness, to render them permanent, to quote Browning, to "shoot/ Liquidity into a mould" (209–210). Music is superior to all other arts because it dredges deeper, drags into day, and gives more honestly "limbs' play and life's symbolence" to the subterranean "marvel and mystery." In short, "save it from chance and change we most abhore!" Browning ends this section with an apocalyptic vision, a pandemonium of musical sound in which one discord is caught up into a mighty symphony: Avison with Bach, Strafford with Pym, past with present. When Browning comes finally to describe that ultimate state toward which all his poetry points—to identify a focusing artifice—he appropriately speaks of a symphonic movement of musical sound.

The epilogue, "Fust and His Friends," along with the

prologue, "Apollo and the Fates," provides the cosmic framework for this great metaphysical poem. A soul journey that begins in the nether world of Greek legend culminates in a modern printing shop. Browning rejects both the fables of Greece and the superstitions of the medieval church to concentrate upon the life which man lives now in an ordinary workaday world. He is concerned not about gods and devils but about men and women.

Browning's epilogue is constructed against the background of the famous medieval Faust legend. Daniel Defoe is credited with first linking Johann Fust with Dr. Faustus, but Browning perhaps had Goethe's *Faust* in mind when he wrote his poem. There are parallels between Fust and Faust. Fust, like Faust, is accompanied by a dog. He is credited with making wine flow from tables, and he allegedly had an affair with Helen. In the discussion of *Fifine at the Fair* some of the affinities between Goethe and Browning were pointed out. There are differences, also. Browning displays a greater awareness of human limits and responsibilities. Perhaps the greatest difference between Goethe's *Faust* and Browning's *Parleyings* is found in the contrasting settings within which the poems conclude: Goethe's in heaven and Browning's in a printing shop. Browning is eager to dissociate his Fust from every vestige of medieval superstition. His great dog is the devil in disguise only in the befuddled minds of his ignorant friends. Fust insists that those who reported having seen wine flow from the table were simply drunk and irresponsible, and he cynically reminds his listeners that a man with money can buy a beautiful woman. Browning is obviously making no attempt to unite past and present in a new synthesis. Goethe, in contrast, accepts without intellectual comment the miraculous elements of the legend and uses them to achieve poetic ends. Although Browning's vision, like Goethe's, must ultimately culminate in eternity, he chooses in his poetry to remain solidly on earth, preoccupied with man as he now is. He remains concerned with the human scene and with the process of man's growth and development by painful stages toward some possible future transcendent state.

That Browning chooses to make a modern printing press the summarizing symbol of a metaphysical poem is both ingenious and appropriate. Its very disparateness, its "unpoeticality," and its contemporaneity reinforce Browning's conviction that man is most interesting in his human struggles. The press also represents an important advance over the past. No medieval scribe, regardless of his skill, could hope to rival the accuracy of the new press. The press, like art, functions primarily to communicate "words," the Word; and, like art, it arrests and fixes man's momentary visions, preserving them from the ravages of time and from the error of ordinary transmission. Fust is sobered by the realization that this instrument for great good may also be used by bad men for great evil. Even this possibility, however, he turns to advantage, once more asserting the interdependence of type and anti-type and their mutual contribution to some over-all purpose.

Browning concludes the poem with a characteristic idea. Fust's clerical friends are terrified by the possible destruction which the press may work upon established thought and traditional institutions. It can so easily, they recognize, become the instrument of heresy. Fust, by indirection, clearly places himself on the side of the heretics, eagerly anticipating that destruction of the old which must precede the new reconstruction. Fust's friend quotes John Huss, the fourteenth-century reformer, who was burned by the Church for heresy, as saying, " 'Ye burn now a Goose: there succeeds me a Swan/ Ye shall find quench your fire!' " To this Fust replies, "I foresee such a man."

In many respects, Browning himself was such a man.

❧ ❧ ❧ NOTES

All quotations from Browning's poetry are taken from the first London edition and are identified by line numbers unless otherwise indicated.

❧ PREFACE

1. *The Poetry of Experience* (New York: Random House, 1957).
2. *Browning's Characters: A Study in Poetic Technique* (New Haven: Yale University Press, 1961).
3. Browning's essential modernity has already been established. In addition to Langbaum and Honan, others have written with penetrating insight about Browning and the modern tradition. Two indispensable studies of the intellectual and spiritual crisis of the nineteenth century are: Morse Peckham, *Beyond the Tragic Vision* (New York: George Braziller, 1962), and J. Hillis Miller, *The Disappearance of God: Five Nineteenth-Century Writers* (Cambridge: Harvard University Press, 1963).
4. Arthur Symons expresses this view in his generally excellent critical study, *An Introduction to the Study of Browning,* first published in 1886. Reviewing Symons' book in *The Guardian,* November 9, 1887, Walter Pater stated the opinion more emphatically than had any critic before him: "We think also that Mr. Symons in his high praise does no more than justice to *The Ring and the Book. The Ring and the Book* is at once the largest and the greatest of Mr. Browning's works, the culmination of his dramatic method, and the turning-point more decisively than *Dramatis Personae* of his style. . . . Noble as much of Mr. Browning's later work is, full of intellect, alive with excellent passages (in the first volume of *Dramatic Idyls* perhaps more powerful than in any earlier work); notwithstanding all that, we think the change here indicated matter of regret. After all, we have to conjure up ideal poets for ourselves out of those who stand in or behind the range of volumes on our bookshelves; and our ideal Browning would have for his entire structural type those two volumes of *Men and Women* with *Pippa Passes*."
5. I have already referred to Peckham and Miller. See also: M. H.

Abrams, *The Mirror and the Lamp* (New York, Oxford University Press, 1953).

6. Morse Peckham summarizes his situation precisely when he says:

> The Romantic experienced a sense of profound isolation within the world and an equally terrifying alienation from society. These two experiences, metaphysical isolation and social alienation—they are of course two different modes of the same perception—were the distinguishing signs of the Romantic, and they are to this day. To symbolize that isolation and alienation and simultaneously to assert the Self as the source of order became one task of the Romantic personality. To find a ground for value, identity, meaning, order became the other task. (*Romanticism: The Culture of the Nineteenth Century* [New York: George Braziller, 1965, 19].)

7. "Hence," Carlyle says in *Sartor Resartus,* "the folly of that impossible Precept, Know thyself; till it be translated into this partially possible one, Know what thou canst work at."

8. Browning's poetry records the development of his own soul; it is the organic, dynamic artifice of his own great immensity. In tracing its evolution we must remember, if we are to avoid distortion and misrepresentation, that Browning's ideas were never static, that they were in a constant flux of change and development. Knowing when and in what context Browning made a particular statement is crucial to our proper understanding of it.

9. Browning's problem, of course, was shared by his contemporaries. John Ruskin, for example, talked convincingly in the early volumes of *Modern Painters* about J. M. W. Turner's efforts to realize his "free" and "sincere" spirit in his landscapes. So long as his subject remained fairly limited, Ruskin could defend art on the grounds that it was psychologically functional. When he turned from the individual painter to the whole of Venetian society, however, he faced a totally different problem. He chose, in *The Stones of Venice,* to trace the spirit, the "soul" of Venice, from its birth through its rise and fall as it was revealed in its architecture. Architecture, certainly as Ruskin conceived it, was communal rather than private. Ruskin needed to believe that "free" and "sincere" workers would combine their efforts and produce a great Gothic cathedral, but he knew at the same time that such an achievement required in addition to willing workers the directive oversight of an architect and the specifications of

his blueprint. How to achieve the latter without enslaving the former was his dilemma. He never satisfactorily solved it. Eventually he arbitrarily imposed upon his socio-aesthetic theory a structuring moral system. He was never able, however, to ground his morality in a metaphysics that was consistent with his vision of the creative, self-creating worker.

❧ CHAPTER I

1. See: Park Honan, *Browning's Characters: A Study in Poetic Technique* (New Haven: Yale University Press, 1961), 15–17. I should like to acknowledge my indebtedness to Professor Honan's excellent study. His influence is perceptible throughout my work in ways which often make specific acknowledgment difficult. Hereafter referred to in text as *Browning's Characters.*
2. See introduction to Donald Smalley, ed., *Browning's Essay on Chatterton* (Cambridge: Harvard University Press, 1948). Professor Smalley's study is the finest yet written on the subject of Browning's use of historical personages as subjects for literary creation.
3. The most helpful article published recently on the poem is: Robert R. Columbus and Claudette Kemper, "Sordello and the Speaker: A Problem of Identity," *Victorian Poetry,* II (1964), 251–267.
4. William Clyde DeVane, *A Browning Handbook* (New York: Appleton, Century, Croft, 2nd ed., 1955), 71–87. Hereafter referred to in text as DeVane, *Handbook.*
5. *Romanticism,* 15.

❧ CHAPTER II

1. *The Diaries of William Charles Macready,* 1833–1851, ed. by William Toynbee, 2 vols. (London: Chapman and Hall, 1912). References identified throughout in text by date of entry.
2. In this chapter passages are identified by act, scene, and page number in the original edition unless otherwise noted.
3. *Letters of Robert Browning, Collected by Thomas J. Wise,* ed. by Thurman L. Hood (London: John Murray, 1933), 5. Hereafter referred to in text as Hood, *Letters.*
4. W. Hall Griffin and H. C. Minchin, *The Life of Robert Browning* (New York: Macmillan, 1910), 125.
5. James P. McCormick, "Robert Browning and the Experimental Drama," *PMLA,* LXVIII (1953), 982–991.

6. In the original edition the passage read:

> Shall to produce form out of shapelessness
> Be art—and, further, to evoke a soul
> From form be nothing? This new soul is mine—(Part II, p. 10).

By "my own Psyche" Jules obviously means his statue, but, I suggest, Browning intended the word to refer ambivalently to Jules' soul also.

7. *Letters of Robert Browning and Elizabeth Barrett, 1845–1846*, 2 vols. (New York: Harper and Brothers, 1889), I, 467. Hereafter referred to in text as *Love Letters*.

8. *Robert Browning and Alfred Domett*, ed. by Frederic G. Kenyon (New York: E. P. Dutton and Company, 1906), 36.

9. Arthur Symons, *An Introduction to the Study of Browning*, new edition, revised and enlarged (London, J. M. Dent and Company, 1906), 94.

❦ CHAPTER III

1. See Park Honan's treatment of this subject in *Browning's Characters*, especially pp. 104–128. For a discussion of the development during the nineteenth century of the dramatic monologue as the structure organic with a "poetry of experience" see Robert Langbaum's *The Poetry of Experience*.

2. Browning in a letter to Isa Blagden in 1870, said of Tennyson's *The Holy Grail and Other Poems:* "Well, I go with you a good way in the feeling about Tennyson's new book: it is all out of my head already. We look at the object of art in poetry so differently! Here is an Idyll about a knight being untrue to his friend and yielding to the temptation of that friend's mistress after having engaged to assist him in his suit. I should judge the conflict in the knight's soul the proper subject to describe: Tennyson thinks he should describe the castle, and effect of the moon on its towers, and anything *but* the soul." Hood, *Letters,* 134.

3. I have treated this poem more fully in *The Bow and the Lyre: The Art of Robert Browning* (Ann Arbor: University of Michigan Press, 1957), which also see for extended explications of "Andrea del Sarto," "Fra Lippo Lippi," and "Bishop Blougram's Apology."

4. For a discussion of this essay and its relation to the poems here under discussion, see: Thomas J. Collins, *Robert Browning's*

Moral-Aesthetic Theory, 1833–1855 (Lincoln: University of Nebraska Press, 1967), 113–122.

5. *The Letters of Elizabeth Barrett Browning,* 2 vols., ed. by Frederic G. Kenyon (London: Smith, Elder, and Company, 1898), I, 449.

6. I have treated this poem more fully in "Browning: 'Mage' and 'Maker'—A Study in Poetic Purpose and Method," *Victorian Newsletter* 20 (1962), 22–25. Reprinted in: Philip Drew, *Robert Browning: A Collection of Critical Essays* (London: Metheun and Company, 1966), 189–198.

7. Katherine deKay Bronson, "Browning in Venice," *Century Magazine* LXIII (1902), 578.

8. Edward Dowden, *The Life of Robert Browning* (London: J. M. Dent, 1904).

9. See: John Howard, "Caliban's Mind," *Victorian Poetry,* I (1963), 249–257. Reprinted in: Philip Drew, *Robert Browning: A Collection of Critical Essays* (London: Metheun and Company, 1966), 223–233.

10. See: Michael Timko, "Browning Upon Butler; or, Natural Theology in the English Isle," *Criticism,* VII (1965), 141–150.

11. Mrs. Sutherland Orr, "The Religious Opinions of Robert Browning, *Contemporary Review,* LX (1891), 879.

12. See: Philip Drew, "Henry Jones on Browning's Optimism," *Victorian Poetry,* II (1964), 29–41. Reprinted in *The Browning Critics,* ed. by Boyd Litzinger and Kenneth L. Knickerbocker (Lexington: University of Kentucky Press, 1965), 364–380.

❦ CHAPTER IV

1. Translation from title page of C. W. Hodell, *The Old Yellow Book, Source of Browning's "The Ring and the Book"* (New York: Everyman's Library, 1911).

2. Edward McAleer, *Dearest Isa* (Austin: The University of Texas Press, 1951), 134.

3. Mrs. Sutherland Orr, *Life and Letters of Robert Browning* (Boston: Houghton Mifflin and Company, 1908), 250. Hereafter referred to in text as Orr, *Life.*

4. George Wasserman, "The Meaning of Browning's Ring Figure," *Modern Language Notes,* LXXVI (1961), 420–426.

5. Richard Curle, *Robert Browning and Julia Wedgwood* (New York: Frederick A. Stokes Company, 1937), 149.

6. For a statement about the historical accuracy of Browning's treatment of Molinos see: William Coyle, "Molinos: 'The Subject of the Day' in *The Ring and the Book*," *PMLA*, LXVII (1952), 304–314.

❧ CHAPTER V

1. André Gide, *Journals*, Vol. III, tr. by Justin O'Brien (New York: Alfred Knopf, 1949), 107.
2. Obviously Browning had by this time become intensely interested in speculations about the nature of one's being, particularly that of the creative artist. In his preface to the selected poems of 1872, written perhaps while he was writing or shortly after he had finished *Prince Hohenstiel-Schwangau,* he said: "In the present selection from my poetry, there is an attempt to escape from the embarrassment of appearing to pronounce upon what myself may consider the best of it. I adopt another principle; and by simply stringing together certain pieces on the thread of an imaginary personality, I present them in succession, rather as the natural development of a particular experience than because I account them the most noteworthy portion of my work. Such an attempt was made in the volume of selections from the poetry of Elizabeth Barrett Browning: to which—in outward uniformity, at least—my own would venture to become a companion." One suspects that Browning turned to that "imaginary personality" for confirmation of his own reality. In doing so, he anticipated questions raised in many of his later poems and at least partly answered in such works as "House" and "Shop."
3. Cited in Dowden, *Life,* 203.
4. *The Diary of Alfred Domett,* 1872–1885, ed. by F. A. Horsman (London: Oxford Press, 1953), 5.
5. Quotations from *Fifine at the Fair* are identified by stanza numbers.
6. W. O. Raymond, *The Infinite Moment,* 2nd ed. (Toronto: The University of Toronto Press, 1965), 121.
7. *Ibid.,* 105–128.
8. *Faust,* Part II, tr. by Philip Wayne (The Penguin Classics, 1959), 282.
9. *Ibid.,* I, 41.
10. Symons, *Introduction,* 103.
11. Betty Miller, *Robert Browning: A Portrait* (London: John Murray, 1952), 252.

12. A. Symonds, Review of *Aristophanes' Apology*, *Academy*, VII (1875), 513.
13. Donald Smalley, "A Parleying with Aristophanes," *PMLA*, LV (1940), 389.
14. Frederick G. Kenyon, *The Works of Robert Browning* (London: Smith, Elder, and Company, 1912), VIII, x–xi.
15. See Browning's letter in response to Edmund Gosse's request that he select four poems "of moderate length which represent their writer fairly," Hood, *Letters*, 235–236. Browning included: Lyrical: "Saul"; Narrative: "A Forgiveness"; Dramatic: "Caliban on Setebos"; Idyllic: "Clive." Perhaps Browning chose these poems much as he made selections from his poetry for the 1872 edition. See note 2 immediately above.
16. A good explanation of the thought of *La Saisiaz* is F. E. L. Priestley's "A Reading of *La Saisiaz*," *University of Toronto Quarterly*, XXV (1955), 47–59. Reprinted in Philip Drew, *Robert Browning: A Collection of Critical Essays* (London: Methuen, 1966), 242–256.

❦ CHAPTER VI

1. Cited in DeVane, *Handbook*, 430.
2. An obvious printing error which was corrected in the 1889 edition to read, "and Hob, do you the same!"

❦ CHAPTER VII

1. The best extended treatment of this subject and, indeed, of the poem as a whole is William C. DeVane's *Browning's Parleyings, The Autobiography of a Mind* (New Haven: Yale University Press, 1927).

❧ ❧ ❧ BIBLIOGRAPHY

❧ I. INDIVIDUAL WORKS (FIRST PUBLICATION)

Pauline: A Fragment of a Confession. London: Saunders and Otley, 1833.

Paracelsus. London: Effingham Wilson, 1835.

Strafford: An Historical Tragedy. London: Longman, Rees, Orme, Brown, Green and Longman, 1837.

Sordello. London: Edward Moxon, 1840.

Bells and Pomegranates

    No. 1. *Pippa Passes.* London: Edward Moxon, 1841.

    No. 2. *King Victor and King Charles.* London: Edward Moxon, 1842.

    No. 3. *Dramatic Lyrics.* London: Edward Moxon, 1842.

    No. 4. *The Return of the Druses.* London: Edward Moxon, 1843.

    No. 5. *A Blot in the 'Scutcheon.* London: Edward Moxon, 1843.

    No. 6. *Colombe's Birthday.* London: Edward Moxon, 1844.

    No. 7. *Dramatic Romances and Lyrics.* London: Edward Moxon, 1845.

    No. 8. *Luria and A Soul's Tragedy.* London: Edward Moxon, 1846.

Christmas-Eve and Easter-Day. London: Chapman and Hall, 1850.

Men and Women. London: Chapman and Hall, 1855.

Dramatis Personae. London: Chapman and Hall, 1864.

The Ring and the Book. London: Smith, Elder, and Company, 1868–1869.

Balaustion's Adventures: Including a Transcript from Euripides. London: Smith, Elder, and Company, 1871.

Prince Hohenstiel-Schwangau, Saviour of Society. London: Smith, Elder, and Company, 1871.

Fifine at the Fair. London: Smith, Elder, and Company, 1872.

Red Cotton Night-Cap Country. London: Smith, Elder, and Company, 1873.

Aristophanes' Apology. London: Smith, Elder, and Company, 1875.

The Inn Album. London: Smith, Elder, and Company, 1875.

Pacchiarotto and How He Worked in Distemper: With Other Poems. London: Smith, Elder, and Company, 1876.

The Agamemnon of Aeschylus. London: Smith, Elder, and Company, 1877.

La Saisiaz and The Two Poets of Croisic. London: Smith, Elder, and Company, 1878.

Dramatic Idyls. London: Smith, Elder, and Company, 1879.

Dramatic Idyls, Second Series. London: Smith, Elder, and Company, 1880.

Jocoseria. London: Smith, Elder, and Company, 1883.

Ferishtah's Fancies. London: Smith, Elder, and Company, 1884.

Parleyings With Certain People of Importance in Their Day. London: Smith, Elder, and Company, 1887.

Asolando: Fancies and Facts. London: Smith, Elder, and Company, 1890.

❦ II. EDITIONS

The Poetical Works of Robert Browning. 16 vols. London: Smith, Elder, and Company, 1889. (The first eight of these volumes appeared in 1888 and were reprinted in 1889 with corrections by the author).

The Complete Works of Robert Browning. (Florentine Edition). 12 vols. Ed. Charlotte Porter and Helen A. Clark. New York: Crowell and Company. Issued first in 1898 and reissued frequently. It appeared in 1910 as the De Luxe Edition and in 1912 as the Pocket Edition.

The Works of Robert Browning (Centenary Edition). 10 vols. Ed. by Frederick G. Kenyon. London: Smith, Elder, and Company, 1912.

New Poems by Robert and Elizabeth Barrett Browning. Ed. by Frederick G. Kenyon. New York: Macmillan, 1915.

The Complete Works of Robert Browning: With Variant Readings, Annotated. 13 vols. Ed. by Roma A. King, Jr. (General Editor) and Park Honan, Morse Peckham, Gordon Pitts. Athens: Ohio University Press. Vol. I, 1968. Others to follow at intervals.

❦ III. LETTERS

The Letters of Robert Browning and Elizabeth Barrett Browning, 1845–1846. 2 vols. New York: Harper & Brothers, 1899.

Robert Browning and Alfred Domett. Ed. by Frederick G. Kenyon. New York: E. P. Dutton & Company, 1906.

Letters of Robert Browning, Collected by Thomas J. Wise. Ed. by Thurman L. Hood. London: John Murray, 1933.

Robert Browning and Julia Wedgwood. A Broken Friendship as Revealed by Their Letters. Ed. by Richard Curle. New York: Frederick A. Stokes Company, 1937.

New Letters of Robert Browning. Ed. by William Clyde DeVane and Kenneth L. Knickerbocker. New Haven: Yale University Press, 1950.

Dearest Isa, Robert Browning's Letters to Isabella Blagden. Ed. by Edward C. McAleer. Austin: University of Texas Press, 1951.

Browning to his American Friends: Letters Between the Brownings, the Storys, and James Russell Lowell. Ed. by Gertrude Reese Hudson. London: Bowes and Bowes, 1965.

❦ IV. BIOGRAPHY

Orr, Mrs. Sutherland. *Life and Letters of Robert Browning,* new edition. Revised and in part rewritten by Frederick G. Kenyon. Boston: Houghton, Mifflin and Company, 1908.

Griffin, W. Hall, and H. C. Minchin. *The Life of Robert Browning.* New York: Macmillan, 1910.

Miller, Betty. *Robert Browning.* London: John Murray, 1952.

Irvine, William, and Park Honan. A detailed comprehensive critical biography of Robert Browning to be published by McGraw-Hill, perhaps in 1969.

❦ V. REFERENCE WORKS

Broughton, Leslie N., Clarke Sutherland Northup, and Robert Pearsall, comps. *Robert Browning: A Bibliography, 1830–1950.* Ithaca, New York: Cornell University Press, 1953.

Broughton, Leslie N., and B. F. Stelter. *A Concordance to the Poems of Robert Browning.* 2 vols. New York: G. E. Stechert & Company, 1924–25.

Browning Society Papers. 3 vols. London: N. Trubner, 1881–91.

Cook, Arthur K. *A Commentary upon Browning's "The Ring and the Book."* London: Oxford University Press, 1920.

DeVane, William Clyde. *A Browning Handbook,* 2nd. ed. New York: Appleton-Century-Crofts, 1955.

Litzinger, Boyd, and Kenneth L. Knickerbocker. *The Browning Critics*. Bibliography from 1951 through May, 1965. (Supplements Broughton, Northup, and Pearsall.) Lexington: University of Kentucky Press, 1965.

Orr, Mrs. Sutherland. *A Handbook to the Works of Robert Browning*. London: George Bill & Sons, 1890.

❧ VI. STUDIES AND CRITICISM

DeVane, William Clyde. *Browning's Parleyings: The Autobiography of a Mind*. New Haven: Yale University Press, 1927.

Drew, Philip, ed. *Robert Browning: A Collection of Critical Essays*. (Contains essays ranging in time from 1880 to 1964 by the following critics: Henry James, George Santayana, Percy Lubbock, H. S. Davies, Edwin Muir, Kingsbury Badger, W. C. DeVane, W. O. Raymond, Robert Langbaum, Robert Preyer, J. S. Mill, E. E. Stall, Roma A. King, Jr., Richard D. Altick, Isabel Armstrong, John Howard, Watson Kirkconnell, and F. E. L. Priestly). London: Methuen and Company, 1966.

Duckworth, Francis R. G. *Browning: Background and Conflict*. New York: E. P. Dutton and Company, 1932.

Honan, Park. *Browning's Characters: A Study in Poetic Technique*. New Haven: Yale University Press, 1961.

Johnson, E. D. H. *The Alien Vision of Victorian Poetry* (pp. 71–143 devoted to Browning). Princeton: Princeton University Press, 1952.

King, Roma A., Jr. *The Bow and The Lyre: The Art of Robert Browning*. Ann Arbor: University of Michigan Press, 1957.

Langbaum, Robert. *The Poetry of Experience: The Dramatic Monologue in Modern Literary Tradition*. New York: Random House, 1957.

Litzinger, Boyd. *Time's Revenges: Browning's Reputation as a Thinker, 1889–1962*. Knoxville: University of Tennessee Press, 1964.

Litzinger, Boyd, and Kenneth L. Knickerbocker, eds. *The Browning Critics*. (Contains essays ranging in time from 1891 to 1964 by the following critics: Henry James, George Saintsbury, John J. Chapman, George Santayana, G. K. Chesterton, Paul E. Moore, Dixon Scott, Frances T. Russell, William Clyde DeVane, F. E. L. Priestley, Donald Smalley, Hoxie N. Fairchild, W. O. Raymond, Richard D. Altick, Kenneth L. Knickerbocker, Robert Langbaum, Roma A.

King, Jr., B. R. Jerman, Laurence Perrine, Robert Preyer, and Philip Drew.) Lexington: University of Kentucky Press, 1965.

Miller, J. Hillis. *The Disappearance of God: Five Nineteenth-Century Writers*. Cambridge: Harvard University Press, 1963.

Pottle, Frederick A. *Shelley and Browning: A Myth and Some Facts*. Chicago: Pembroke Press, 1923.

Raymond, William O. *The Infinite Moment, and Other Essays in Robert Browning*, 2nd ed. Toronto: University of Toronto Press, 1965.

Santayana, George. *Interpretations of Poetry and Religion* ("The Poetry of Barbarism," pp. 201–38). New York: Charles Scribner's Sons, 1900.

Smalley, Donald, ed. *Browning's Essay on Chatterton* (introductory materials). Cambridge: Harvard University Press, 1948.

Symons, Arthur. *An Introduction to the Study of Browning*, new revised edition. London: Cassell & Company, 1906.

🌱 🌱 INDEX

Numbers in heavy type immediately following a title indicate
a major entry or an explication.